# Money Mastery

## 10 Principles That Will Change Your Financial Life Forever

by
**ALAN M. WILLIAMS**
**PETER R. JEPPSON**
**SANFORD C. BOTKIN**

CAREER
PRESS
Franklin Lakes, NJ

**Money Mastery**
Copy edited by Dianna Walsh
Typeset by John J. O'Sullivan
Cover design by Design Concept
Printed in the U.S.A. by Book-mart Press

To order this title, please call toll-free 1-800-CAREER-1 (NJ and Canada: 201-848-0310) to order using VISA or MasterCard, or for further information on books from Career Press.

The Career Press, Inc., 3 Tice Road, PO Box 687
Franklin Lakes, NJ 07417
**careerpress.com**

**Library of Congress Cataloging-in-Publication Data**

Williams, Alan M.
  Money mastery : 10 principles that will change your financial life forever /
by Alan M. Williams, Peter R. Jeppson, Sanford C. Botkin.
    p. cm.
  Includes index.
  ISBN 1-56414-610-3 (pbk.)
R. II. Botkin, Sanford C. III. Title.

HG179 .W5336 2002
332.024—dc21

2001058427

# Acknowledgments

*M*oney Mastery is a work of the ages. Its ideas, principles, and methods are the accumulated time-value works of the financially secure from ancient to modern times. It is precisely for this reason that Money Mastery cannot be considered the work of just a few and to recognize all that have contributed to this book would be impossible—it is truly the work of many. However, the authors wish to acknowledge those individuals who have been instrumental in the creation of this work and who have inspired and enlightened us as we have sought to bring the power of the Money Mastery ideas to you, the reader.

We must first acknowledge George S. Clason's ageless compilation of *The Richest Man in Babylon* as the wonderful philosophical basis for the Money Mastery principles. The essence of paying oneself, dealing forthrightly with debt, and seeking financial mentors is what this book is built upon.

To Larry Adamson, a friend and partner, we express thanks for his technical expertise and inspiration in helping create a total financial management system that helps people make the most of the money they already have and aids them in finding additional wealth they never dreamed possible.

We wish to acknowledge Suzanne Kimball, the managing editor of this book, for her expert skills in the creative direction, composition, and overall tone of the work. This book would not have been possible without her capable management of the project from start to finish, and her understanding of the greater purpose and impact of the Money Mastery principles in people's lives. Suzanne has immersed herself in those principles, and lives the work. The book could not have been written without her.

We express appreciation to Gary Weinberg, the CEO of National Seminars, whose life's work has been to educate hundreds of thousands of people about how to have a better and more effective life, and who encouraged us to bring the Money Mastery concept to the masses.

A special thanks goes to Tom Murphy, author and writer, who saw the need for a good "how to" publication on financial management and who encouraged us to write this book. His experienced perspective has guided its development.

To Financial Health Educators' formative partners, Glen Willardson and Lyle Shamo, we give thanks for their long pursuit of a satisfactory means to convey their spending and debt management ideas. We will always be grateful for their friendship.

We acknowledge Jim Christensen and Clint Coombs, the authors of *Rich On Any Income*, who have contributed to the Money Mastery program with class and dignity. Their sincere help and support of our complete development and presentation of the tracking systems is greatly appreciated. We will always be grateful for their inspiration.

We especially wish to thank the thousands of clients and seminar participants who have personally validated the principles and concepts presented in this book. Almost every strategy found within has come from observing these participants' financial lives. Without our clients, these strategies would be mere thoughts, but from their experience we have seen the absolute legitimacy and inspiration of the Money Mastery principles and Tax Strategies taught herein.

Not the least of those to be acknowledged are our family and friends who have contributed to, made suggestions for, and lived the Money Mastery and Tax Strategies systems and tested them to the maximum. Your patience and love has been empowering.

Finally, we express our thanks to you, the reader, for taking the time to seek out this book. You are our purpose.

Alan Williams
Peter Jeppson
Sandy Botkin

# Contents

## Part II:

# Foreword

I met Peter Jeppson and Alan Williams more than seven years ago when they flew into Kansas City to discuss with National Seminars Group the development of a Money Mastery audio cassette series and seminar. I had reviewed the Money Mastery program, but only had talked to Peter and Alan a few times before meeting them. Our previous conversations had focused on the marketing potential of the program and they were now trying to get me to understand why Money Mastery was different from all the other boring budgeting systems on the market—systems that people don't use. I have to admit, I was a little skeptical about our ability to market another "budgeting" program and their ability to deliver on their promises. Boy, was I surprised when I finally learned what Money Mastery was all about.

Money Mastery is not just another "budgeting" program. It shares financial success secrets in such a powerful way that it can, and does, change lives. If you will take the time to read this book *and* do what it says, it will change *your* life. "More marketing hype," you may be saying. . .well, read on only if you want to be financially independent. Otherwise, close this book and go buy a novel.

Here's a sneak peak at some of Money Mastery's secrets:

- Money budgeting has a reputation for being boring and tedious, requiring you to do something about what you spent last month *after* you've already spent it. With the Money Mastery system, every time you spend a dime, you know exactly what you've spent, where you've spent it, and how much you have left to spend for the rest of the month. It's not a system that makes you go back and look at the past—it helps you track *instantly* what you've spent and gives you information about your life when you need it. What is tracked is controlled, giving you immediate decision-making ability. And Money Mastery will even show you how to find a significant amount of money in what you now think is a tight budget.

- Not only does Money Mastery teach you how to control your spending, it teaches you how to eliminate your debt. Too good to be true? With the "Power Down" approach, Money Mastery will show you how to get rid of debt, including your mortgage, in as little as nine years.

- Money Mastery also teaches you how to reduce your tax load. The key to investment success is your net return after taxes. This program can show you how to get the largest net return on all the money that will become available to you through following all the other Money Mastery techniques.

Before I met Peter and Alan and really understood the program, I felt the way you might be feeling now: skeptical that it can really make a difference. But you see, we all have to break through old paradigms. I can tell you that if you want to change your life, if you are tired of the status quo, if you want a program that deals with *your* realities and your problems, then Money Mastery is your ticket to financial success. I hope when you are done reading this book and applying the principles found in it, you will write me and tell me what it did for you. I would like to add your name to the list of testimonials from people just like me who are living their lives in a much more satisfying way because of Money Mastery.

—Gary Weinberg
Chief Operating Officer
Rockhurst University
Continuing Education Center, Inc.

# Introduction

# Why You Should Read This Book

This book is unlike any other you'll ever read about money and its management. That's because it isn't really about money; it's about the emotional hold money has over you and how those emotions affect how you spend, borrow, and save.

This book is also a message of hope. Its primary purpose is to help you more deeply understand your emotional perceptions about money and to give you a complete system for managing your personal finances that will totally change your life. It can teach you how to:

- Get out of debt, including your mortgage, in nine years or less.
- Gain immediate control of your personal finances.
- Improve your relationship with your spouse and never argue about money again.
- Understand how to legally pay up to 50 percent less taxes every year.
- Save 10 percent of your gross income and be able to predict how much money you will need to retire.

Within the pages of this book you will begin to learn a system that will help you get on the road to personal financial freedom and greater self-esteem. You will also be lead down an emotional path, one that will help you more clearly see yourself and the way you look at money. Counter to what you may have learned over the years:

***Money is emotional, not mathematical.***

In our seminars and coaching sessions, we ask people to respond to the following searching questions. Take a moment to note the answers for yourself:

1. How often do you argue with your spouse about money?
   a) Seldom
   b) Weekly
   c) Monthly

2. Do you know exactly how much money you spent in the last week? On what exactly did you spend it?

   _____

   _____

   _____

3. How much money do you save each month?
   a) none
   b) 1 percent of gross income
   c) 6 percent or more

4. What percent of your income goes toward paying off debt?
   a) More than 50 percent
   b) Less than 30 percent
   c) Less than 20 percent
   d) Have no debt

5. What percentage of your income goes toward paying all taxes required of you?
   a) About 10 percent
   b) About 20 percent
   c) About 30 percent
   d) More than 40 percent
   e) Have no idea

Most of the answers our clients give are startling:
- "We argue every day about money; it's always an issue."
- "I couldn't tell you every single item I bought last week. I mean that seems awfully tedious don't you think?"
- "We have more than $15,000 in credit card debt."
- "Everyone buys on credit today; no one can survive without going into debt."
- "I don't ever put anything into savings; how can I? I barely have enough to pay my bills and all my taxes."

- "We live from paycheck to paycheck; it seems like we'll never get ahead."
- "I have no idea how much of my paycheck goes towards paying taxes. I haven't ever really given it any thought."

If your answers are similar to these, it's clear that you're like thousands of other Americans today: You know your debt load is high, that you overspend, you're not saving enough for the future, and that your tax load is excessive.

***Perhaps now is the time to stop and ask yourself, "Why?"***

Let's meet a couple whose struggle with finances caused them to stop and ask what they were doing wrong and how they could overcome their problems:

Case History

# Mark and Joyce: Out of Control

Mark and Joyce* came to Money Mastery for help at the height of an emotional power struggle over their family finances. Both were in their mid-30s, raising two children in northern Idaho, and struggling to deal with their financial situation. Their "discussions" on money had evolved into arguments and were becoming more frequent. Both Mark and Joyce worked and made similar incomes. Mark was a pharmaceutical rep, working a fairly new territory in Idaho and Oregon. Joyce was a dental hygienist. Both made more than enough money to support the family, yet they knew they were out of control. They couldn't understand why.

At the height of their financial struggles, Mark and Joyce had accumulated $15,982 in consumer debt alone. This figure, of course, did not include their mortgage. When it was combined with their consumer debt and all the interest, their total debt load came to a whopping $306,000. They had accumulated debt on two credit cards and were only making the minimum monthly payment. Although together they had an after-tax monthly income of $3,000, Mark and Joyce always spent more money than they made. To compound the problem, each insisted on using their own system for paying bills and managing their finances. Neither shared this system with the other. Any communication about finances came in the form of emotional outbreaks, finger pointing, and failure to take personal responsibility.

*Names have been changed to protect privacy.

"I began to hate driving to my parents' house on Sundays," says Joyce. "During that 45-minute drive, it was either stark silence or constant arguing over our finances. I began to wonder if we would ever be friends again, like we had been when we first got married."

"I had just about given up," recalls Mark. "I hated the confrontation. I worked hard for every bit of money I earned, but we never could seem to make it. I made as much money, if not more, than my neighbors and I just couldn't understand why we never had enough at the end of the month. We couldn't talk about it either with any sort of mutual understanding, and I eventually just wanted to avoid the whole situation and pretend it wasn't there."

• • •

Sound familiar? Mark and Joyce's situation is typical of many U.S. households today. Their struggle wasn't about how much money they made. It wasn't even about their excessive debt. It wasn't based on the numbers, but rather on a lack of understanding about the emotions behind their spending and borrowing habits.

Many people are doing their best to manage their finances, but based on our experience, we have found 93 percent of them are struggling. It's ironic that in an age of relative prosperity and unbelievable opportunity, a majority of Americans are suffering financially due to overspending and excessive debt. An additional few, while not burdened with debt, worry constantly that their savings and investments will not be secure, that they will experience a loss in income due to reduced interest rates on their savings programs, and that taxes will ultimately devour all of their assets. We believe that these worries stem from a lack of understanding about how various forces at work in the world today can affect our emotional perceptions about money, and consequently our ability to control our finances. Many people are victims in today's economy because they are not aware of these powers and how they influence our lives. Let's take a closer look at three of these forces.

# Consumerism:
# Caving in to Relentless Media Hype

In today's sophisticated and highly technological world, we are constantly bombarded by emotional media messages suggesting that in order to be successful, we must adopt a particular standard of living. These media forces urge us to embrace extravagant lifestyles regardless of whether we can afford to or not. Billboards, magazines, television, the Internet, and other forms of media subtly insist that we must do everything we can to keep up with the Joneses. We must wear the right labels, prevent the most facial wrinkles, and drive the hippest car. Countless individuals are victims of today's product-oriented society, one that screams for attention and demands that we buy. Americans have caved into the emotional media hype, becoming so accustomed to spending and borrowing in order to answer consumerism's siren call that they never question whether something should be purchased. They only ask themselves if there will be enough money to make the minimum monthly payment. Even if there aren't enough funds to cover a monthly payment, many Americans will buy a product anyway. We call this reckless spending the "disease of consumerism."

Victims of this disease cannot blame the media entirely for their illness. While media messages are often prevalent, passionate, and persuasive, they are not accompanied by a taskmaster with a whip. We have the choice whether to listen to these messages or not, but unfortunately, many Americans do not comprehend this because very few have ever had to go to bed hungry or be out of work for two or three years at a time. Instead many feel driven to consume by a taskmaster of their own creation that is born of guilt, greed, pride, materialism, and expectation.

This greed and materialism stem from a lack of respect toward money, a respect that's been lost as a whole from our society since the ending of the Great Depression 60 years ago. The generation who suffered through the Depression carried a real fear of not having the basic necessities of life because most people of that era went many years without being able to provide adequately for themselves or their families. The Depression taught people a profound respect for money and its power over life. It also taught them the value of self-reliance, the importance of self-denial, and the danger of overindulgence. Unfortunately, as America came out of that great economic trial into the most prosperous time in all of history, it did not teach subsequent generations to fear and respect money as it ought. Instead, it taught its children to hold their hands out in expectation. Because of that, we now live in a time of great self-indulgence and very little financial self-control.

> *Today's generation, instead of fearing that it will not have* **anything,** *fears that it will not have* **everything.**

Many people today spend money out of fear that they won't be able to keep up with everyone else if they don't. They spend money to reduce their fears and as a way to feel powerful and capable of meeting any and all desires. This kind of spending is usually impulsive and acts as an emotional release, helping such individuals feel better about themselves and their personal circumstances. Did you know that 25 to 50 percent of all consumer purchases are unplanned and unneeded? And here's another terrifying statistic: The average American will retire with just $57,000 at age 65—that's after making more than $1.6 million over their lifetime![1] As a nation, we've been saving less than 3 percent.[2] In fact, in recent years, the personal saving rate has hovered around a negative .02 percent![3] In other words, Americans are spending more than they're making, something the nation hasn't struggled with since the stock market crashed in 1929. That's why more than two-thirds of all Americans who have reached retirement age today are not sufficiently prepared to retire,[4] and why many older Americans are going back to work after age 65.

A lack of respect for money, combined with the absence of a system for handling personal finances, largely accounts for our nation's financial unhappiness. So many Americans do not yet see how the force of consumerism is eating away at their lives. Is it eating away at yours? Perhaps it's time to take a hard look at how consumerism might be affecting you.

# Indebtedness:
# Becoming a Slave to Lenders and Easy Credit

Another force at work in many people's lives goes hand-in-hand with consumerism. It's called indebtedness, and unless its power to control you is completely understood, you will fall victim to credit card companies, lending institutions, banks, and other entities that wait with bated breath to put to work for them the compound interest they collect from you.

Unfortunately, most people don't realize that when the initial loan amount is combined with double compound interest, they can end up paying three times the amount they actually borrow!

Credit card companies and other credit issuers are keenly aware of this fact. These entities know that double compound interest is the way to make money. That's why they send out more than two billion offers for new credit cards each year, even to those with bad credit, no credit, or those who have declared bankruptcy.

After being seduced into spending through emotional media messages, those sick with the disease of consumerism seem driven to further compound the problem by adding an interest payment to their load. Is it any wonder that the majority of Americans cannot keep most of the money they make? Even though personal income has increased by 72 percent over the past decade, personal debt has increased by 123 percent![5] Consumer credit debt in the United States now stands at a whopping $1.6 trillion![6]

This type of debt enslavement is similar to taking one step forward and two steps back; it's impossible to get ahead so long as you fail to understand the power that credit issuers can have over you if you let them. As John Cummuta of Illinois-based Financial Independence Network notes: "We are seduced into using credit by the illusion of prosperity and the short-term pleasure. We don't think about the long-term pain."[7] The inability to fully and completely comprehend the enslaving power of compound interest, combined with the lack of a system for getting out from underneath this enslavement, is what keeps people chained to the credit-issuing institutions that control them. Are you being deceived by the false notion that debt is a normal and expected part of life and that there's no other way to live other than as a slave to those with money to lend? If so, it's time to free yourself!

# Excessive Taxation: Allowing Ourselves to Be Sheared by the Tax System

A third force at work today that can have a powerful effect on your emotions and lifestyle is excessive taxation.

Over-taxation is one of the most subtly destructive forces in your life, but it's unlikely you realize just how much it is affecting your long-term financial well-being. If you do realize its impact in your life, you may feel you have little power to control it. Most Americans believe a myriad of tax myths that keep them perpetually yoked to a relentless tax machine that marches forward, with precision and intimidation to seize what it believes will be necessary for its survival. But it doesn't have to be that way.

What are some of the myths you may be embracing that keep you under the control of this powerful force?

One of the most pernicious is the assumption that a huge tax burden is inevitable and inescapable. Less than 100 years ago, the average taxpayer forked over $60 annually in taxes.[8] Through the continual expansion of government, however, more taxes are extracted from you each year in order to sustain growth, only adding to the belief that there's nothing that can be done to reduce such a burden. Under recent tax laws, the government is limiting the amount of employee deductions that can be taken, and raising Social Security taxes. This results in both spouses feeling compelled to work in order to keep the family going. Even then, with tax laws such as they are, a two-income household rarely brings the desired financial relief it seeks.

*Did you know that taxes have become the largest expense for most people, exceeding what they pay for food, clothing, rent or mortgage, and transportation combined?![9]*

In fact, the average American pays a whopping 39 percent of their gross income in taxes,[10] which represents about $8,000 per year.[11] For some, their tax bill can represent 50 percent of their income.

With that kind of money being paid by seemingly unquestioning taxpayers, is it any wonder that the Internal Revenue Service (IRS) and other government entities are unsympathetic and relentless in their efforts to ensure that the cash continues to roll in? While many Americans grumble over the high cost of taxes, few seem to question what they can do about it, assuming they must pay such ridiculous sums of money. All of this makes many Americans feel like sheep being led silently and helplessly into a pen for shearing.

But the truth of the matter is, you don't have to be a sheep.

The government gets away with taking far more money from you than is required by law simply because you don't know any better. One way Uncle Sam keeps the money coming in is by keeping you in the dark about what he can actually exact from you. It is up to you to come out of the dark and get informed about how to change this unacceptable situation.

Another tax myth that keeps us chained to excessive taxes and goes hand-in-hand with the previous myth is the idea that a large and complex government is necessary. Through an attitude of "entitlement," many Americans are unknowingly subjecting themselves to larger and larger tax burdens. Over the last 60 years, post-Depression generations have held their hands out in expectation, demanding more services and greater benefits from government than at any other time in the history of the United States. Walter Williams, a professor of economics at George Mason University, explains:

> *Americans from all walks of life, whether they realized it or not. . . have decided that government should care for the poor, the disadvantaged, the elderly, failing businesses, college students, and many other "deserving" segments of our society. It's nice to do those things, but we have to recognize that government has no resources of its own. Congressmen and senators are not spending their own money for these programs. Furthermore, there is no Tooth Fairy or Santa Claus who*

*gives them the resources. The only way the government can give one American one dollar is to confiscate it first. . .from another American.*[12]

You may be thinking, "But, I don't have my hand out looking for government assistance. I'm the poor sucker who pays the taxes for all those other people who expect the government to take care of them." What you may not realize, however, is that it isn't just those on welfare who have their hands outstretched in anticipation to receive government benefits. You do not have to receive a welfare check to get federal "assistance" in some form or another. This assistance ranges from small things like reduced entry fees into federally controlled national parks to larger benefits such as subsidized education and federally funded health care. If you are in favor of such entitlements, that's fine, but remember someone has to pay for them, and that someone is you.

Many people today want to receive government benefits without considering how much they will cost. The greater number of benefits we are willing to receive, the larger government grows and the greater the tax burden we must expect to pay. Is it possible that the mentality that leads some to buy the cell phone in the mall, even when they have no real way of paying for it, is the same mentality that leads some to embrace more government programs even though they will not be able to afford the taxes required to support these programs?

While the idea that a large tax bill and big government are inevitable is a hazardous one, the most dangerous tax myth of all is one that never gets any attention and isn't discussed at round tables in Washington. It is one of the worst wealth killers today and is only seven words long. These seven words make more money for the IRS and steal more people's wealth than almost anything else—and the funny thing is, you'll never see them mentioned in any other financial management book. These seven words are:

### My accountant takes care of my taxes.

We equate this myth to the equally absurd notion that a doctor takes care of your health. To believe such a notion assumes that you can eat all the cholesterol and fattening foods you want, never exercise, and then once a year have a doctor give you the equivalent of a plumbing job to clean out your clogged arteries. The idea that your accountant can magically clean up your tax life is just as preposterous.

If you don't know the rules for good "tax health," you can't expect your accountant to save you thousands of dollars in taxes at the end of each year. If you believe that your accountant takes care of your taxes, you will pay more to the government than even it requires! Only you can keep your tax bill fully under control. Unless you begin to understand the importance of taking personal responsibility for your own taxes and learn how to take advantage of the good tax laws that are available to you, you will always pay more than is required by law. Excessive taxation is only excessive because you lack the knowledge to fix the problem. Without a system for eliminating unnecessary taxation, you will forever be subject to a powerful force to which you have unknowingly yoked yourself. In fact, the subject of taxation is so important and so misunderstood, that we have devoted the entire second part of this book to tax planning and audit-proofing strategies.

## The Time/Value of Money

These three forces—consumerism, indebtedness, and excessive taxation—are largely taken for granted by most Americans, and their casual attitude towards such powers leads to victimization. They know there must be something wrong with their impulsive spending habits, but they have not yet linked those habits to their inability to tune out the media hype that urges them to consume, at any cost. These same people long to have more money for retirement, for their children's education, for vacations, and yet they realize they're not saving anything. Unfortunately, they have not yet seen the correlation between their enslavement to credit issuers and their inability to save for the future. These people feel overwhelmed by the amount of taxes extracted from their paycheck each month, and by the way that estate and death taxes eat into their savings and investment nest eggs, but have not yet connected big government shearing with their own ignorance about the way the tax system really works. These people see tremendous financial opportunity in the world but lack the skills necessary to control these powerful forces and harness the wealth and prosperity all around them.

Without a big picture view of how these forces can affect us over time, we may be forever trapped in the moment, failing to understand what we call the "Time/Value of Money." For those who live from paycheck to paycheck, the daily struggle to survive inhibits the ability to see the true *value* that money can have over *time* and the kind of return it can bring over the course of several years. Those who choose to remain in debt do not understand that the *time* it takes to pay off compound interest is affecting the long-term *value* of their money. The money that they could be using wisely to give them a return over *time* is instead being paid to creditors, completely stripping their money of any *value* it could bring them. Those who continue to pay excessive taxes, are in a similar fashion, failing to see the time/value of money because they don't realize the *value* that their money will bring them over *time* if they paid their taxes correctly so they continue to let it slip through their fingers even though they don't need to.

People weighed down by consumerism, indebtedness, and excessive taxation have a difficult time understanding the exponential value that money can have if given a little time to grow. The time/value of money can only be explained to a point, and then it must be experienced in order to fully comprehend it. Many of the people we work with are so caught up in the worry and frustration of the moment that they can't see what's waiting for them in the future. Others think they already have all the answers about money management. Some of the hardest people we try to help are the financial planners and accountants who have an intellectual base of knowledge on how to deal with money, yet are thousands of dollars in debt because they do not fully comprehend the power of these forces, the emotional impact they can have on lives when they are taken for granted, and how a casual attitude affects the value of their money over time. Are you one of them?

*Are you limited by the things you don't know you don't know because you're wrapped up in the daily struggle for survival?*

**OR**

*Are you blinded by your own brilliance in thinking that you already know everything you want to know about money and its management?*

It's been said that if all the money in the world was pooled together and then divided equally among each man, woman, and child, each person would have more than $1 million. However, in less than 10 years, the majority of people would misuse that money so that they would end up with the same amount they started with. Amazing as this sounds, such loss of wealth is a direct consequence of the mind-set and attitudes about money that most of us struggle with today.

# A Message of Hope

As we have promised, the intent of this book is to inspire and motivate you to see that there is a logical and simple way to solve financial problems. The first step is to help you see the negative habits you may be engaging in so you can be aware of your own situation, whatever it is. We have seen countless people improve their lives the minute they became aware of their own behavior. The next step is to help you learn the system for eliminating any negative behavior and accentuating the positive habits you may already have.

Mark and Joyce are just one couple that have been helped by the Money Mastery system you will learn in this book. Let's go back to their story to see how this system and the principles it teaches totally changed their lives.

When they first came to Money Mastery, Mark and Joyce were thousands of dollars in debt and constantly fighting about money. Once they were made aware of how consumerism and indebtedness were eating away at them, they made a conscious decision to stop unnecessary and impulsive spending and to get out of debt, including their mortgage. Instead of paying off their house in 29 years, if they stick to their current plan, they will eliminate their mortgage and become completely debt-free in just eight years. This quick debt elimination is saving them over $131,000 in interest alone. By investing that saved interest money, they will accumulate over $971,000 at retirement. With their understanding of how to avoid excessive taxation, they are also protecting that retirement money. And best of all, they're doing all this without any additional out-of-pocket expense. If you're thinking this kind of wealth is only possible through slick financial wheeling and dealing, think again. Because Mark and Joyce now understand their emotions behind money, and approach money with the respect it deserves, retiring with close to a million dollars is totally possible for them. It can be totally possible for you, too.

How can you make it happen? First you must learn how to limit the power of consumerism, indebtedness, and excessive taxation in your life. To do this, you must be aware of just how much they influence you and your emotions. Next, you must understand the importance of having a system that will help you deal with each of these forces. Putting this system in place is much like baking a cake. You need a proper recipe if you expect to get the results you want.

First, you must have all the proper "ingredients" if you expect the "cake" to turn out just right. That means you must be aware of what it takes to become financially successful before you even begin creating that success. We will give you those ingredients within the pages of this book.

Second, you must have the correct amount of these ingredients—too much or too little of one particular thing can spoil the result. We'll tell you how much of which ingredients to include.

Third, you must add the ingredients in the right order. A cake will not turn out right if you try to add the egg, for instance, after the cake is baked. The same holds true for personal financial happiness; you must do what is expedient first, then add more ingredients later. We can show you how to do "first things first."

Many experienced people have attempted to share the recipe for financial happiness and success, but unfortunately, most information sources do not include everything necessary to help you. Some provide all the ingredients but don't tell you in which order to bake them. Others know the order, but don't tell you how much of one particular ingredient to include. Contrary to what we're taught, the best information on how to bake the perfect financial cake is not found on Wall Street. It isn't locked behind the doors of bankers or financial counselors. It isn't available in schools.

***The secret to successful money management is understanding first, that money is emotional, and second, that because it is emotional, it requires a system for carefully controlling it.***

In these pages we will begin to explain the powerful secrets behind true money mastery. You will learn the meaning of the Time/Value of money and how financial security can release you from being nickled and dimed to death by tedious daily financial concerns. Isn't it about time that you stopped living in fear of tomorrow because you don't have control over today?

We invite you to stay with us as we explain how you can stop being a victim of the system and become a victor over it instead. We will give you the tools you need to get your emotions and your money under control. Meet other struggling couples like Mark and Joyce, and see how these people overcame their own ignorance and inability to deal with the emotions surrounding their money. Read how they learned to take the emotion out of their financial decisions and how this totally changed their lives.

Make a commitment to change your own. Decide now to remove yourself from the cycle of failure that has kept you in a pattern of unhappiness. Read as if you know nothing about money because from an emotional perspective you may not!

To help you get enthused about making that commitment, we invite you to consider one of the most powerful arguments for committing yourself to change that has ever been recorded:

> *Until one is committed there is hesitancy, the chance to draw back, always ineffectiveness. Concerning all acts of initiative (and creation), there is one elementary truth, the ignorance of which kills countless ideas and splendid plans: that the moment one definitely commits oneself, then providence moves too.*
>
> *All sorts of things occur to help one that would never otherwise have occurred. A whole stream of events issue from the decision, raising in one's favor all manner of unforeseen incidents and meetings and material assistance, which no man could have dreamt would have come his way.*

*I have learned a deep respect for one of Goethe's couplets: "Whatever you can do, or dream you can, begin. Boldness has genius, power, and magic in it."*

— W. H. Murray
(The first man to photograph the top of Mt. Everest)

# Our Promise

If you stay with the book, "definitely committing yourself," as Murray puts it, you'll learn a system of financial success and happiness that will open you to all the following possibilities:

- Understand how to get out of debt, including your mortgage, in nine years or less.
- Gain immediate control of your finances.
- Learn immediately how to live within your income.
- Understand how to prioritize money so you can have anything you want.
- Learn how to legally pay up to 50 percent less taxes.
- Understand how to forecast the dollars you will need for retirement and how to maximize that retirement money.
- Learn how to spend your way to financial freedom.
- Never argue with your spouse or yourself again about money.
- Find an extra $300 a month.
- Learn how to begin saving at least one percent of your gross income and work your way up to 10 percent or more.
- Double and even triple your retirement income.

Best of all, you can learn how to do all this without any additional money from your pocket and without any additional risk!

Now let's get started!

# Part I   The Money Mastery Principles

# Chapter 1

# Money Is Emotional

We began this book with a bold statement: Money is more about emotions than it is about math. With that in mind, let's begin examining the ways that emotions affect your money by taking a look at the first Money Mastery Principle:

 ## Principle #1: Spending is emotional.

Think back to the last time you spent money. Perhaps it was yesterday or even a few hours ago. Perhaps you can't remember the last thing that you bought. If so, think hard until you can pinpoint what you spent money on.

Ask yourself the reason for making that spending decision. Did you buy something necessary such as groceries or medication? Was the item something you needed or just wanted at that moment? Did you worry about having enough money to pay for the item? Did the purchase cost more than you thought it should or did you even worry about the price? Will this spending decision have a big effect on whether you'll be able to purchase other things later? Did spending the money make you feel guilty or did it give you pleasure?

Now, try to recall a particular incident where spending money had a strong emotional impact on your life or the lives of your family members. What made that incident so emotional?

*One of the most important questions you can ask is:*
*"How does spending money make me feel?"*

Through years of counseling thousands of people, we have heard countless reasons why people spend money. Many of those reasons have more to do with a person's circumstances and the way they feel about those circumstances than whether there is, or is not, enough money to spend. Let's take a closer look at what we consider the three most significant reasons people spend money.

## Impulsiveness

As we noted in the Introduction, we live in a world full of emotional media messages. These messages often play upon people's deepest psychological needs pointing out all the things a person may lack in his or her life. Responding to this supposed lack, many individuals spend money impulsively without thinking as a way to meet unfulfilled desires. Without the proper respect for money our current society has become notorious for impulsive, reckless spending. According to Richard A. Feinberg, professor of Retail Management and director for the Center of Customer-driven Quality at Purdue University, up to 50 percent of all consumer purchases are made on impulse.[1]

Here are some of the responses we get from people who spend money on impulse:

- "Spending money fills an emotional void in my life. . .I just feel like I can't get the things I really desire, so I acquire material things to fill myself up."

- "I like to give my children what they want because it gives me joy. Sometimes I feel like it's the only thing I can really do right for them."

- "Having the money I want to spend, when I want to spend it makes me feel important. I know my Dad never could feel that way and I always felt sorry for him."

- "I can't say no to my children. . .they pester me until I give in and get them what they want. They're just plain stronger than I am."

The Haywood* family is a perfect example of how emotions can trigger impulsive spending. They had a habit of going to All-a-Dollar, a bargain chain store that sells every bit of stock for $1 or less. Purchasing little items such as candy or inexpensive toys for the children gave the Haywoods pleasure without making them feeling guilty, especially with the store's low prices, which made the trips seem so innocent. But once the family started to keep track of how much they were spending at All-a-Dollar they were shocked to find it was more than $300 per month. Low prices combined with their impulsive desire to please their children cost the Haywoods some serious cash they would rather have spent elsewhere.

Most people are trapped in an impulsive mentality that prevents them from keeping much of the money they make for any length of time. Remember the time/value of money we discussed in the Introduction? Impulsive spending completely eliminates the possibility of increasing the *value* of money over *time*. Did you know that 85 percent of all Americans who win lotteries spend every penny of their winnings on consumable goods rather than investing it in high-yield programs?[2] Based on this statistic, it's plain that the majority of Americans do not understand the profound power of the time/value of money and are destroying their future because of it. Are impulsive emotions affecting the way you spend money?

## Economic Hardship

Experiencing a financial disaster is another thing that can greatly affect feelings about money and how it should be spent. Have you ever lost a job and had to come home to your spouse with the bad news? What kind of an emotional impact did that have on your family? After the trauma of losing a job, or some other economic hardship such as illness or divorce, we often hear responses like these about the way spending money makes people feel:

- "I just hate not feeling like I have enough money for the things I want. I get so depressed just thinking about it."
- "Spending money makes me feel guilty, like I don't deserve the thing I bought or that it will come back to haunt me later."
- "My divorce has wiped me out financially. I have nothing left after I pay child support and alimony for anything I might want to get myself."

Doug* was a young father of three when he experienced the economic trauma of divorce. Within 12 months of the divorce, he began paying more than $900 a month for alimony and child support. Having recently graduated with a degree in graphic design, Doug wasn't advanced enough in his career to make the kind of money he needed to support his three children and an ex-wife. He was forced to move in with his parents and sell his car. Even then, he barely made enough to meet his financial obligations. The only thing he indulged in was music, buying a CD or two every once in a while. Doing so made him feel extremely guilty because he worried that indulging himself would somehow affect the happiness of his children. Doug's economic hardship was an emotional situation that had a huge impact on the way spending money made him feel.

When we are forced into a bad financial situation due to some kind of economic disaster, spending money can be a highly emotional issue that causes friction in marriages and personal unhappiness.

## Daily Financial Obligations

The struggle for daily survival can also affect why and how we spend money. Even those who are frugal and don't spend impulsively have heavy debt loads and excessive taxes and are impacted emotionally by the sheer effort of just making ends meet from day to day. We have counseled hundreds of clients who have felt burdened and depressed by this daily struggle:

- "I feel angry that I have to fight just to pay taxes and my debts. It leaves me nothing left over to spend on myself or kids."
- "We were just audited recently and I felt so intimidated by the IRS. Taxes are the first thing that comes out of my paycheck and it just makes me sick that I still feel like the government controls my life."
- "We were so poor growing up. I promised myself I would never make my kids wear hand-me-downs, but we don't have enough money after all of our other expenses are paid for me to really give my kids what I dream of."
- "I can't believe that I have to work almost six months out of the year just to pay my taxes. It really upsets me just thinking about it."

The Martinellis* are a good illustration of how this daily struggle to survive can greatly affect the emotional well-being of a family. Don and Keisha Martinelli were struggling to make ends meet on the East Coast where the cost of living is high. The couple had three boys younger than the age of 7 and were concerned about financing their children's college education. Don was working 14-hour days as a controller for a corporation in Manhattan, but even with the long hours, they weren't able to find enough money to build a savings program for their sons' future education. In an attempt to earn extra money, they had invested in a business opportunity that never took off because they didn't have the time to put into it, forcing them into further debt and farther away from the boys' educational funding. This daily struggle simply to survive was draining the Martinelli family and was killing the fun times they wanted to have with their boys because they never dared spend money to take them anywhere or go on any vacations.

## Emotional Events Affect Money

Impulse purchasing, economic hardship, and daily financial obligations are just some of the things that affect the way people spend money. Because of these emotional events, whether we end up with anything to show for all our hard work has less to do with the math behind the money, (that is, how much we make), but rather with how well we understand that these emotional events can affect our money over time.

Many people mistakenly assume that if they only had a job where they "made the big bucks," they wouldn't have to deal with these emotional issues. They think that more money would eliminate the problems that their impulse spending causes or that more money would alleviate the burdens of economic hardship and the daily struggle to survive. But more money doesn't usually solve the problem. "In our seminars on money management," says Jim Christensen, co-author of *Rich on Any Income*, "we often quote a George Gallup survey which highlights four groups of workers (farmers, factory workers, business executives, and doctors). These four groups were asked if they felt they needed more income to make ends meet, and if so, how much. Every income group, from $15,000 to more than $200,000 annually, responded that they needed about 10 percent more income to work things out."[3] From this, we can see that financial happiness has nothing to do with making a large income. Individuals making more than $200,000 a year are just as likely to be financially stressed as those who make a modest income. That stress is not caused because people don't bring home enough pay, but because they do not understand their own emotional reasons for spending money or because they have become a victim of financially draining events due to poor planning.

When our clients are tempted to blame their salary for their financial problems, we like to point out the following:

*It matters not how much you make,* → ITS HOW MUCH YOU KEEP
*only how well you manage your money that counts.*

Now let's meet a couple who were unable to manage their finances because they did not understand the emotional reasons for their spending:

Case History

# Doug and Sally Hamilton: Victims of the Disease of Consumerism

Doug and Sally Hamilton* had married young. They made a modest living in a rural community in the Southwest, Doug working at a parts supply house for a trucking company and

Sally working in a dental office. They had three children. Both Doug and Sally had grown up without a lot of material security and both wanted to provide their children with the things they never had as kids. This led to over-indulgence of their children giving them virtually everything they wanted, even if the family couldn't afford it. The Hamiltons had inherited some land from Doug's father and when they were first married had built a modest home on that land without going into debt. But due to poor spending habits, they had been forced to borrow money against the house and had a mortgage hanging over their heads. They were also alienating other members of their family because Doug's parents continually bailed the Hamiltons out of financial problems. Every month they spent $500 more than what they brought home and were close to $16,000 in consumer debt.

At the height of their financial distress, the Hamiltons came to Money Mastery for help. Their coach, Peter, began working with them to figure out exactly how they were spending their money. As he sat at their kitchen table finalizing an overall picture of their spending habits and counseling them on how they would need to start cutting back, the Hamilton's 16-year-old daughter came home asking for money.

"We had just finished talking to Peter about the huge financial mess we found ourselves in when Katie* came home," says Sally. "She wanted $5 to go with her friends to McDonalds. Dinner for that night was cooking on the stove. I had a roast and vegetables waiting to serve my family after we finished our session with Peter, and Katie wanted extra money to go out with her friends. Doug and I looked at Peter and then at Katie and all I could say was 'We can't afford it Katie.'"

"She looked at me like I was crazy," says Sally, "and started arguing with us and coaxing and claiming that $5 was not going to break us. She said she couldn't understand why we were making such a big deal out of her asking for money. 'C'mon Mom, be serious, it's only $5.' What she didn't know was that Doug and I had just been made to realize that we literally didn't have $5 to give her because of the way we had mismanaged our finances throughout our entire marriage. I continued to explain that dinner was already prepared and that she couldn't go to McDonalds, but she wouldn't stop arguing. Doug tried to reason with her, but she wouldn't listen. Finally, she said 'Mom, you've never told me "no" before!' and slammed the door in a huff. After she left, I turned to Doug and Peter and said in astonishment 'Gosh Peter, that's our problem. . .we just can't say no, can we?'"

• • •

We introduced you to Doug and Sally because we want you to think about how their situation applies to you. Are you like the Hamiltons, even in a small way? They were totally unaware of the impact that reckless spending was having on their lives over the course of their marriage. How about you?

When we are unaware of the long-term consequences of our spending decisions, we are pulled in a variety of emotional directions, spending money for all the wrong reasons.

> *When we spend money, even for seemingly inconsequential things,*
> *we are at a crucial moment in time that will affect the rest of our lives.*

If we make the decision to spend money for something now, we will not have that money later. We must decide if the purchase has more *value* to us now than the money would have later if left alone to work for us over *time*. Spending money emotionally eventually forces us into a survival mode rather than a planning mode. Usually this reckless spending causes us to burn up more than we make and ultimately limits what we can do for ourselves and others in the future. It also puts a lot of pressure on a family. When we define our own needs and desires and learn how to meet those needs appropriately, we can then create surplus to help others. That surplus is the absolute emotional thrill—ultimately more meaningful than the brief excitement that comes from impulse spending, and certainly more joyful than the terrible feelings of fear and guilt that come from spending more than we have.

# Get in Control—You Can Do It!

Understanding that spending is emotional is the first step toward financial control and the key to true contentment and happiness. The remaining nine Money Mastery principles are based on understanding this first most important idea. Having come this far with us already, you're obviously making an effort to better understand your own emotional approach to money. And that means you're beginning to take control. Taking control is tremendously rewarding and we encourage you to continue!

To see just how rewarding it can be, let's go back to Doug and Sally Smith. As they worked with their coach, the Smiths began to understand how their emotions were affecting their spending. They realized that they had a problem telling their children no. They understood that they were spending money to make themselves feel better in the short term and jeopardizing their long-term financial security. They began making changes by denying their children when it was necessary. This was not easy to do in the beginning. The children were not used to their parents' new behavior and resisted it. But in a short time, they began to accept their parents' new way of doing things. When the Smith's daughter had the opportunity to go to Europe for a high school academic event, instead of stressing out about how they would send her, Doug and Sally encouraged her to get a job and earn the money to go herself. Once she realized her parents were not going to hand her the money, she got a job and earned her own way. Later, she commented to her parents that she had actually enjoyed the satisfaction of making her own money for the trip and had appreciated her experience in Europe much more than if Doug and Sally had just given her the money.

Today the Smiths have stopped overspending and have actually begun saving an extra $300 each month. They have begun to look at every expenditure as an emotional decision, determining whether the object of their spending is something that fits their financial priorities or not.

We encourage you to think deeply about the first Money Mastery principle by looking at how you emotionally spend your money. Take the challenge to complete the following short assignment before going on to Chapter 2. It will help you go further in your commitment to make important changes to your life. Go ahead! Take the challenge! You're worth it!

## Challenge #1

# Look at Your Own Emotions Behind Spending

Pinpoint the last time dealing with money became a dramatic experience that deeply impacted you. It could be the last time you made a major purchase such as a car, or sent a child off to college—or the last time you examined your paycheck and realized how much you're paying in Social Security and federal income taxes. *Note: The experience may or may not be negative; it simply needs to be significant.*

1.  Write down at least three emotions you felt during that event.

    _____

    _____

    _____

2.  What was your attitude toward spending money at the time the event took place? Were you affected by consumerism and/or economic hardship?

    _____

    _____

    _____

3.  Who or what was responsible for the way the event turned out? How much did your monthly take-home pay affect the outcome?

    _____

    _____

    _____

# Chapter 2

# Track It! Control It!

We hope you have given some thought to the first Money Mastery principle: Spending is emotional. At the end of Chapter 1, we asked you to identify some of the feelings you had during a significant event in your life that involved money. This exercise should have helped you determine how emotions affect the way you spend your money. Understanding why you spend will help you become more aware of how and where you spend. This leads to the second Money Mastery principle:

 ## Principle #2: When you track your money, you control it.

Have you ever taken your car for a tune-up and received a test result form similar to the one on page 35?

The value of this kind of analysis is that it allows you to visualize exactly how your money was spent in getting your car tuned up. Without it, the only thing you may know when you pay the mechanic is that $75, for example, seems like too much. Or you may not even consider what the $75 was worth to you at all without something to verify the value of that expenditure.

Having a clear picture of exactly where you spend your money is extremely important in today's consumer-driven society. The constant barrage of emotional media messages often lures us into spending more money than we have. That's why it is more crucial than ever that you learn the value of keeping track of where and how you spend your income.

## ENGINE PERFORMANCE ANALYSIS

| BEFORE | | | ROAD TEST | | | | | | AFTER |
|---|---|---|---|---|---|---|---|---|---|

### VISUAL INSPECTION

| | OK | SERVICE | | OK | SERVICE |
|---|---|---|---|---|---|
| Air Filter | | | Throttle Body | | |
| Breather Element | | | Carburetor | | |
| Cold Air Intake | | | Choke / Pull-Off | | |
| TAC Motor | | | Canister / Purge | | |
| Heat Riser Tube | | | Dist. Cap / Rotor | | |
| PCV Valve | | | Mech. / VAC Adv. | | |
| Fuel Filter | | | Ignition Wires | | |
| Fuel Pump | | | Rocker Cover Gskt | | |
| Fuel Lines | | | Batt. / Hold Down | | |
| Radiator / Cap | | | Cables / Ends | | |
| Antifreeze Electrol | | | VAC Hoses | | |
| Radiator Hoses | | | Oil Level | | |
| Heater/Bypass Hoses | | | Missing Parts | | |
| Clamps | | | Systems Inop | | |
| Belts | | | A/C Duct. Temp. | | |
| Fan Clutch | | | Hood Struts | | |

### COMPUTER CONTROL

| TROUBLE CODE | CODE DESCRIPTION |
|---|---|
| | |
| | |
| | |

### STARTING / CHARGING

| | OK | SERVICE | SPECIFICATIONS | TEST |
|---|---|---|---|---|
| Cranking Vacuum | | | | |
| Cranking Current | | | 300 amps Max. | |
| Cranking Voltage | | | 9.6 volts Min. | |
| Battery Capacity | | | 12.2 volts Min | |
| Charging Current | | | | |
| Diode Pattern | | | | |
| Regulator Voltage | | | 14.2 Average | |

### PRIMARY IGNITION

| | OK | SERVICE | SPECIFICATIONS | TEST |
|---|---|---|---|---|
| Dwell / Timing Variation | | | / 10% | / |
| Primary Pattern | | | | |

### ADDITIONAL DIAGNOSTICS NEEDED / COMMENTS:

- ☐ Timing Belt
- ☐ Fuel System
- ☐ Computer
- ☐ Diagnostics
- ☐ Electrical
- ☐ Compression
- ☐ Air Conditioning
- ☐ Other

### SECONDARY IGNITION

| | OK | SERVICE | | TEST |
|---|---|---|---|---|
| CAP / Rotor KV | | | 5 KV Max. | |
| Coil / Pack / Output | | | | |
| Ignition Wires | | | Wire No. | |
| Idle KV | | | 8-12 KV | |
| Snap KV | | | | |

### CYLINDER PERFORMANCE

| | OK | SVC | TEST | | | | |
|---|---|---|---|---|---|---|---|
| Firing Order | | | | | | | |
| Cylinder Output | | | | | | | |
| Carb. Balance | | | | | | | |

### TIMING CONTROL SYSTEM

| | OK | SERVICE | SPECIFICATIONS | TEST |
|---|---|---|---|---|
| Basic Timing (Idle) | | | | |
| Mechanical Advance | | | | |
| Total Advance | | | | |

| Carburated ☐ | | | | | Fuel Inj. ☐ |
| Adjustable ☐ | FUEL DELIVERY SYSTEM | | | Catylst ☐ |
| Non adjustable ☐ | | | | Non catalyst ☐ |

### FUEL DELIVERY SYSTEM

| IDLE | SPECS | | | TEST | OK | SVC |
|---|---|---|---|---|---|---|
| CO | | CO | | | | |
| HC | | HC | | | | |
| CO2 | | CO2 | | | | |
| O2 | | O2 | | | | |
| NOX | | NOX | | | | |
| Vacuum | | Vacuum | | | | |
| Acc. Pump | | Acc. Pump | | | | |
| Idle Speed | | Idle Speed | | | | |
| Fast Idle | | Fast Idle | | | | |

| CRUISE | SPECS | | | TEST | OK | SVC |
|---|---|---|---|---|---|---|
| CO | | CO | | | | |
| HC | | HC | | | | |
| CO2 | | CO2 | | | | |
| O2 | | O2 | | | | |
| NOX | | NOX | | | | |
| Vacuum | | Vacuum | | | | |

### REMOVE INFRA-RED PROBE

Analysis By:

When you fail to do so, you can easily consume every penny you earn on impulse and without any real awareness.

Tom and Shannon* are a perfect example of this. Shannon liked music and was a member of a club that offered discounts on CDs purchased through its mail order catalog. Shannon bought multiple CDs in order to take advantage of what she thought were cost savings. Tom was into computers and thought nothing of buying himself a new video game every week to play on his PC. Neither Tom nor Shannon tracked these expenditures and were often overdrawn in their checking account because of them. Shannon decided to take money from their savings account to cover the bounced checks she had written, but she didn't tell Tom. In turn, Tom decided he would dip into their savings to bail himself out of all his overdraft fees but didn't know Shannon had already used all their savings to cover her problems. Because they didn't keep track of how they were both spending money, Tom and Shannon had not only overdrawn their checking account, but had devoured all their savings as well.

As we mentioned in the introduction, many Americans today are avidly pursuing their every want with the expectation that somehow it will be fulfilled. Individuals who had parents that satisfied each childhood desire often grow up expecting that they can continue to have everything they want as adults. Even with the knowledge that the money supply is not endless, some people continue to spend as though their decisions will have no consequence. It is not until a person learns to track his money that he begins to see that all spending decisions have repercussions. Remember the Haywoods who enjoyed frequenting All-a-Dollar? Once they began keeping track of how much they were actually spending at the bargain store, they were shocked to discover they were wasting $300 each month.

Consider this statement by George Clason from the book *The Richest Man in Babylon*:

### *"Learn to live on 90 percent of your income."*

In today's consumer-driven society, is it feasible to spend less than 100 percent of what you earn so that you can have a surplus for the future? It is, even for those who have become accustomed to devouring every penny they earn and living on credit. We have seen countless individuals do it, but they first learned how to track how much money they spent so they could contain that spending where necessary.

Multibillion-dollar sports associations know the value of tracking. The NBA, the NFL, and other organizations keep very close track of each athlete's playing statistics so that when it comes time to trade or negotiate contracts, they will know the value of that player. They also keep track of player statistics and make them known to the public to heighten awareness. This awareness creates interest, which in turn creates profits. A system of tracking is vital to any big corporation that wants to stay in business.

Consider the example of a California-based computer hard disc drive manufacturer that was notorious for not keeping track of its inventory. The company constantly had problems filling orders and usually took an average of three weeks to find parts in order to ship products to its customers. The company's distributor got tired of waiting such long periods and went to a competing supplier. The business lost $12,000 and the distributor never came back. How big was this company's actual loss? In reality, its damages were much greater than $12,000 because it lost a valuable distributor who took his business to the competition.

And what about the IRS? Collecting taxes is a nasty business and without a system for collecting those funds the government knows it wouldn't stand a chance. That's why taxes are taken directly out of payroll so that no one cheats the system. Without your own system for tracking your finances, you could be cheating yourself out of valuable money or be cheated by others.

"But," you may find yourself saying, "I really detest keeping track of the way I spend my money. It seems so tedious!" We have found over the years that most people want to get on the road to financial control but initially hate being "restricted" when it comes to tracking money, so they play emotional games with themselves.

Have you ever played any of the following games with yourself?

**Game #1: Avoid balancing your checkbook monthly.** Many of our clients have expressed to us that they simply don't want to know how far out of control they are or how bad things have actually become. Fear and guilt are often the reasons for this stubbornness. In fact, one of our clients was so overwhelmed by the thought of balancing her checkbook that she simply opened a new account every six months.

**Game #2: Blame employers or others, and/or think you are not making enough income.** Many people trick themselves into thinking that their overspending and debt load should be blamed on their jobs and/or their employers. These people convince themselves that true financial happiness can only be found in a larger salary. They assure themselves that pastures are greener elsewhere, and incur further expenses when they change jobs, uproot their families, and move across the country.

*Remember, it matters not how much you make,*
*only how well you manage money that counts.*

Even major league athletes who have not yet learned to track their spending think they don't make enough to support themselves. The Associated

Press, reporting on the National Basketball Association's 1998 labor strike, quoted Jazz player Greg Foster as saying, "It hurts missing a paycheck—especially for a guy like me," who was scheduled to make more than $500,000 in 1998. After missing close to 30 games due to the strike, Foster and other NBA players felt they just couldn't make ends meet. "I mean, I'm not Patrick Ewing or one of those guys who gets the big bucks. I need every penny."[1]

 **Game #3: Claim that you never dreamed anything could go wrong when emergencies hit.** This is the ultimate gaming strategy, which transfers every bit of personal responsibility onto a "natural disaster" that you couldn't possibly foresee. We counsel with hundreds of clients who have no idea where the money goes each month and yet cannot see the correlation between this lack of tracking and the total devastation that a basic emergency can bring to their family. One of our clients mysteriously lost her hard contact lenses, which would have cost her approximately $350 to replace. However, because she did not want to feel restricted, she had not tracked her money and therefore could not find the extra funds to purchase new lenses. This small amount of money put her into a state of total financial and emotional panic.

At the outset, tracking your money and how it's spent may appear tedious and restrictive. But we know from years of helping people gain control of their finances that it's actually wonderfully rewarding. Let's meet a couple who learned those rewards:

# Stan and Arlene Harbrecht: "We're Already Tight. We Won't Find Any More Money!"

Case History

Stan and Arlene Harbrecht* were from Tennessee. Stan was a truck driver, making a modest income of about $24,000 a year. Arlene was a schoolteacher. The Harbrechts had a daughter in college who was in real need of money but Stan was concerned because he just didn't feel they had anything to send her. The daughter's housing had come due and they needed an additional $110 a month to cover this expense. The Harbrechts had come to Money Mastery for some basic coaching but Stan was only mildly interested and as their coach explained Principle 2, Stan said "I know how tight we are with our money. I can't believe that you think tracking our spending is going to help us find extra cash. That's bologna!"

Their coach promised the Harbrechts that they would be able to find the extra money they needed and then told them that on average, Money Mastery clients find 1 percent of their annual income each month that they are wasting on unneeded items. That means that a person making $30,000 annually will easily find $300 per month extra if they will learn to track their expenditures. Because Stan was making $24,000 a year, his coaches knew he could easily find the $110 he needed for his daughter.

Stan and Arlene agreed to give it a try and his coach committed Stan specifically to this challenge. She asked him to send her a copy of his expenses once a month so she could review his progress. Stan sent in his first month's spending but it was only partially filled out, so his coach challenged him on it. "I just think this is really boring and time-consuming, and frankly, I don't want to do it," said Stan. The coach then reminded him of his need to come up with an additional $110 for his daughter's college expenses and Stan reaffirmed that he desperately wanted to keep her in college. His coach promised him again that if he would keep track of his spending faithfully, that he would find the money he needed. At this point he replied, "Well, what if I don't find the money?" The coach promised the Harbrechts that if by tracking their expenses they couldn't find an additional $110 in wasted money, that Money Mastery would make up the difference. Surprised, Stan said, "You've got a deal!"

Once Stan had given the coach his full attention, she explained to him again that he would have to keep track of his spending very carefully every day. He agreed. It was only two days later when Stan called the Money Mastery offices. He was excited about a discovery he had made. He had pulled into a 7-11 store for his daily visit to buy a Big Gulp and some snacks while he talked with other truckers. He paid $.84 for his 32-ounce drink and as he had promised, recorded the expense. He had been keeping track all day of his spending and when he totaled his expenditures they came to $11. Stan quickly realized that it was $11 of miscellaneous money that he didn't need to spend. He was clearly shocked at the amount and realized that he had been spending that kind of needless money for years. He said "I can tell you right now, I know I am going to find that extra money I need for my daughter." As he meticulously kept track of his spending, the Harbrechts found that Stan had spent $78 that month just on Big Gulps alone. As he proceeded over the next two months to carefully track his money, he found well more than $180 a month that was being wasted on Big Gulps, Twinkies, and other junk food. Containing this unnecessary spending kept the Harbrecht's daughter in school.

• • •

Many people are like Stan Harbrecht, objecting to a system of tracking. What are your reasons for resistance?

## Tracking Takes Too Much Time

Over the years, we have found that in the absence of a system of tracking, people end up quadrupling the amount of time spent on taking care of finances! According to Douglas LaBier in his book, *Modern Madness*, the focus on money at the expense of personal fulfillment drove 60 percent of his study subjects to suffer from depression, anxiety, and other job-related problems.[2]

Our experience shows that when you have a system of tracking, you will spend one-fifth of the time you're used to spending worrying about personal finances.

We have also found that when people don't keep track of their money they think they are actually saving time. "I don't want to waste the time on all that, I trust the bank, and I think I have a pretty good feel for what I spend anyway so I don't feel it's necessary."

Meet Tony and Angie*, a couple who didn't think tracking was necessary until they were introduced to Principle 2. While examining their financial records they found that they had paid $1,850 in bounced check charges during the previous year. Big shock! It made them both sick. They thought they had bounced a "few" checks, but had no idea they had both been so careless with their money. When they took the time to track their money, they became immediately aware of how their reckless spending was costing them thousands of dollars in annual bank fees. With this new emotional awareness they were motivated to make changes by spending cash only. Today Tony and Angie are easily saving $900 per month.

With a good system, tracking your spending can actually take as little as seven seconds for each transaction. If you compared how much you are paid on an hourly basis against that seven seconds of time, you might find that tracking your spending will actually be the *most money* you have ever paid yourself in the *shortest* amount of time because of all the things you will discover about your spending habits, your emotional needs, and your actual monetary losses.

When you take the time to track your money, those monetary losses may become so appalling that you will be compelled to make some serious changes. For instance, some families after taking a close look at their financial situations, have begun to realize that having both spouses work outside the home is actually costing the family money because taxation contributes to the loss of most of the income of a two-income household.

This is illustrated in Jane Bryant Quinn's *Woman's Day* article, "How to Live on One Salary."[3] Quinn noted that the husband of the family in the article was earning $40,000 per year, and his wife, Lori* wasn't working.

Every month the family was short on funds so this prompted Lori to get an administrative job for $15,000 per year. When Quinn examined the economics of getting this extra income for the family, the results were startling!

Lori had to pay federal and state taxes on her new income. Because they filed jointly, the family's combined income was what established their tax bracket. She paid $4,500 in new taxes, most of which was non-deductible for federal and state income tax. Lori had Social Security withheld from her paycheck at the rate of 7.65 percent, which amounted to an additional non-deductible amount of $1,148 being extracted from her salary. She also has to commute to work 10 miles round trip, resulting in non-deductible commuting costs (in 1995) of $696 per year.

Lori also had child-care expenses, which gave a partial tax credit, but Quinn figured that the amount spent over the tax credit was $4,250 per year. Lori also ate out each day with colleagues, spending an average of $5 per day, five days a week. This resulted in a non-deductible expense of $1,250 a year. Now that Lori had a job, she had to have better clothing and purchase more dry cleaning. Quinn assumed that Lori's increased expenses here were an extra $1,000 per year, non-deductible, of course. Finally, with both spouses working, Lori wasn't in the mood to cook. Thus, there were more convenience foods and more eating out. This resulted in increased food costs of a non-deductible minimum of $1,000 per year.

Add it all up and Lori's take-home pay was a paltry $1,156 a year, for which she had to put up with the commute and a boss and the corporate hassles. Her children also suffered by spending the majority of their day without either one of their parents. Families who begin to track often find that working for that extra money doesn't always bring desired results, especially in the face of today's tax laws. Without taking a close look at what really happens to our money once we earn it, we may be causing our families more harm than good.

What are some other things that happen when we don't take the time to track? When people are overdraft in a checking account, for example, or when tax day rolls around, or when it's time to take a vacation, they realize they don't have the money to do what's necessary and talk themselves into fixing the problem later. In the meantime, they use credit cards to bail themselves out, compounding the problem and certainly adding to the time it will take to actually resolve the problem. As we have already stated, the amount of time it takes to track your spending is minimal and brings great rewards. Make the time to do it today! Learn the secrets behind your own emotional spending by taking that challenge.

*Tracking your money creates awareness, which helps lead you*
*to the emotional reason you spend money in the first place.*

## Tracking My Money Takes the Joy Out of Spending

We hear many people object to tracking because they feel it makes them a slave to their money, taking the spontaneity out of buying something. This "month-to-month" mentality, although very easygoing now, leads to lots of stress later when there's no money for retirement, children's college educations, or vacations. A spend-now-worry-later attitude has forced many older Americans back into the workplace after retirement. In an article by Tony Pugh of the *Mercury News*, a study by the Consumer Foundation of America and Primerica found that "one-quarter of Americans believe their best chance to build wealth for retirement is by playing the lottery, not by patiently saving and investing."[4] Decide today that tracking, rather than taking the joy out of spending, will lead to long-term happiness.

## I'm Already Tight With My Money—
## Tracking It Isn't Going to Help Me Find Anything Else

Many people are already living frugally, trying to make ends meet by not buying expensive cars or going on fancy vacations; they may even avoid eating out and buying themselves the latest clothes. But just like Stan Harbrecht, they are probably wasting more money than they know. That's because most people usually only keep track of the big expenses. Without a system for tracking all of your money, all of the time, you may not have as good a feel for what's going on with your finances as you think. Big Gulps add up, even if they only cost $.84 each.

A good system of tracking is like a rudder on a boat. It helps steer you in the direction you want to go, not in the direction that mindless spending will take you. A good system of tracking helps you predict the outcome and eliminates the "spend as you go" and "live month-to-month" attitudes that make it impossible to understand the time/value of money and that stamp out the wonderful possibility of future financial freedom. We cannot emphasize enough the power that tracking your spending will bring into your life.

*Keeping track of your money builds a powerful level of awareness*
*that leads to emotional control.*

Adopting a system, any system of complete and total tracking, will bring huge rewards, both financially and emotionally. Learn to love keeping track of your money. We want to help by giving a challenge and making you aware of some of the tools that can help you set up a system of complete and total tracking.

## Challenge #2

# Track All Your Expenditures

**Forecast your spending by creating a spending planner worksheet.** One of the most important ways to get control of your money is to forecast your spending. To help you get started, we have included Money Mastery's Spending Planner Worksheet as an example. (For information on how to obtain the Money Mastery Worksheet and other tracking tools, please refer to Appendix A.) We use this worksheet to help our clients see how they have spent their money over the previous 12 months, and then use it to help them forecast their spending on paper. On page 45 is a worksheet for Mark and Joyce, the couple we profiled in the Introduction.

**Step 1:** Write in your gross monthly income, then subtract from that how much you pay in Social Security tax, federal income tax, and state tax. What's left is your net spendable monthly income. This is the amount of money that you fully control. As shown on Mark and Joyce's worksheet, they have a total of $3,053 they can spend each month.

**Step 2:** Create categories for spending such as groceries, car payments, entertainment, and so on. To do so, we recommend reviewing your last 12 months of expenses to determine these categories and how much you have spent in the past. A good way to do this is to review all your credit-card statements, bank statements, check registers, canceled checks, and receipts. Doing this will be a very eye-opening experience and you might find yourself asking, "Why did I do that? That was a waste of cash." This process will be an emotional experience that we can assure you will alter your future spending decisions. It will also teach you how to reprioritize your spending so that you can stop the waste.

**Step 3:** Once you have determined how you have spent money over the last 12 months, total the expenses for each category, and then divide each by 12. This will give you the average amount of money you have spent per month in each category. With these averages in place, you can now use them to estimate what will be needed in each category for the next 12 months. You may decide that you spent way too much money on eating out last year and will cut the amount you will allow in this category for the next 12 months.

**Step 4:** Once you have figured the amount of money you want or need to spend in each category for the next 12 months, total those figures. Compare this total with your net spendable monthly income. These two figures must match as shown in the example for Mark and Joyce where their total monthly income figure of $3,139 matches with the total amount of money they spend in each category per month. If you find that your monthly expenses exceed your total spendable monthly income, then you are overspending and will need to adjust things. Remember, tracking has two purposes:

1.  to help you see exactly how and where you spend money, and
2.  to help you see if you are spending more money than you actually bring home.

**Track all your income and expenditures for one week, including cash.** This includes every cup of coffee, every package of gum, and every can of soda. To do so, we recommend using a check register to write down all expenses, even those things you purchased for which you did not write a check. (Money Mastery Spending Booklets allow you to record, by category, each expense; refer to Appendix A for information on how to obtain the booklets.)

• • •

Plan to be shocked by how this exercise makes you feel. You may even find like Stan Harbrecht, that you are wasting more money than you ever thought possible. Don't wait any longer to become more aware of what's really going on in your financial life. Get started today!

# Mark & Joyce
## Spending Planner

**A. SPENDABLE MONTHLY INCOME:**

| | Current | Projected |
|---|---|---|
| Gross Monthly Income | 3,550 | 3,650 |
| Less Taxes (Income & FICA) | 497 | 511 |
| Total Spendable Monthly Income | 3,053 | 3,139 |

**B. SPENDING CATEGORY EXPENSES:**

| Spending Category | Last 12 Months Totals | Last 12 Mo. Avg Per Mo. | Next 12 Mo. Avg Per Mo. | Fixed Expense | Variable Expense | Amount to Spend | His $ | Her $ |
|---|---|---|---|---|---|---|---|---|
| Auto - Gas & Repair | 1,500 | 125 | 130 | 0 | 130 | 130 | 70 | 60 |
| Charitable Contributions | 600 | 50 | 50 | 0 | 50 | 50 | 0 | 50 |
| Cleaning & Laundry | 144 | 12 | 12 | 0 | 12 | 12 | 0 | 12 |
| Clothing | 1,320 | 110 | 110 | 0 | 110 | 110 | 30 | 80 |
| Debt Payment | 20,880 | 1,740 | 1,740 | 1,740 | 0 | 1,740 | 1,685 | 55 |
| Eating Out | 480 | 40 | 40 | 0 | 40 | 40 | 20 | 20 |
| Family Activities | 300 | 25 | 25 | 0 | 25 | 25 | 0 | 25 |
| Gifts | 420 | 35 | 35 | 0 | 35 | 35 | 0 | 35 |
| Groceries | 4,800 | 400 | 400 | 0 | 400 | 400 | 0 | 400 |
| Home Maintenance | 300 | 25 | 25 | 0 | 25 | 25 | 25 | 0 |
| Insurance | 1,140 | 95 | 95 | 95 | 0 | 95 | 95 | 0 |
| Medical, Dental | 300 | 25 | 25 | 0 | 25 | 25 | 25 | 0 |
| Miscellaneous | 300 | 25 | 25 | 0 | 25 | 25 | 10 | 15 |
| Property Tax - Car, Home | 600 | 50 | 50 | 50 | 0 | 50 | 50 | 0 |
| Recreation/Entertainment | 600 | 50 | 50 | 0 | 50 | 50 | 25 | 25 |
| Savings | 960 | 80 | 150 | 0 | 150 | 150 | 150 | 0 |
| Utilities | 1,392 | 116 | 127 | 0 | 127 | 127 | 127 | 0 |
| Vacations, Trips | 600 | 50 | 50 | 0 | 50 | 50 | 0 | 50 |
| **Total Expenses** | 36,636 | 3,053 | 3,139 | 1,885 | 1,254 | 3,139 | 2,312 | 827 |

# Chapter 3

# No Such Thing
# As "Savings"

**A**wareness. It's a powerful tool against foolish behavior and by taking our challenge in Chapter 2 you may have discovered, like Stan and Arlene Harbrecht, that perhaps you have been wasting money on unneeded items. Did you spot any spending patterns of which you were not aware? Were you shocked by some of the things you learned about yourself and the way you treat money? Tracking spending is always a very emotional experience because it makes us immediately aware. We have found over the years that as people become more aware of the way they spend money, they will change the way they think about money. Changing the way you think and spend is the next step to financial happiness and the secret behind the third Money Mastery principle:

 ## Principle #3: Saving is actually delayed spending.

What does this mean exactly? At Money Mastery we teach that there is actually no such thing as "savings" and that all money is to be spent—what matters most is when and how you spend it. Allocating money to savings is actually "spending" money by putting it aside to use at a later date for necessary needs and wants. Because your money is going to be entirely used up at some point, it is important to understand the concept of "delayed spending" so that you can be sure all of it will be spent in a way that will bring you and your loved ones the most satisfaction and happiness.

You can begin to look at savings as delayed spending by tracking your money as we have already encouraged you to do. This will get your spending under control, which in turn will lead you to find more money. This is good. But it is not the end result! Now your focus must be turned to the future and what you are going to do with the newfound money. Usually what people do once they see that controlling spending brings in a surplus of funds is to consume that extra money the minute they get it. This is wrong! What they should do is put this money away for "future spending" so it will be available later when it is needed. Unfortunately, most people do not understand the importance of this concept. Instead, they are seduced into believing the notion perpetuated by a consumer-oriented society that they can have everything they want right now *and* everything they need and want later. The actual truth is that if we want to spend all our money on consumable goods and high-interest credit card purchases, then we cannot assume we will have much of anything we will want in the future, including a financially secure retirement. At some point we all have to make a choice: We can either prioritize the way we spend our money so that we will be prepared for the future or we can recklessly spend every extra penny and have nothing for the future. Bear in mind:

> ***You can have* anything *you want,***
> ***you just can't have* everything *you want.***

People who understand this concept know how to prioritize their money so that they will be able to have the things they want and need right now, as well as what they will need and want in the future. This often requires them to sacrifice in one area of spending so that they can have what is necessary in another area. For example, a man may feel that taking his wife and children out to eat twice a week is an important family activity. It's perfectly fine for this man to use his money this way if he wishes but he must also realize that he may have to cut down on groceries, entertainment, or other items if he wants to have extra money available to spend on eating out and for the future.

Perhaps eating out isn't as important to you as buying a new outfit every month. Naturally, the choice is up to you. However, the key is that you must make a choice because it's impossible to have everything. As simple as this might sound, we are amazed by the number of people who somehow believe that they can buy a new outfit every month, for example, and eat out as well when they have no way of paying for both. This kind of behavior not only keeps people in a cycle of perpetual overspending, but it also eliminates all possibility of seeing money grow in *value* over *time*.

Now is the time for you to decide what is important and what is not, and then spend money according to those desires and not according to the notion that you don't have to make a choice at all. To help you make those decisions, we asked you in Chapter 2 to create spending categories for such things as groceries, entertainment, and house payments. With these spending categories in place, you can see exactly where you spend money, what your priorities are, and what you truly value. To have the things you want right now (like the new outfit), and still be able to have what you need in the future (comfortable retirement), you may have to prioritize your spending by cutting down in some categories. Doing so will help you use your money more wisely, which in turn will lead you to find surplus funds. The next step is to prioritize the spending of these surplus funds by creating additional categories that will be used for "delayed" or "future" spending. Most people call these categories "savings accounts," but these savings categories should be viewed no differently than any other category in which you allocate funds for the month. You must learn to "spend" money for savings just as you would spend money for groceries. Remember:

*Saving is actually "delayed spending."*

To help you learn how to create these "delayed spending" categories, take a look at the pie chart on the right.

Notice that it is divided into three categories: Emergency, Emotional, and Long Term (Investments). Each section of the chart represents a percentage of money that you should be "spending" for emergencies, emotional needs, and long-term retirement. We have learned that at the very

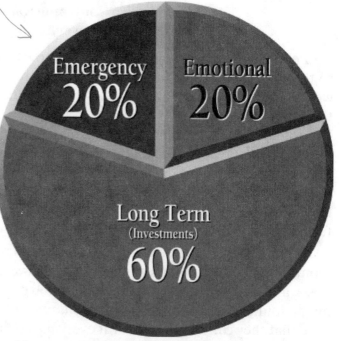

least, a person should save 10 percent of his gross income throughout his life in order to create a money-making machine that will generate the income he will need as he grows older. Even though the ultimate goal is saving at least 10 percent of your monthly income, if you are not already doing that, we suggest beginning with just 1 percent. We have found that anybody can save 1 percent. Some of our clients do not believe this initially, but as they track their money and learn to control it, every single client finds at least 1 percent they are wasting that can be "spent" into saving categories.

For example, if a person makes a gross annual income of $30,000, then saving 1 percent would require finding $25 each month that can be spent into savings. Is it likely that a person will find $25 they have been wasting? Absolutely! We guarantee that if you aren't already saving some percentage of your monthly income, that by tracking your spending you can find at least 1 percent that you've been using unwisely elsewhere. Once you have found that 1 percent, commit a portion of it to the three savings categories we outlined in the pie chart using the 60/20/20 rule: 20 percent for emergencies, 20 percent for emotional needs, and 60 percent for long-term investments.

Following is an example of how to spend that 1 percent using the 60/20/20 rule:

Let's suppose that Hayden and Rose have a combined gross monthly income of $6,000. After tracking their spending, they find an extra $60 a month (or 1 percent of their gross monthly income) that they can use for delayed spending. Using Principle 3, we suggest that Hayden and Rose do the following:

- **Emergency Spending:** Deposit $12 per month (which is 20 percent of $60) into a low-risk fund such as a certificate of deposit, money market account, utility stocks, and so on.
- **Emotional Spending:** Deposit $12 per month (which is 20 percent of $60) into any type of savings or investment account.
- **Long-term Investments:** Deposit $36 per month (which is 60 percent of $60) into any long-term retirement account such as 401(k), Roth IRA, and so on.

As Hayden and Rose see their money grow in each of these savings categories, their confidence will increase and their ability to manage and control their finances will be enhanced. This will help them realize that it is easy to begin saving 2 percent, then 3, and then 10 percent. With time, and as you implement the Money Mastery principles you are learning in this book, it will be totally possible for you to save at least 10 percent every month.

Now that we have established the importance of setting aside a certain percentage of income for future, or "delayed" spending, let's examine the significance of each of the emergency, emotional, and long-term categories.

# Emotional Spending

We have already discussed at length that money is more about emotions than it is about math, so it goes without saying that we will often spend money for purely emotional reasons. This, in and of itself, is not a bad thing. It is simply something we should plan for, especially in today's product-oriented society where we are often enticed to make impulse purchases. We have found over the years in working with our clients that people spend money whether they have it or not. Saving money for emotional spending takes into consideration that there are many times we need to spend money for reasons that go beyond the categories we have assigned for basic daily survival. Tracking your money will help you balance your spending to your income, but it will not be enough when an emotional event occurs. You must put aside even more money into an "emotional spending account" so that you will be prepared when these events arise. Remember, you can have anything you want, you just can't have everything you want—and that means you must learn to prioritize your spending so that you can fulfill your emotional needs without jeopardizing the future.

What are some of the emotional needs for which you should be saving? Typically these include such things as family vacations, holidays, or new recreational vehicles. Some people use their emotional spending money to purchase clothing for a special occasion, to buy novelty decor for their home, or to treat a family member with a surprise gift or getaway. Whatever the money is used for, it is important that it be spent on something fun, and not for routine, daily sustenance. If you are married, emotional money should be spent on your family and not someone outside the household.

Have you ever had these kind of conversations with yourself?

- "I work hard for my money and I owe myself these new clothes!"
- "Why shouldn't I splurge to buy all these beautiful flowers for my garden? It's the one thing that brings me pleasure."
- "I never buy myself anything. I'm always spending money on the kids. I want this new DVD player and I'm getting it now."

Wouldn't it be wonderful if you could meet your emotional needs when these kinds of desires pop up by dipping into your emotional spending account? Wouldn't it make you feel sensational to spend money for these needs when you've actually put it aside expressly for that purpose? Preparing for the need to spend money for purely emotional reasons eliminates reckless spending of the money that has been set aside for daily survival or for long-term investments. It helps curb debt, and it brings wonderful psychological rewards into your life and the lives of your family members. For those who don't overspend but constantly deprive themselves and their family members of those things that would help build lasting family memories and close emotional ties to loved ones, emotional spending can be a lifesaver. It gives these people exhausted by the daily struggle for survival a chance to play, relax, and enjoy themselves a little bit when they would not otherwise feel justified in doing so.

The only time it is not proper to spend money for emotional wants is when you have not planned for them or allocated funds for that purpose. Otherwise, it is totally appropriate to set aside money for the sheer purpose of providing pleasure to you and your family members. Doing so will give you a sense of peace and satisfaction and eliminate the guilt feelings that come from spending money on emotional impulse purchases when you have not planned adequately for them.

Now let's meet a family that learned the value of saving money for emotional needs and see how they were rewarded for their self-discipline.

# Barb and Russell Bellfrey: Learning How to Spend "Emotional" Money

Case History

Barb and Russell Bellfrey* had been deeply in debt for many years. Even though they were both working full-time jobs, they never had enough money to make ends meet. In addition, their family, which included four children, had never been on a vacation together because the Bellfreys knew they could not afford it. They came to Money Mastery desperate for a way to get their debt under control, but also looking for ways to relieve the emotional strain and put fun back into their family life. As they were taught Principle 3, Russell had a hard time accepting that they would ever be able to find even a little extra money they could put away for emotional needs. With their debt load such as it was, saving even a little money for this purpose seemed impossible to him. But as the Bellfreys began tracking their money, Barb and Russell discovered $100 a month that they had been wasting on unnecessary items that they could now spend into their emergency, emotional, and long-term categories. Barb began putting away 20 percent of that $100 (or $20 a month) into an emotional spending account. With time, as they got their spending and debt even more under control, the Bellfreys began depositing $60 a month into their emotional account. Little by little, the cash began to build up and Barb and Russell started to get pretty excited with the results. They finally reached a point where they could do something for the family of which they had always dreamed. Their plan was to fly to California, rent a house on the beach, and do nothing but play in the sand and sun for a whole week.

Barb and Russell decided to secretly prepare for the trip without their children's knowledge. They packed each child's suitcase and hid the bags in the trunk of their car. They then told their children that they were going to the airport to pick up an aunt who visited them regularly. When they arrived at the airport, instead of parking the car they pulled up to the unloading zone and the children began to ask questions. Barb and Russell then told their kids they were all going on a vacation by the sea to spend a full week body surfing and playing in the sand. The children couldn't believe it. So Barb reached for one of her girls' suitcases and pulled out the child's clothes. "Are these your clothes?" she teased. Her little daughter said yes. Barb then handed the suitcase over to the sky cap and led the children onto the plane. The family spent a wonderful week on the beach and have since spent other wonderful vacations together because they learned how to save money each month for family outings. The pictures and memories they have of these activities have strengthened their family over the years. All of this was possible because the Bellfrey's realized the importance of emotional spending and prepared for it.

$$\bullet \ \bullet \ \bullet$$

Learn how and when to spend emotionally because the need to use money for reasons other than for daily survival is certain to occur.

## Emergency Spending

Emergencies come at us in so many ways. We might experience illness, accidents, job layoffs, technological changes, bad investments, divorce, increased taxes, inflation, and even death. You've probably experienced at least one of these economic hardships over the course of your life. The key to dealing with these problems is to be prepared with money to meet these emergencies when they arise. When we don't plan for emergencies, we get blind-sided by them and that's where the real stress begins! It isn't enough then to simply balance your spending to your income, which will naturally occur when you track your money. You must also learn to balance your spending *and* provide even more money for these surprises just as you must for emotional needs.

Case History

# Joseph and Gentry Meckling: Living on the Edge

The Mecklings* were a family that liked to play. Joseph Meckling made a good living and had been used to giving his wife and children expensive gifts. The Mecklings felt fairly secure with their current lifestyle because they had all the necessary life and medical insurance, paid their taxes on time, and kept up with their mortgage. However, they spent all the surplus money that came into the household on watercrafts and extra cars. Joseph also liked to take his wife, Gentry, on exotic vacations every year, even though they would usually go into further debt for at least four months to pay for the trips. The Mecklings felt like they had life pretty much under control, despite their extravagant tastes, until Gentry became ill with cancer. Within two months, her medical expenses had exceeded $30,000. Even though the Meckling's out-of-pocket expense for Gentry's initial surgery and subsequent treatments was only $3,000, it actually blew them apart financially. This was because the family was not aware of their real financial situation and had been living closer to the edge than they thought, just barely making ends meet but not realizing it.

"All I could think of was how I was going to come up with $3,000," said Joseph. "These medical bills were so totally unexpected...I mean how could we have known anything like this would happen to us? We felt like we were living life pretty much like everyone else around us. All our neighbors were doing the same things. I couldn't really see how we could have prepared for anything like this."

Although Gentry's prognosis was very good, and most of her medical treatment had been completed, the family was totally stressed out. At a time when Gentry needed to be concentrating on getting well, she and Joseph were actually considering bankruptcy because they had not saved even $3,000 to cover the medical costs she had incurred over the previous four months. What's more, it had not occurred to the family that they could resolve their financial concerns immediately if they were to sell one of their two motor boats.

• • •

There's no doubt that Joseph and Gentry found it easy to spend money. Their problem was that they had not "spent" that money in the right place, allocating some of it for emergency needs. As we mentioned in Chapter 2, claiming that you never dreamed anything could go wrong is the ultimate game people play with themselves to avoid taking responsibility when emergencies occur.

Financially secure individuals understand the power of preparing for emergency situations by living within their means and putting money away for a rainy day. In Tony Cook's article "Secrets from 'The Millionaire Next Door,'" which appeared in *Money* magazine and *The Reader's Digest*, Cook reports on the best-selling book *The Millionaire Next Door* by Thomas J. Stanley and William D. Danko. Cook notes that in order to learn what today's millionaires have in common and how they accumulated wealth, Stanley and Danko sent questionnaires to affluent Americans. They found that "about two-thirds of those millionaires aren't trust-fund babies; eight out of 10 accumulated their riches themselves. Most are extremely frugal. Although their average net worth is $3.7 million, they generally live so modestly that even their neighbors don't have a clue about their wealth."[1]

Unlike these millionaires, the Mecklings certainly weren't living frugally and were very intent on maintaining the same lifestyle as their neighbors. So when things went wrong, the family was devastated. The Mecklings made $72,000 a year, which means that after 40 years of work, $2.4 million will have passed through their hands. With that in mind, we have to ask why $3,000 should hurt so much. If they had actually declared bankruptcy, they would have cheated their creditors simply because they wanted extra boats, jet skis, and other toys. Would declaring bankruptcy be fair in this case? Would it be honest?

In order to be prepared for emergency needs, it is advisable to accumulate at least three months of spendable income, and ideally to save one year's worth of net earnings. As we have already stated, the best way to do this is to commit 20 percent of your savings to this emergency category.

# Long-Term Spending (or Investing in Your Future)

Another event that is sure to happen in most of our lives is that we will get old. Our bodies will begin to wear out and our ability to work and earn money will slowly diminish. We will need money in the future in order to be prepared for this event. The solution to this problem, as we have noted about emergency and emotional spending, is not just to balance our spending to our income today but to set aside more money in order to have what we will need as we get older.

One of the ways to provide ourselves with this extra money is to do as George Clason in *The Richest Man in Babylon* admonishes:

### *"Learn to live on 90 percent of your income."*

The best way to live on 90 percent is to track your money, as we have already advised. Once you get your spending under control through tracking you will find that you have more money to "spend" into a long-term savings program.

Unfortunately, what we often find is that many of our young clients do not really think that living on 90 percent of their income is even necessary, especially when they can't envision old age ever happening to them.

Many younger Americans survive from day to day knowing they do not have enough money for the future but are still not seeing the urgency of doing anything about it. Instead of fearing what the future might hold, they are more fearful of the present—they worry unceasingly that they will not be able to have the latest technology gadget or the most expensive car. Our society is so caught up with its present-day consumption that it refuses to see the danger lurking in the future. We have seen many people refuse to make change because to them, nothing matters but "right now." With that kind of attitude it should not be surprising that national statistics predict that by the year 2015, 77 million Americans will be over the age of 50,[2] and only about one-third of those people will be financially secure enough to retire.[3] That may be because like many young people today, the Baby Boomer generation has lived by the "spend as you go" philosophy and has taught it to their children.

Consequently, very few are prepared for retirement when it hits them because they believed in the false notion propagated by media hype that they could have everything they wanted in their younger years and would still be able to retire comfortably. Most of these people do not want to face the fact that they are getting older and that Social Security income will not be enough, if it is available at all. In a world that screams at us that we deserve to have everything, living on 90 percent and saving 10 percent is totally inconceivable.

This attitude is illustrated in a recent *USA Today* article that reported that Americans have been spending more than they've earned, resulting in the first negative personal-savings rate since the Great Depression. The report went on to say that "although Wall Street [boomed] during the 1990s, economic statistics suggest that only a small slice of society has benefited from the run-up in stock prices. According to a study by New York University economist Edward Wolff, the average net worth of the richest 1 percent of families was $9.7 million in 1997, while the bottom 40 percent averaged just $3,000."[4]

Bill & Betty Wright* were some of the first wave of Baby Boomers to reach retirement age, but they had not worried about putting money away for the future when they were younger. Suddenly it seemed, at age 55, neither one of them was prepared for what was ahead of them. In relatively poor health, the couple lived on a combined disability income and only had $30,000 in the bank. The Wrights came to Money Mastery in fear of the future, realizing they barely had enough money to pay rent on their modest apartment in a Southern California suburb. The Wrights were taught to track their spending, and as they did, determined that the best way to save money would be to manage an apartment complex where they could earn free rent. This arrangement did wonders for their self-esteem and made it possible for them to meet their future financial challenges with confidence. However, the Wrights could have had even more financial freedom, allowing them to travel and retire in comfort, if they had taken more seriously the need to plan for the future when they still had the time during their younger years.

No matter how old or young you are at this moment, spending money into a long-term investment program is extremely important. Doing so will eliminate the fear and dread of getting older and will help you feel confident and more empowered. Because you will need more money for this spending category than either of the other two, it is important to allocate at least 60 percent of available savings funds into this category.

# Finding Money to Save

Although the arguments are sound for saving emotional, emergency, and long-term funds, some people still resist "spending" into these categories because they labor under the idea that the only people who can save money are those with lots of extra cash. They often think, "I can't possibly put any money away when I struggle just to pay the bills!" Are you one of these people? If so, we encourage you to change your way of thinking. Within *The Richest Man in Babylon*, George Clason teaches a wonderful way to begin that change by making the following part of your thought process:

*"A part of all you earn is yours to keep."*

Think of that statement often. Turn it over in your head until you can begin to believe it. It is false to assume that just because you have a lot of financial obligations that others are entitled to every penny of your income. If you feel like you can't find even one additional penny to "spend" into any of these savings categories, don't give up. There is hope! As you track your money, as we have already affirmed, you *will* find at least 1 percent of your income that you can begin saving. Remember the Harbrechts in Chapter 2? They didn't think they could find even one additional penny, but through tracking realized they were wasting as much as $180 per month on junk food! By keeping track of your spending, you will easily find an extra 1 percent per month that you could be setting aside for "delayed spending." We guarantee it and challenge you to begin looking for that money today if you haven't already found it.

If you are a person that has become infected with the disease of consumerism, believing that you are entitled to have everything you want whenever you want it, it may be a bit difficult at first for you to find that 1 percent. You may still be spending more than 100 percent of your net income, making it next to impossible to keep a part of what you earn because you are forced to give up that money in compound debt interest. But don't give up.

It doesn't matter at first that you may be only saving 1 percent. What is important is that you start the process. And as you follow the principles set forth in subsequent chapters of this book, you will learn how to find even more money that you can save.

To help you get on that road, we invite you to take the following challenge.

## Challenge #3

# Find 1 Percent of Your Income to Allocate to the Three Savings Categories

1.  Carefully review how you have tracked your money; be sure to look at all of your spending categories.

2.  Determine, based on your monthly income, the amount of money you will need to equal 1 percent, then deposit 20 percent (of that 1 percent) to an emergency fund and 20 percent to an emotional fund. Sixty percent should be set aside every month (regardless of how small it may be right now) to eventually invest in a high-yielding certificate of deposit, a tax-free municipal bond, an IRA account, or other long-term saving program.

3.  If possible, set up a system for having funds automatically transferred from your checking account into these three separate savings accounts (but be sure the bank doesn't charge for this service).

As you begin this challenge, we hope you will find encouragement in the following statement by A.F. Bannerman:

> *"Your savings, believe it or not, affect the way you stand, the way you walk, the tone of your voice—in short, your physical well-being and self-confidence. A man without savings is always running. He must take the first job offered. He sits nervously on life's chairs because any small emergency throws him into the hands of others.*

> *"Without savings, a man is often fearful of the present and the future. Being in a constant state of fear is a horrible place in which to live. A man with savings can walk tall. He may appraise opportunities in a relaxed way, have time for judicious estimates and intelligent decisions. He need not be rushed by life's problems or economic necessity.*

*"A man with savings can afford to resign from his work, if his principles so dictate. A man who can afford to change his work is much more valuable. He can afford to give his company the benefits of his most candid judgments.*

*"A man always concerned about the immediate necessities, such as food, rent, school, and medical needs, cannot afford to think in long-range career goals.*

*"A man with savings can afford the wonderful privilege of being generous in family or other emergencies. Emergencies become opportunities for service; they help shape personality and develop character.*

*"Schools do not teach thrift. Schools do not teach work habits. However, a man with savings can teach his children by example how to have a more successful and worry-free life.*

*"The ability to save has nothing to do with the size of a man's income. Many high-income people spend it all, and are forever on a treadmill, always working—never able to rest. Many years ago, the dean of American bankers, J. P. Morgan, advised a young broker, 'Take waste out of your spending, and you'll drive the haste out of your life.'*

*"If you don't need money for college, a home, or retirement, then save for your self-confidence and you can take a level stare from the eyes of any man, whether he be friend or stranger. Start paying yourself regularly, because the state of your savings does have a lot to do with how tall you stand and how relaxed you walk."*

# Chapter 4

# Power Down Your Debt

S tanding taller. It's something we challenged you to do in the last chapter by taking our challenge to apply Principle 3. We're confident that by now your new spending and saving habits are helping you stand quite a bit taller. In Chapter 3, we noted that as people become more aware of the way they spend money through tracking, they are inclined to want to use that money more appropriately by putting it away to be consumed at a later date for emergency, emotional, and retirement needs. As you learn to "spend" part of your money into funds that will cover these needs, rather than using it all on consumable goods, you will be able to stand taller, experiencing a feeling of tremendous freedom and control. Continuing on the road to financial freedom requires that tracking and proper spending be coupled with the next Money Mastery principle:

 ## Principle #4: Power down your debt, and power up your fortune.

It goes without saying that today, both nationally and personally, we are tangled in a trap of debt. As a nation our collective credit-card bill, which was $240 billion in 1990, has now climbed to a whopping $677 billion.[1] And total U.S. household debt now stands at $5.4 trillion.[2] Debt in this country has risen as a percentage of disposable income from 35 percent in 1952 to 100 percent in 1998.[3] That means that as a nation, every penny of our income is going towards debt, leaving nothing to save for the future.

Our product-oriented society most assuredly contributes to all this debt entrapment. Americans have become so accustomed to spending and borrowing that they never question whether a purchase should be made, but only if they can cover the minimum monthly payment, falling victim to what debt counselors call the "minimum-payment" syndrome. This reckless spending has infected the majority of Americans. James Clayton, a history professor and U.S. economics researcher confirms this point in his best-selling book, *The Global Debt Bomb:*

> *Along with the lowest savings rate in the industrial world, the United States has the highest consumption rate. To illustrate, in 1965 the rate of personal consumption as a percentage of net national product was 68 percent; by 1991 that figure had risen to 77 percent. This substantial increase comes at the expense of everything else...As Peter Peterson, who was secretary of commerce during the 1970s has long argued, this strong desire to consume is part of our policy of growth maximization and entitlement mentality....Our rapidly expanding entitlements are a derivative of this larger desire to consume [and] debt is the vehicle by which greater consumption is made possible.[4]*

If it weren't for easy credit and the widespread acceptance of debt (once broadly shunned as an immoral and shameful method of acquiring goods), Americans would not be infected so seriously with the disease of consumerism. Debt helps makes the entitlement and material acquisition possible on a scale in the United States that has never before been seen in any country or at any other time in the history of the world. Savvy media moguls know how easily available credit has become, counting on it as a means to further seduce Americans into purchasing more goods and services through emotional advertising messages. Not only do those who are sick with the disease of consumerism listen to these messages and make purchases they cannot afford, but they further compound the problem by going into debt for them, adding an interest payment on top of the expense. This triples the amount of money they should actually be paying for an item. Is it any wonder that the majority of Americans cannot keep most of the money they make? In the United States, consumer spending has risen twice as fast as income, and individuals have been withdrawing more money than they put into savings for the first time since the 1930s.[5]

In addition to consumerism, a prosperous and seemingly strong economy during the 1990s added to the notion that high levels of personal debt are acceptable. A somewhat artificial euphoria has floated over the United States for years because of a 10-year economic boom, a boom that dampened the stigma of borrowing on credit and contributed to a sense of "entitlement" that many people possessed during that decade. Most Americans didn't worry about getting into debt, believing that it wouldn't really hurt them because they could not imagine an economic downturn. But history proves otherwise: Where there is a boom, there will always be a bust that will follow it. James Clayton notes that the euphoria surrounding Americans has given them a false sense of well-being and he warns that being in debt without fear of economic risk is a very dangerous place to be:

> The message conveyed. . .by Congress is that Americans no longer need to worry about rising public indebtedness—that a growing economy and a continually rising stock market will solve the debt problem that has plagued the nation for several generations. This euphoric outlook is even more evident regarding the rising private-sector debt. Private-sector debt in the United States in 1999 was about 130 percent of the gross domestic product (GDP), the highest level on record. Equity prices, which have risen faster in the U.S. than in any other major nation since 1990, are often used to justify this level of private indebtedness and unprecedented optimism. A rapidly rising stock market is thought to have increased the net worth of corporations and households, thus justifying historically high levels of debt. This stock-inflated net worth is also used to justify a zero household savings rate.[6]

Without fear and respect for money, our current generation is sinking itself into greater debt enslavement by its "gotta-have-it-now" attitude. In 1998, consumer credit as a ratio to after-tax income reached 21 percent in the U.S., the highest on record.[7] The average American now has 11 credit cards, up from seven in 1989. And the number of credit cards in circulation increased 34 percent between 1988 and 1994, the number of transactions increased 55 percent, and the overall value of credit card transactions increased 98 percent.[8] James Clayton, again, makes a very stark observation about this level of debt: "Americans, who invented the shopping mall and the credit card, believe they deserve more than they have. So why shouldn't they continue to prosper even if they do not earn it."[9]

Debt penetrates every part of our lives, with the potential of ruining far more than just our credit ratings; it can break up marriages and destroy future financial happiness. This indebtedness, naturally, is counter to the principles we have already taught about getting spending under control so that you can save for the future. And it eliminates any possibility of preparing for the emotional, emergency, and retirement events we mentioned in the last chapter.

To better see the negative effect that debt and its accompanying compound interest can have, let's review the case of Mark and Joyce, the couple we profiled in the introduction. Take a look at Mark and Joyce's "Real Debt Report," which was created using Money Mastery's Master Plan software:

# Mark & Joyce
## Current Debt

REAL DEBT REPORT
For: Mark & Joyce

| Description | Monthly Payment | Interest Rate | No. of Payments | Remaining Debt | Real Debt |
|---|---|---|---|---|---|
| VISA | 55.00 | 18.000 | 9 | 460.00 | 495.00 |
| Medical/Dental | 215.00 | 12.000 | 12 | 2,420.00 | 2,580.00 |
| AT&T Credit Card | 110.00 | 16.500 | 24 | 2,236.00 | 2,640.00 |
| Auto | 325.00 | 9.500 | 16 | 4,866.00 | 5,200.00 |
| Furniture | 220.00 | 12.000 | 32 | 6,000.00 | 7,040.00 |
| Home | 815.00 | 7.500 | 354 | 116,032.00 | 288,510.00 |
| | 1,740.00 | | | 132,014.00 | 306,465.00 |

*The interest you will pay is: $174,451.00*

From this report, we can see that Mark and Joyce have six debts, totaling $132,000. If they were to pay all six of their debts using a monthly minimum payment, they will pay an additional $174,451 in interest, bringing their actual total to $306,465! That's nearly two and a half times what they borrowed!

Unfortunately, most people don't realize that when the initial loan amount is combined with compound interest, a person can end up paying up to three times the amount they actually borrow! This bears repeating:

*When you accumulate debt, you can end up paying*
*up to three times the amount you actually borrow!*

Credit card companies and other credit issuers thoroughly understand this fact. They know that compound interest is the way to make money. That's why they send out more than 3.54 billion offers for new credit cards each year, even to those with bad credit or to those who have declared bankruptcy. Unless you more fully understand the power that compound interest can have over you, you will fall victim to credit card companies, lending institutions, banks, and other entities that wait with bated breath to put to work for them the compound interest they collect from you.

David and Wendy* are a good example of how compound interest can ruin a family financially. This couple had 18 credit cards and thought nothing of using them to pay for everything, even groceries. When asked how much they owed on their cards, Wendy said quickly, "Around $17,000." But David said, "No, I pay the bills, and it's around $22,000 to $24,000." When we finished adding up all their credit card debt, it was more than $47,000! They were shocked and completely unaware their debt was so high. Their interest expense alone to service these debts was $950 a month! They had to earn $1,450 each month so that after taxes they would have the $950 left just to pay the interest.

## A Systematic Approach to Paying Off Debt

We have painted a fairly bleak picture of the debt problem in the United States, and if you are like the majority of Americans buried under a load of debt, you need to be aware of just how grim your own situation is before you can ever hope to do anything about it. While things may seem overwhelming, there is hope. We can promise that Principle 4 will have the most power to change your situation because it teaches a direct method for getting out from underneath debt. When you learn how to "Power Down" debt, you will be able to eliminate compound interest much more quickly and begin accumulating the money you need for future events.

What does it mean to power down your debt? Powering down is a method of eliminating debt through a systematic approach to paying bills. Through this technique, you prioritize your debt, then work to entirely pay off the first obligation in your prioritized list. Once this debt with the highest priority is paid off, you then apply that debt's payment amount to the next obligation on your list. As you work through your list of debts, paying off each one, you will continue to add the previous debt payment amounts on top of each other, allowing you to more rapidly pay off your loans by gradually increasing the amount available to you to make those payments.

To more fully understand how the power down method works, let's go back to Mark and Joyce. Take a look at their "Get Out of Debt" Report on page 65. This report is Money Mastery's way of showing our clients the benefits of the Power Down method of eliminating debt as quickly as possible.

Mark and Joyce prioritized by putting the debts that can be paid off the quickest at the top of their list. You will notice on the report that the first

# Get Out of Debt Report

GET OUT OF DEBT REPORT
For: Mark & Joyce

| Loan Description | Principal | Regular Payment | Power Payment | Interest Rate | Total No. Payments | Estimated Payoff Date |
|---|---|---|---|---|---|---|
| VISA | 460.00 | 55.00 | 0.00 | 18.00 | 9 | 11/23/99 |
| Medical/Dental | 2,420.00 | 215.00 | 55.00 | 12.00 | 11 | 01/23/00 |
| AT&T Credit Card | 2,236.00 | 110.00 | 270.00 | 16.50 | 14 | 04/23/00 |
| Auto | 4,866.00 | 325.00 | 380.00 | 9.50 | 15 | 05/23/00 |
| Furniture | 6,000.00 | 220.00 | 705.00 | 12.00 | 19 | 09/23/00 |
| Home | 116,032.00 | 815.00 | 925.00 | 7.50 | 103 | 09/23/07 |
| | | 1,740.00 | | | | |

|  | Standard Debt Repayment- 29.5 Years | Accelerated Debt Repayment- 8.7 Years |
|---|---|---|
| Original Debt | 132,014.00 | 132,014.00 |
| Total Payments | 306,465.20 | 180,673.52 |
| Total Interest Paid | 174,451.20 | 48,659.52 |
| Savings Balance | 0.00 | 971,155.06* |

*If you save 1,740 per month for 20.7 years at 7.00%

debt listed is a VISA credit card. They began working to pay off the VISA card by applying a $55 monthly payment. When that was accomplished after nine months, instead of using that $55 they had been paying to VISA on other needs and wants, they began applying it to the second bill of $215. By applying the $55 to the $215 medical/dental payment, they were able to pay off this second debt in 11 months instead of 12. If they continue this process, adding the combined amounts from each of the previous paid-off debts to the next prioritized debt, they will be completely debt-free in 8.7 years instead of the 29 years it would have taken them had they not powered down.

In addition to applying money from one paid-off debt to the next on their list, Mark and Joyce could also apply an "Accelerator Payment" to their debt. For instance, should they find through tracking their spending that they have an additional $158, they could add this $158 on top of each of the accumlated debt payments, decreasing further the time it will take to get completely out of debt. They could also sell an asset and apply the proceeds from the sale toward their debt. Regardless of which of these additional methods for powering down debt that Mark and Joyce choose, applying them will only add to the amount of interest they will save.

*It has been our experience that by using the Power Down method of eliminating debt, you can drop your interest expense to one-third the cost.*

At the end of the 8.7 years, when all of Mark and Joyce's debts are completely paid off, they will continue to take that same amount they have been applying to debt reduction and put it into a savings plan, which will accumulate interest providing them with a very serious nest egg. That savings in interest of $125,792 that they didn't have to pay to creditors can be used to increase their net worth at retirement.

Naturally, in a real-world setting many things can occur financially that are not reflected on the reports we have just discussed. For example, it is unlikely that Mark and Joyce will go 29 years without incurring some other debt. Things such as cars eventually wear out and will need to be replaced, requiring new debt. When this occurs, instead of getting out of debt in 8.7 years, for instance, it may take nine. But using the Power Down method Mark and Joyce can see their debt and potential savings as a snapshot in time and by applying Principle 4 can save an enormous amount of money, even if the plan does change over time.

Now, of course, Mark and Joyce could choose not to power down. Will they be out of debt in 30 years? Yes. But if they power down their debt, they will not only be out of debt 30 years down the road, but they will also have close to $1 million in the bank. Which should they choose? Which would you choose? The answer is obvious. Using the Power Down method, the money you save by not paying interest for years and years can be put to work in the form of compound interest, which over time will make you more money for the future. One of the greatest minds of our time, Albert Einstein, certainly understood the power of compound interest—he looked upon it as the greatest discovery of the 20th century.

*We like to point out that compound interest is also the greatest opportunity of this century!*

That's because it doesn't just work for the bill collector. It can work in your favor as well if you understand how to harness its power.

## But what about the discipline it will take to stop reckless spending and eliminate debt?

Most people are successful at some sort of orderly approach to paying off debt, and are usually vigilant enough to stick to that system until at least one debt is paid off. But minus a full Power Down approach, they might think, "Well, I paid off that debt, now I have extra money I can spend." This is wrong! Without understanding the full impact that interest has, many people lack the discipline it takes to remain committed to debt elimination and are tempted to spend. As we have already noted, that kind of mindset will force them to pay three times the amount they actually borrow. Consider the following statement made in 1938 about the relentless nature of compound interest:

> "Interest never sleeps nor sickens nor dies. Once in debt, interest is your companion every minute of the day and night; you cannot shun it or slip away from it; you cannot dismiss it; it yields neither to entreaties, demands, or orders; and whenever you get in its way or cross its course or fail to meet its demands, it crushes you."

— J. Rueben Clark Jr.

What happens when we let interest expense silently multiply?

**Situation:**
- Amount owed on a credit card is $3,100.
- The card company charges an interest rate of 19.9%.
- Cardholder only pays the minimum monthly payment of $51.43.

**Question #1:** How long will it take to pay off the card?

**Answer:** 39.4 years!

**Question #2:** How much principle will be paid on the above debt in the first year?

**Answer:** $0.29!

**Question #3:** How much interest will be required to pay the card off?

 **Answer:** $21,216.10!

As *Consumer Reports* has admonished, "Remember, cards are designed to keep you in debt forever."[10] And that's exactly what they will do if you do not understand the importance of the Power Down method of eliminating debt.

Now let's meet a couple who were being choked by indebtedness and through the Power Down method, were able to take control of their lives and begin investing in their future.

# Tim and Sherri Collins: Plunging Deeper into Debt

Case History

Tim and Sherri Collins* should have had everything money could buy. Tim was a dentist who had graduated from a top dental school and had been practicing for seven years in California. Sherri had a master's degree with a successful career in interior design. They had been married three years when they came to Money Mastery seeking help in 1996. Although their gross annual income was close to $600,000, they owned no home, had no savings, and didn't feel like they could afford to have the child they so desperately wanted. They were burdened with 26 credit card debts totaling more than $59,000 in real debt, which did not include interest. The Collinses were also in arrears three years in income taxes. To make matters worse, they had used eight credit cards attempting to pay for the back taxes they owed.

Tim had come from a wealthy family who had paid for his dental schooling. As a child, he had never been denied anything he wanted and had never been taught any self-discipline when it came to money. To compound matters, Tim had been single for several years before meeting Sherri, so all the money he made as a dentist he felt he could spend entirely on himself. He also admitted that as a medical professional, he labored under the delusion that he would always have an endless supply of money, much like he had as a child growing up. Once he graduated from dental school, his family felt he was equipped to manage his own financial affairs, leaving Tim to manage money without any skills to do so. In addition, as a person with a passive personality, Tim sometimes let urgent matters slide. Spending to Tim was something he did without thinking, because it felt good and because he had been raised to think that he didn't need to deny himself.

Sherri, on the other hand, was a fastidious, detail-oriented person with a proactive personality who had fallen in love with a man that was already thousands of dollars in debt. In 1996, when the Collinses first came to Money Mastery, Sherri was 36 years old and very concerned about bringing a child into such a financial mess. To compound matters, they were renting an apartment in a desert region of California and their home was constantly plagued by scorpions. The Collinses could not imagine bringing a baby into such a situation, yet they had no way of leaving due to their financial burdens.

"I felt so completely burdened," says Tim. "It was unbelievable to me that we could be making $600,000 a year and still be so completely behind. To me the dollar figures said it all. With that kind of money I didn't feel any urgency to hold back on spending. I kept insisting that the figures should have been enough so I couldn't understand why we were so far behind. With as much education as I had, I had never been taught to consider the emotional side of money. Instead, I just spent without thinking of the consequences."

Finally, at their wits end, Tim and Sherri began tracking their spending and learned just exactly where all the money was going. They also began working with Money Mastery coaches to prioritize their huge list of 26 credit card debts. Using Principle 4, Tim and Sherri were able to apply Power Down payments to their debt load. Using the "Get Out of Debt" Report, the Collinses projected that they would be debt-free in 2.8 years if they used power down techniques as opposed to 15.5 years if they only used a minimum monthly payment plan.

With 15 years of debt ahead of them, should they have chosen not to power down, they would never have been able to get their spending and borrowing under control to the point that they could start a family. Three years later, in 1999, the Collinses had purchased a house and were expecting their first baby. Today, after the birth of their son, the Collinses are well on their way to total financial freedom, having paid down every single credit card and meeting their IRS tax obligations. They are now saving $21,000 a year.

"It was difficult to sort out all our debt issues at first, but we are so thankful for the principles we learned through Money Mastery," says Sherri. "We are so grateful to have been empowered by these principles [which help us make] serious decisions about our financial future. Now we are looking with hope at where we are today, and where we can be tomorrow, and it means so much to us!"

• • •

Fortunately, the Collinses were able to get out of debt and get their lives under control. But let's stop and ask why the Collinses found themselves in such a financial bind in the first place. Because most people don't make $600,000 a year, you might find it hard to believe that they could be in debt to 26 credit card companies. You can probably think of a lot of things you would be able to do with that kind of money. But that's precisely what Tim and Sherri were thinking, too. They mistakenly thought that because they made that much money, there should always be enough regardless of how they spent or borrowed.

As we instruct our clients about Principle 4 and the power it can have in their lives, there are two very important messages we like to emphasize:

1. **The Long-Term Picture:** As you get your spending under control and pay off the first debt in your prioritized list, you must choose to think long-term so you can pay off the next debt. Only you can decide if you want to continue to be in debt or out of debt with a lot more money in the bank. You must learn to think about what kind of long-term emotional impact the choices you make today will have on you tomorrow. Remember:

   *Every dollar paid in interest, is one less dollar*
   *to invest in your own future.*

2. **Opportunity Cost:** Spending money always comes at a cost. If you choose to spend money on more consumable goods rather than toward paying off a debt, you must understand the consequences of that decision because it eliminates opportunities for the future. Remember the time/value of money and that debt decreases our ability to put money to work for us over *time* so that it can have more *value* in the future. As we noted in Chapter 3, it is up to you to make a choice about how your money will be spent. Remember:

   *You can have anything you want, you just can't have everything.*

If you choose not to power down, not only will you remain in debt but you will extinguish future opportunities to make money because you will continue to pay interest to someone else. As James Clayton notes, "Traditionally, persistent increases in public debt levels have often been compared to termites in the house. You can ignore these pests for quite a while, but eventually you will have a very big problem."[11]

How big is your problem? To find out, ask yourself the following questions:

1. Do I argue with my spouse over bills?
2. Is an increasing percentage of my income being used to pay off debts? Am I near or at the limit of my lines of credit?
3. Am I extending repayment schedules—paying bills in 60 or 90 days that I once paid in 30?
4. Am I chronically late paying my bills?
5. Am I borrowing to pay for items I used to buy with cash?
6. Do I put off medical or dental visits because I can't afford them?
7. Do I know my total debt, or am I afraid to add it up?

If you are struggling with any of these concerns, now is the time to get your debt load under control. It's your choice. You can continue spending like crazy while trying to pay down debt for another 30 to 40 years, or you can be empowered to get out of debt now so you can reap the following wonderful rewards:

- Get completely out of debt within nine years, including your home mortgage.
- Begin saving, on top of eliminating debt, at least 2 to 4 percent of your monthly income.
- Begin to maximize your retirement income by making compound interest work for you instead of against you.

All this is possible if you want to make it happen! If you have five or more debt items, it is mathematically predictable that you can be out of debt in nine years or less, even including a 30-year home mortgage. And the best part is that it's easy and effective, requiring no additional out-of-pocket money. What's more, it's literally worth "millions" once you learn how to stop paying someone else so you can begin paying yourself! Decide today that you will no longer be a slave to the power of compound interest! Incorporate the Power Down system today by taking the challenge on page 75.

As you begin this challenge to power down your debt, we hope you will find great strength and encouragement from the personal and inspiring story of one of the Money Mastery authors, Peter Jeppson. Peter tells, in his own words of how, through a tragic accident, he learned firsthand the power and peace that comes from eliminating debt.

"As a young man just starting college, I was in a serious car accident. I was hit head on by another car and trapped in my Volkswagen Bug almost burning to death, until three drivers in passing automobiles stopped and pulled me from the wreckage. I spent more than two years in the hospital, depressed, broken, blind, and burned beyond all recognition.

"At first I went in and out of a coma, fighting for my life. The doctors told my mother privately that I had no chance of living. Once I did stabilize, the doctors informed me that I would never walk again, and that there was no chance I would ever see again having lost my eyelids and most of the skin on my face.

"As the days came and went, I recovered enough to be out of danger of losing my life. But I became very despondent and discouraged. While in this terrible situation I received help from so many caring people who read to me, bathed me, played chess with me, and gave me pep talks to buoy up my spirit. From this service, I learned some of the most important lessons in life. I learned that self-worth and self-esteem come from within and that beauty is what is on the inside.

"Over time my health gradually began improving. Eventually I did walk again and thanks to the many doctors who worked with me, my eyesight was saved. But as I lay in ICU for months, the medical bills began to pile up. I did not have health insurance and every Friday the hospital accounting office came to my room to review my bill with me. After every Friday's meeting I would become so upset about the thousands of dollars of debt I was incurring and knowing there was nothing I could do about it, that I would schedule a morphine shot for pain relief. Just a little calculation and anyone can figure that seven months in ICU times $1,500 (at the time) per day was costing me a literal fortune. Add to this another two years mostly in the hospital and 28 major surgeries, and I began to stagger under the weight of this tremendous financial burden. It was while under this incredible pressure that I learned the lesson that would change my life forever.

"While in the hospital, my brother Bil brought me the book *The Richest Man in Babylon* by George S. Clason. The chapter on the 'Clay Tablets' about powering down debt was so impressive to me. At first, the methods described in the book seemed too simple and too good to be true. I couldn't fathom ever paying off all my debt. But then I found myself asking, "Yes, but what if this system really works? I certainly have nothing to lose! It's easy to test the math—I can do that in my head." What I found by doing the math was that if I applied a Power Down system to my debt load, I could completely eliminate it in five years. Then I had different members of my family write down the math when they came to visit. Their numbers checked out what with what I had figured in my head. In time, I was released from the hospital. But even with those debt-reduction methods still fresh on my mind, I was so overwhelmed by what I owed (besides my hospital bill I owed money to seven different doctors), I didn't know if I could ever get out from underneath it all. However, I once again tested the figures and found that I could indeed, be out of debt in five years if I applied Power Down principles.

"Bankruptcy was mentioned over and over by friends and family members as a way to start a new life financially. My own father, who now had been divorced from my mother for three years, told me he was going to file bankruptcy himself. Because I was still a minor when the accident happened, I could be included in his bankruptcy if I wanted and wipe my slate clean.

"His suggestion caused me to review all the work the wonderful doctors and nurses had done to save my life and restore my eyesight, and I realized there was no way that I could bail out on my obligation to them. As I declined my father's invitation, he told me he thought I was making a stupid decision, but I then thought about how money had ruined his marriage to my mother. I thought of all the arguments he had had with her about money. I thought about how upset it made me feel every time I heard them fight and I was determined to do something different financially with my own life. It was then that I committed myself to applying the systematic Power Down approach to my debt.

"Five years later, I paid off my last medical bill. Even though my body was terribly scarred, those scars began to stand as a symbol of victory over my own personal debt and as a sign of triumph at beating impossible odds, both physically and financially.

"Although most people do not carry any outward scars, so many individuals today have scarring on the inside caused by a lack of self-esteem due to financial worries and crushing debt. I have learned, over 30 years of taking every opportunity to teach thousands of people about the Power Down approach, that if you have five or more debts it is mathematically possible to eliminate all of them in nine years or less using this method. I learned it for myself personally all those years ago and I have seen it work over and over again in the lives of countless people. It simply works—no matter how much debt you have, no matter how bad it is, no matter how high the interest rates are, no matter what! It works! If I can do it, you can, too! Gaining the victory over debt is a huge accomplishment that I strongly encourage you to work towards. Begin now! Don't wait another day to relieve yourself of this terrible burden that scars, destroys, and maims your life."

## Challenge #4

# Prioritize Your Debt

This week, gather information on all your debts including interest rates, monthly payments, and balances. Then begin to prioritize each debt using one of the three following choices:

1.  List debts by maturity (shortest to longest debt period).
2.  List debts by interest rate (highest to lowest).
3.  List debts by size of debt (smallest to largest).

We usually suggest that debt be prioritized by maturity date. Once you have prioritized debts for payoff, determine to begin paying off the first debt on your list by allocating an amount of money toward the bill that will eliminate it as quickly as possible. Also, you may want to review your spending to see if you can find additional money that you are wasting on unneeded items that you could apply as an accelerator payment.

Money Mastery's Master Plan software is specifically designed to help you prioritize debt and to visualize the impact that interest will have on your finances over time. It was used to create Mark and Joyce's debt reports featured in this chapter and can help you play "what if" scenarios to determine the best way to power down your own debt. (Please refer to Appendix A for more information on how to obtain the Master Plan software.)

# Chapter 5

# Know the Rules
# of the Game

**W**hen Einstein said that the greatest discovery of the 20th century was compound interest, he was right. That's because compound interest has made millions of dollars for some people. It has also cost others a fortune in debt interest. Whether it works positively or negatively in your life depends on how well you understand its power. As the old saying goes:

> *"Those that don't understand interest pay it,*
> *and those that do understand it, earn it."*

At the end of Chapter 4, we gave you the challenge to prioritize your debt and then begin powering it down so that you can learn how to stop paying compound interest and instead start earning it. Once you see how quickly you can actually become debt free, you will begin to feel more and more empowered. You will become appalled at the thought of paying someone else and work to begin paying yourself instead!

Remember Mark and Joyce? As they began looking at their real debt situation, it became apparent that they had a choice. They could choose to just be getting out of debt after 29 years, or in the same time frame, they could be totally debt free with $971,000 for retirement from the debt interest they saved by Powering Down. Just like Mark and Joyce, you too can become more informed about the reality of interest working either for you, or against you, and then make some important changes in your life. Taking advantage of the tremendous benefits that being informed can bring to your life leads to the next Money Mastery principle:

# Principle #5: Know the rules.

Initially, this principle may seem very obvious, but it isn't. If it was an idea that more people truly understood, there would not be nearly the amount of emotional heartache over finances that most Americans are experiencing.

Take a look at the picture below of a die.

Notice the four dots on the front side of the die. How many dots are on the opposite side of the four dots? If you're familiar with dice, you probably know. The answer is three. What is on the opposite side of one? The answer is six. The rule with dice is that opposite sides of a die always add up to seven. Therefore, on the opposite side of the five are two dots. When you know the rules, it is really easy to predict what will be on the back side of the die.

How many times do you make a financial decision when you are *not* able to really examine the decision—pick it up, so to speak, turn it around, and look at what is on the "back side"? Many financial decisions are very difficult; not being able to see the final result can make us feel very frustrated, even out of control. Has it ever made you feel at the mercy of what others know over your own basis of knowledge? You can see from this little example with the die that knowing the rules can be very powerful.

Here's another example of why it is so important to know the rules. Sandy and Bart Owen* came to us very upset about refinancing their debts. They found as they went through the process of consolidating some of their debts that a pre-payment penalty of $2,200 had been written into the agreement for one of their loans. This stipulation was clearly stated in the agreement the Owens had signed when they obtained the loan. It was easy to read and understand, yet Sandy and Bart had never known it was there because they didn't take time to read the contract before signing it. Now, when it came time to consolidate they could not do so without paying the $2,200 penalty.

Not knowing the rules in this case cost the Owens. Knowing the rules is just like playing the game of tic-tac-toe. If you have played it before, you can pretty much predict who will win within the first few plays of the game. If both parties know how to play tic-tac-toe usually there won't even be a winner; the end result is a tie. In the case of the Owens, the lending institution was adept at the game it was playing, while Bart and Sandy never took the time to learn the rules of the game. If they had learned the rules, even if they couldn't win, they could have at least had an equal advantage. In this case, they ended up the losing.

*When you know the rules of the game, you have
a much higher chance of winning or at least playing even.*

Now let's meet another individual who lost big time because he did not know the rules of the game he was playing.

# Michael Marchant: Paying a High Price for Not Knowing the Rules

Case History

Michael Marchant* provided financial planning for medical and dental professionals. For more than 25 years he counseled many people who had improperly invested their money and lost large portions of their retirement funds. To better serve his clients, Michael became licensed in insurance and securities and placed the license with a broker whom he had worked with in financial planning. Over the years, this broker helped Michael with securities issues and Michael helped the broker with insurance and real estate issues. At one point in their working relationship the broker asked Michael to perform some simple functions as the secretary/treasurer of a small, private investment fund. His duties in this position were simply to pay out money when clients asked to redeem their shares. But as Michael says, "Never in my wildest imagination did I realize the tremendous liability in which I had placed myself by accepting the broker's request to become secretary and treasurer of this fund."

That's because over time the broker began making improper trades on the stock market. When the market crashed in October of 1987, a large portion of the money the broker had traded was lost. He did not disclose this to Michael or his clients. The clients just continued to redeem their shares with the money that was left until it finally ran out. The last few clients couldn't get their money so they filed complaints and lawsuits. An investigation by the state division of securities was then launched.

When Michael was first approached by the securities division, he had no clue about the fraudulent behavior of the broker. Michael was helpful, and discussing openly all activity of all involved. He wasn't in a position to invest this money nor control it; he was not an owner of the fund and did not serve as a director of this fund, so he didn't see any reason to be concerned about the investigation. Michael was completely unaware that anyone had ever lost any money until the securities team came calling. He had not been involved to any degree requiring himself to be responsible for the investments, so he didn't see the danger he was placing himself in by not knowing everything that had happened up to that point. Answering each inquiry started a chain reaction, like a "domino effect," which only made matters worse. Michael recalls, "This securities team then began asking me searching questions for which I had no answers."

In the end, Michael paid out more than $160,000 for attorney's fees and court costs in order to defend himself against the filed lawsuits and has endured incredible humiliation and pain because of the damage to his reputation. "Unfortunately there are so many people that, like me, don't realize how serious it is when they don't know the rules," says Michael. "Take time to understand the rules of the game you are playing before you begin to play it. Put forth the effort to find out what is happening on the inside. Hire an attorney, or professional, if necessary, and be sure you read everything before you sign!"

# Financial Games of Choice

As we have pointed out, every game has rules. The games we play in the financial world should not be games of chance; they should be games of choice. If you know that money is emotional and not mathematical, you will be less likely to take your money for granted and will give it the respect it deserves. If you know the rules about tracking your spending, you will begin to use your money more efficiently. If you know the rules behind properly "spending" into appropriate savings categories, you will not be blindsided by emergency and emotional events that are sure to occur in your life. If you know the rules about compound interest, you will become empowered to eliminate debt as quickly as possible and learn how to make interest work in your favor. Knowing the rules has all kinds of valuable consequences, especially in today's complex world.

It wasn't too long ago that the world of personal finance was much simpler. Prices were similar between competing goods and services, taxes were easier to figure, mortgages and loans were structured with less complexity, and there were less consumer products from which to choose and fewer methods by which to buy them. But today we live in a very complicated and dynamic world economy. We have so many choices! There are thousands of vendors and literally millions of products we can choose to buy. What was once purchased at the corner drugstore is now available on the Internet. Not only can we evaluate products and services right in our backyard, but we can choose from those being produced on the other side of the world. All of this complexity makes understanding the following especially important:

*It's no longer possible to simply assume the vendor or the lender*
*have fully disclosed everything that we may need to know*
*to make a wise financial decision.*

Today, more than ever, we must become fully informed about how our spending, borrowing, and tax-paying choices will impact our life over the long term. Historically, sellers of goods and services had the advantage over the consumer because these sellers knew more than the buyer. But today, the tables have turned. With all this available information, we are now in a position to structure financial decisions to best meet our needs, but only if we get informed. Learning the rules can help you become more efficient with the money you already make and shifts the focus away from trying to earn more money to learning how to use more wisely that which we already have.

*Unfortunately, we have found that the vast majority of people we deal with are*
*more concerned with making money than with understanding how to be more*
*efficient with the money they already have.*

Without seeing the value of efficiency and how that efficiency is tied to understanding the rules of the financial games they play, many people are losing those games. This is perfectly illustrated in an article entitled "What We Need to Know about Money" by Lynn Brenner. Brenner notes that a recent test sponsored by the National Council on Economic Education found that many adults and teens in the United States today don't understand the most basic concepts about money. "The economy affects everything in our lives: how we earn a living, how much we earn, the availability, cost and quality of what we buy, and how we invest for our future," says

Brenner. "Unfortunately, its importance is the only thing many of us know about the economy."[1]

The article further notes that 1,010 adults and 1,085 high school students took the National Council's 1998-99 test of their knowledge of basic economic principles. "Both groups flunked resoundingly," says Brenner. "Almost two-thirds of those tested did not know that in times of inflation money does not hold its value. Only 58 percent of the high school students understood that when the demand for a product goes up but the supply doesn't, its price is likely to increase. Half of the adults and about two-thirds of the students did not know that the stock market brings people who want to buy stocks together with those who want to sell them."[2]

Hard to believe isn't it? Those findings are alarming, especially in the face of what we have already noted as a time of complexity and opportunity.

# Working the Game to Your Advantage

Now, with that said, you may be thinking, "Well, the amount of information that is thrown at me on a daily basis is overwhelming. With everything else I have to do, I can't afford the time to stay on top of all this, too!" When we hear such complaints, we like to point out to our clients that they cannot possibly afford *not* to become informed. In today's world of easy credit and consumable goods, many people feel they are entitled to play a very complex economic game, like owning a credit card or mortgaging a house, without paying the price to learn the rules of that game. As they old saying goes:

*"If you want to play, you have to pay."*

What we are required to pay is a little bit of our time and effort so that we will go into the game fully informed and on the same level as all the other players. Those who will not take the time to do this should not be surprised when they are unable to work the game to their advantage. It simply follows that without knowing what you're doing when you enter the playing field, especially where there is a lot of risk involved, that you will probably be trampled by those who do.

Following are some of the typical objections to Principle 5 and how we counsel our clients to overcome them.

## Too Much Information

It goes without saying that we live in an era of information overload. There is so much coming at us each day that it's impossible to take it all in.

We are forced to choose between that which we will absorb and that which we will discard. So how can we possibly learn what we need to know without becoming overwhelmed? What we teach our clients is that they do not have to know *everything*, but it is important that they get on the road to knowing *something*. When people realize that there is a limit to that which they personally need to learn, they begin to relax and feel empowered by their newfound desire to become informed and continue that process. This requires a commitment to continual learning while not requiring that a person learn about everything.

We encourage you to make a commitment to continual learning. Doing so will help you learn a little bit about a lot of things so that you can determine when you need to get extra help. Consumer affairs writer Carma Wadley offers some tips on how to start this learning process: "The important thing is not so much knowing all the answers as knowing where to find them."[3] She suggests keeping a list of resources handy to which you can refer, including favorite Web sites, government agencies, or a list of people you know who have expertise in particular areas. Another way to get on the road to knowing only that which you need to know is to get in the habit of reading all documents related to the product or service you are evaluating. Sources of information about the rules of that product or service are contained in the documents the vendor or lender provides you. Read all documents. The value of Principle 5 is that it motivates you to study all contracts.

In addition to these ideas, we'll discuss more ways to help you understand how to learn what you need to know at the end of this chapter. (Money Mastery also offers coaching services that can help; refer to Appendix A for more information on these services.)

One of our clients, Maria*, learned the importance of knowing the rules and reading all documents after her coach helped her better understand tax forms and tax filing. When Maria received her tax forms from her CPA at tax time, she felt "comfortable" with the documents, but because of Principle 5, decided to look them over carefully. In the process, Maria found a $1,700 error in her favor. The CPA then refiled and instead of receiving an $1,800 tax return from the IRS, Maria got back $3,500. Knowing the rules and reading the documents in this case really paid off!

## Not Enough Time

The second objection to Principle 5 is the notion that there's not enough time to know the rules. What people don't realize is that most of us are very close to knowing what would save us a lot of grief, but we don't want to make that little bit of extra effort to find out the last little bit of information that would save us a lot of trouble. The amount of trouble you will save is disproportionate to the amount of time it will take you to avoid it. That's because we have found that most people are within 30 minutes or $300 from getting all the information they need to make informed financial decisions. It usually takes no more than 30 minutes to thoroughly review a legal document. And, if upon examination of those documents you find that further advice is needed, a $300 fee will usually hire a knowledgeable attorney or specialist to review a financial decision to ensure that it is right.

The following is what can happen when people don't take the time to be responsible for making sure a deal is secured properly.

Two very successful businessmen approached an accomplished CPA and asked for her help in accounting and tax planning to set up their new business. Approaching a professional at this stage of the game was a smart idea. They restructured their business from a sole proprietorship to a Sub-S corporation. The CPA said she had prepared everything required by the IRS that would let them operate legally as a Sub-S corporation, allowing them to receive a better tax rate. Four years later, they began working with Money Mastery coaches in order to more efficiently run their business. As they began getting organized by preparing wills and trusts for estate planning, they discovered their Sub-S election was never filed by the CPA, creating an additional tax liability of $47,000.

After learning Principle 5, they understood the importance of taking the time and money necessary to unravel the problems created over the previous four years. They hired a tax attorney who was successful in relieving $30,000 of the taxes due, but they still had to pay an extra $17,000. If these two men had just taken the time in the first place to do a simple review of the filing papers with a tax attorney, they would not have lost the $17,000.

## Trusting Others Instead of Taking Responsibility

Another reason people don't want to get informed is because they think other people should know the rules for them. They often trust their economic well-being to strangers because they assume that other people will have enough interest to take care of them as well as they would themselves. This is not so. Of course, as we go about making financial decisions, we are required to trust others to some degree. However, trust is composed of two elements:

1. Trust that the person or entity providing the service won't try to cheat us.
2. Trust in the competency of that person or entity to deliver as promised.

Our experience shows that people must be on guard in both areas. Although vendors are not generally trying to cheat the consumer, the biggest risk we take when interacting with providers of goods and services is the incompetence of those providers. Humans make mistakes, as in the case of Maria's CPA. When you know the rules of the transaction in which you are engaging, you protect your dollars and your economic well-being.

# Dale and Shellie Tamaki: Learn the Rules for Yourself

**Case History**      Dale and Shellie Tamaki* are an example of what can happen when you trust others rather than learning the rules for yourself. Dale Tamaki was a professor at the local college and Shellie worked in human resources. After their children were mostly grown, the Tamaki's decided to refinance their home in order to lower their monthly payment and to consolidate their consumer debt. The couple's credit was immaculate and they chose a qualified mortgage lender in their area and proceeded with the loan. Rates at the time were at 7 percent. When it came time to close the loan, they were told the best rate they could get on the refinance was 9 percent. This shocked the Tamakis, because they thought their credit was good enough to get the 7 percent interest rate. The loan officer's response to their shock was, "There were a few glitches on your credit report that caused the interest rate to go up." This embarrassed the couple so they didn't question it, nor did they check their own credit report. They simply closed the loan and started to make the payments.

Dale and Shellie were then introduced to Money Mastery Principle 5. It made them think back to the time they refinanced their home and the 9 percent interest rate they were paying. Their coach counseled them to send all the closing documents to a mortgage specialist for review. Upon examination, this specialist found that with their perfect "A" credit rating, the Tamakis were totally qualified for a 7 percent interest rate, but had been charged three percentage points (which had been completely disclosed at the time of signing) for originating the loan, and six points on the back end, providing a brokerage fee of nearly $14,000 on a loan amount of $126,000. Basically, the Tamaki's "A" credit should have entitled them to pay no more than $1,000 in brokerage fees, but because the broker had disclosed the three percentage points, and Dale and Shellie had been too embarrassed to question the higher rate, the lending broker was able to arrange for a much larger brokerage fee than he was entitled to, basically ripping off an extra $13,000. (Some lending brokers will do this if they can see that the borrower is not going to question it.) The Tamakis then went back to the lender and cried foul, at which point the lender promptly revised the loan and negated the excessive fees, saving the Tamakis nearly $11,000. Not knowing the rules and trusting that others would tell them what they should have known themselves made the Tamakis prime targets. A little bit of research could have saved the couple the emotional trauma of "being taken."

• • •

Knowing the rules and not being afraid to question are vital in today's world, where many people will deal with you legally, but not always ethically.

*Other people who know the rules will often take advantage of those who don't.*

## Not Wanting to Do First Things First

An additional objection our clients sometimes have is that they don't want to learn the financial basics but would rather experiment with more sophisticated and risky financial games before they have taken care of the fundamentals. They are tempted, for instance, to dabble in the stock market before getting out of debt. Knowing the rules suggests that you do "first things first." In our experience, it is a good idea for an individual or family to follow the steps (at right) in the order prescribed.

As you play each of these financial games in the order that is best for you, you will naturally be led to an understanding of the rules governing the next game. Each step you take will build confidence until you understand how to play even the most risky financial games and have the economic wherewithal to afford to play them. Because every financial game we play comes with a certain amount of risk, knowing the rules means un-

### The Basics

- Consider getting an education or learning a skilled trade.
- Secure vocational income.
- Avoid getting into debt (Principle 4).

### Cover Risks

- Buy basic life and disability insurance.
- Build emergency and emotional savings (Principle 2 and 3).
- Purchase a house.
- Minimize taxes (Principle 9; refer to Ch. 9 and Part II for information).

### Invest Surplus Money

- Consider investing in guaranteed investments such as CDs or Money Market accounts.
- Consider investing in low-risk options such as mutual funds.
- Consider investing in individual stocks. (Covered in greater detail in Chapters 8 and 10.)

derstanding what those risks are. Some financial decisions are less risky than others, but nonetheless, each one can be a gamble. (We will discuss these risks in more detail in Chapter 6.)

We have seen too many instances where vital savings have been put in jeopardy due to high-risk investments. In general, we recommend that vital savings be invested in low-risk opportunities and that disposable savings be set aside for higher risk programs, as shown in the following illustration.

**Passbook Savings:** Has most flexibility because it allows you to deposit and withdraw money from one account to another easily; has the lowest interest rates.

**Certificates of Deposit and Money Market Accounts:** Has higher interest rates but usually for a specific term so these are less flexible; requires more money to open than a savings account.

**Mutual Funds:** Spreads risk out over many pools of stock so gamble is less than buying specific stock, but these funds are not guaranteed.

**Individual Stocks:** Allows the buyer to pick something with which they have interest (such as dotcom companies or high-tech industries) with potential for making large sums, but is much more risky; no limit to the downside.

**Start-ups in Closely Held Companies:** Highest risk; only for those who can afford to lose money; examples of such are Angel Investors, venture capitalists, and philanthropists.

From this example, you can see that you can make more money the higher the risk you take, but you can also lose the most as well. That's why a person with debt should not be investing in high-risk opportunities, because they are not in a position to lose money. Too many people, because they do not take the time to know the rules, try to invest their way out of debt. This is unwise. Remember, debt interest is unrelenting and it's not a good idea to borrow money to invest in something else.

*Investment returns for the indebted disappear like smoke.*

Case History

# Sam Bennett:
# Risking Retirement Savings

We see people in their late 50s get panicky about retirement and then become tempted to invest in the high-risk programs instead of trusting in a moderate plan. One of our clients, Sam Bennett*, is a good example of this. At age 58, Sam had accumulated more than $300,000 in savings over the course of his career as a mechanical engineer. While it wasn't a meager sum, Sam and his wife knew they still needed more money before Sam could retire. He planned to continue with his retirement savings until he reached age 65. Right before his 59th birthday, however, three of his friends presented to him an opportunity for investment. While he did not have to contribute any money personally to the deal, he did have to co-sign on the loan to secure the funds they needed to launch the venture. Sam decided to jump at the chance, looking at it as a way to more quickly accumulate retirement wealth.

A year later, the investment went bad and the creditors went after Sam's friends to collect on the loan. None of these men had the money to cover the debt, so they came to Sam looking for money. As the only person with anything to contribute to the delinquent debt, Sam lost his entire $300,000 retirement nest egg. His wife was so hurt and angry that she began divorce proceedings. Sam came to us desperate for help. Using the Money Mastery principles, Sam began tracking his spending and found an extra $3,000 a month he could put into savings. Although he will not be able to retire at age 65, he will have enough money at age 72 to quit working. In addition, he has used his engineering expertise to design slot machines that have been installed in the Las Vegas casinos near his home. He receives a royalty fee from these casinos that will provide he and his wife with a perpetual source of income, even after he retires. Both Sam and his wife are pleased with the results they are getting by applying the Money Mastery principles and have reconciled their marital differences. However, Sam could have avoided all the heartache if he had resisted the temptation to invest in a risky business venture late in his career.

## Getting Rid of Credit Card Debt

Credit card debt is another area where it is important to know the rules and to do first things first. As we have already stated in previous chapters, it is important that you get out of this kind of debt first because it is usually the most costly. If you have ever taken the time to read the unique set of rules that govern a credit card, you know they can be complex and numerous. Of course the banks who provide credit cards know their own interest rules; they know their own averages, and they know their own risks. If you are going to borrow money from these banks you better know those rules as well. Many of these institutions have begun to loosen their requirements and extend the length of credit card loans, causing consumers to go into further debt. Without understanding the gimmicks that can be used to get more money out of you, you're probably losing far more than you think to a credit issuer.

For example, you may already know that credit card companies warn in fine print on their contracts that they will bump up your interest rate by as much as 1.5 percent if they see a derogatory credit report appear on your record. What you may not know, however, is that credit card companies consider any check done on your credit as "derogatory." That means that if you go to the bank seeking a loan for a new car, for instance, and the bank runs a routine credit check as part of the loan fulfillment process, that check could be interpreted by your credit card company as a negative report, which could make them feel legally justified in raising your interest rates. What's more, this happens on a regular basis to many people, but because they don't even check their credit card statement each month, they have no idea the credit card company is getting away with charging them a higher rate.

Upon learning this, many of our clients feel that credit card companies have taken advantage of them. But as we mentioned previously in this chapter, in today's society, you are not automatically entitled to play a very complex financial game, like owning a credit card, without paying the price to learn the rules of that game. Some people feel the solution is to get rid of every card they own. While we strongly recommend that those who are in debt get credit card spending under immediate strict control, there are rules about the value of using credit cards that could hurt your credit if you don't use one. And did you know that you could actually earn interest from a credit card instead of paying it? Selected cards that you pay off completely each month can earn you as much as $.05 on each dollar you spend through that card—the GM card, Ford card, or Discover card are examples. If you were to spend $1,500 per month for 12 months you could earn $900 if you spend wisely.

Of course most of us know that it usually costs us money to use a credit card. That's why knowing the basics about credit card borrowing could save you (or earn you) thousands of dollars. It's worth the effort and we strongly urge you to take the time to learn more about your own credit card situation.

Here are a few startling observations about credit card borrowing, taken from an article in *Consumer Reports*, that may help you see the value of knowing the rules:

> *Say you paid $19 for a pepperoni pizza by charging it to your card. If you carry no balance on your credit card and pay your bill within the 20- to 25-day grace period, the pizza won't cost an extra dime. But consider instead the cost of that pizza if you are already carrying an unpaid balance of $5,000 on your credit card. If you simply add the cost of the pizza as a topping to all your other revolving debt, that "inexpensive" dinner out would have cost a total of $40.04. Did you really want to pay so much for a pizza? Probably not. Next time, [when carrying balances], pay cash. And what about perpetual payment? Lenders would prefer you didn't worry how much a debt will cost or how long it will take you to repay. All they want you to think about is the minimum monthly payment that will keep your account current. At a recent meeting of the International Credit Association in Wilmington, Delaware, Peter McCorkell, senior vice president of Fair, Isaac, warned credit card industry executives of a proposed law that would require lenders to disclose how long it takes to pay off a balance with minimum payments. 'In some cases, the answer would be darn near infinity,' he announced to a ripple of giddy laughter. Paying off balances with the minimum now takes longer than ever because, over the years, credit card companies have downsized monthly minimum payments from between 3 and 5 percent of the balance to between 1.5 and 2 percent.*[4]

The article also urges consumers not to wait for a credit card offer but to choose what's best for them. "That can only be done by getting out your magnifying glass and scrutinizing the terms and conditions in the fine print on the back of the offer. Does the low introductory rate apply to new charges, cash advances, or balance transfers—and how long does that rate last?"[5] Even a low introductory rate on a credit card offer of say 2 percent could end up costing you money if you don't know the rules of the game the credit card company is playing with you.

## Mortgage Refinancing to Consolidate Debt

And what about home mortgage refinancing? In today's credit-laden world it's become very popular to consolidate debt through a home mortgage loan but as the "The New Rules of Borrowing" article suggests, "Even the new math of mortgage refinancing can add up to trouble for many of the hundreds of thousands of borrowers who rolled over a higher-interest-rate-mortgage for one charging today's lower rate. Had you bought a house in 1992 and financed it with a $100,000, 8.3 percent, 30-year mortgage, for example, you would still have $93,020 in principle left to pay by 1999. You could decide to refinance that loan with a cheaper 30-year loan at today's prevailing rate of 7 percent. You would have to pay 2 percent in closing costs, or $1,860. However, your monthly payment drops from $752 to $619—not bad. But what looks like a big win for the borrower can end up costing plenty. If you had left the old mortgage in place, your 360 payments at $752 per months would add up to $270,700 by the time the house was paid off. Your new mortgage will cost $222,800. But that figure doesn't include the nearly $54,700 you already paid over the seven years of your first mortgage. Refinancing restarts the clock on your payments, so that new loan will end up costing a grand total of about $277,500 over a period of 37 years—an additional cost to the borrower of $6,800."[6] The article suggest that if you decide to refinance, try to make the same monthly payment you made under your old loan. "That way you'll shave years—and tens of thousands of dollars in interest payments—off your debt obligation."[7]

In the case of refinancing, most people only care about the immediate, short-term savings, failing to see the real costs they will incur over the long run. This comes from not taking the time to learn the rules.

Following is a summary of how best to start learning the rules:

1. **Don't get overwhelmed by the amount of information you need to know.** Remember, you don't have to know everything, you just need to begin by knowing something.

2. **Take the time to learn the rules.** It usually only takes 30 minutes to learn what you absolutely need to know in order to make informed decisions.

3. **Don't trust others to know the rules for you.** Take responsibility for your own financial well-being and do what is necessary to ensure success; hire a professional if needed to help you understand the rules. This can usually be done for as little as $300.

4. **Do first things first.** Avoid the temptation to dabble in risky behavior before setting yourself up financially to afford that behavior. Pay off high-rate credit card debts first and know the rules of the credit card game before you play it.

Knowing the rules is a simple concept that in today's world is more important than ever. Once again we encourage you to become more proactive and make that little bit of extra effort to protect yourself and your financial future. Take an attitude of continuous reading and learning. The amount of material you will need to learn is not mammoth in size, but an ongoing time commitment is vital. To help you make that commitment, we recommend taking the challenge found on page 92 and to read from the following list. You will be enthused, empowered, and inspired by the books on this list.

## Money Mastery Suggested Reading List

1. *The Richest Man in Babylon*, George S. Clason.
2. *Nine Steps to Financial Freedom*, Susie Orman.
3. *The Millionaire Next Door*, Thomas Stanley and William Danko.
4. *Rich Dad, Poor Dad*, Robert Kiyosaki.
5. *Your Money or Your Life*, Joe Dominquez and Vicki Robin.
6. *Die Broke*, Stephen M. Pollan and Mark Levine.
7. *Tax Strategies*, Sandy Botkin.
8. *Guide to Understanding Your Taxes*, The Wall Street Journal.
9. *Tax Amnesty (A Guide to the Forgiveness of IRS Debt)*, Daniel J. Pilla.
10. *Working from Home*, Paul and Sarah Edwards.
11. *Protect Your Estate*, Robert A. Espert and Renno L. Petterson.
12. *Guide to Understanding Money and Investing,* The Wall Street Journal.

## Challenge #5

# Understanding Your Important Financial Contracts

We challenge you this week to locate all of your important financial documents. These could include home mortgages, credit card agreements, car loans, insurance contracts, tax returns, and so on. Take time to review each of these documents carefully. Make the extra effort to read the fine print where necessary. Once you have reviewed these documents, evaluate your understanding of them based on the following:

1.  Do I understand the rules of the contract?
2.  Do I understand the amount of risk I have taken by agreeing to the contract?
3.  Where the IRS is concerned, do I understand the tax laws surrounding this contract?
4.  Do I know my own priorities and do my priorities fit the contract?
5.  Can I afford to lose part or all of my money by engaging in this contract?

We also encourage you to seek counsel from a professional if needed. Money Mastery offers extensive coaching for those who need more information about how to learn the rules. (Please refer to Appendix A for information regarding coaching services.) In addition, refer to Part II of this book for more information on tax laws and tax relief.

# Chapter 6

# The Rules Are Always Changing

The Arabs have an ancient proverb that affirms:

*He who knows not, and knows not that he knows not,*
*is a fool—shun him.*
*He who knows not, and knows that he knows not,*
*is a student—teach him.*
*He who knows, and knows not that he knows, is asleep—wake him.*
*He who knows, and knows that he knows is wise—follow him.*

Which level of consciousness best describes you? If you've come this far in the book, we're certain you don't belong in the first category. As you have begun tracking and controlling your spending and are now more aware of your true debt situation, you're becoming more conscious of your true financial and emotional state. If you now see the value of Money Mastery Principle 5, "Know the rules," which we outlined in the last chapter, you are probably moving ever closer to knowing what you need to know in order to make wise decisions.

Becoming aware of that which you really need to know is extremely enabling. Examples in every aspect of life demonstrate how this kind of knowledge brings empowerment. Take for instance a college student who, as he goes through the process of learning, either becomes very aware of that which he knows he still needs to learn, or feels satisfied that he now possesses enough knowledge to build a career. Both levels of awareness are key to rising above the foolishness of ignorance. Upon graduating from college, this student has basically learned how to learn. If you, like the student, have "learned how to learn" by embracing Principle 5, you are well on your way to the incredible emotional freedom and financial happiness that come from being in control of your money.

But knowing the rules is only the beginning. For example, if a physician, after completing his education, felt that he could stop learning simply because he thought his knowledge was complete, he would soon be unable to properly heal the human body. Likewise, if you stop learning about money and how it can affect your life simply because you think your knowledge is complete, you will make foolish financial decisions that you cannot afford. Remember the old bumper sticker: "If you think education is expensive, you ought to try ignorance." Knowing the rules coupled with understanding that those rules can change introduces the sixth Money Mastery principle:

 # Principle #6: The rules are always changing.

We live in a world where few things ever stay the same. For example, we can see change in such things as technology, politics, medicine, agriculture, weather, and education. And one of the things that provides the most evidence of change is taxes, where alterations take place insidiously, regularly, and subtly. As we noted in the Introduction, government has grown to an astronomical size over the last 60 years, causing the tax system designed to support it to grow with it. To keep up with this growth, more and more tax laws have been changed, making the overall tax system very cumbersome and complex. Did you know that Americans spend 5.4 billion hours each year just trying to comply with the 46,000 pages of federal tax code? Basically, that equates to three million people working full-time on deciphering tax law each year.[1] According to Walter Williams, professor of economics at George Mason University, "If it were employed in productive activity, the labor now devoted to tax compliance would be worth $232 billion annually."[2] To see just how much tax law has changed over the last several years, take a look at only some of the major tax changes that have occurred since 1984.

### 1984: Deficit Reduction Act (DEFRA)
- Limited life insurance and annuity benefits.

## 1986: Tax Equalization Reform Act (TEFRA)

- Broadened the definition of gross income subject to tax, reduced deductions.

## 1987: Revenue Act of 1987

- Limited the deduction of qualified residence interest.
- Created five tax brackets (11 percent, 15 percent, 28 percent, 35 percent).

## 1988: Technical and Miscellaneous Revenue Act of 1988 (TAMARA)

- Introduced eventual elimination of deduction of consumer interest expense.
- Reduced tax brackets to 15 percent and 28 percent (5 percent surtax created 33 percent bracket).

## 1989: Omnibus Tax Act

- Standard deduction indexed to inflation.

## 1990: Omnibus Tax Act

- Personal exemption indexed to inflation.

## 1993: Revenue Reconciliation Act of 1993

- Created four tax brackets (15 percent, 28 percent, 36 percent, 39.6 percent).
- Retroactive taxation.
- Further deduction limitation and phase out of personal exemptions.
- Increased Estate Tax.
- Reduced Qualified Retirement Plan Compensation limit.
- Social Security included in gross income for tax purposes.

Other less obvious tax administrative changes that have had major impact on Americans include:

## Treasury Regulation

- Amplify, supplement, and interpret Internal Revenue Code.

### Revenue Rulings

- Court decisions given varying weight; can be revoked by IRS.

### Revenue Procedures

- Internal management and State procedures the IRS will follow in specific situations.

### Private Letter Rulings

- Issued to particular taxpayer by the IRS.

### Technical Advice Memoranda

- Issued to IRS personnel with application to Code.

Although legislators are trying to cut down on tax laws, a 1999 Associated Press article reported that the U.S. tax code "now stands at more than 1.5 million words...thanks to more than 12,000 changes enacted by Congress...in the past two years alone."[3] The report went on to say that the IRS developed 11 new forms and revised 177 others in one year alone. Of course, all those changes can make the average American feel very overwhelmed by what they know they don't know. As we noted in Chapter 5, information overload and the sheer amount of material we must understand can make us feel very anxious. But our intent in sharing tax law changes is not to discourage you, because as we also noted in the last chapter, you can get a handle on that which you need to understand personally in order to make informed decisions; we'll talk more about that later in this chapter and in Part II of the book. For now, we simply want to illustrate the importance of at least being aware that the rules don't stay the same, and that it's vital that we know how changes will affect us financially.

## Changes Affect Our Money

Subtle shifts in the banking world also demonstrate how the rules are always changing. Years ago, when a person bounced a check, the bank would charge a dollar or two for overdraft fees, which is the actual hard cost for the bank to provide the service of returning the check and informing the customer that funds were insufficient. Today, however, banks charge on the average $20 for bounced checks plus an additional interest fee if the charge goes on a credit card. Banks have found by experience that people are embarrassed when they bounce a check so the customer will not usually challenge the high cost of these fees. Consequently, these fees have grown over the years; the change has been slow, but it has also been dramatic. Customers who took for granted that banks have changed the rules subtly over time are now locked into paying ultra-high bounced-check fees because those fees are now accepted as the "new rule" and nobody disputes them.

Of course taxes and the banking system aren't the only thing that can affect our money over time. Other changes in our world, which seemingly have little to do with financial matters, can also have a huge impact on what happens to our cash flow. For example, with advances in medical technology, people are living longer. This longevity is now introducing the possibility that most people will actually outlive their available money. Individuals in their 40s today will add another 10 years onto their life expectancy, which means most people will live well into their 90s. Will they need money past age 65? Of course—30 more years worth! This need for more money is greatly affecting the way people are forced to plan for retirement and whether they will be able to retire at all. Explosive changes introduced by the growth of the Internet and e-commerce have altered the way we buy and sell goods and services, opening up opportunities to more rapidly make or lose a profit. Fortunes in the high-tech computer and consumer electronics industries are made and lost every day. And what about travel? The world is a much smaller place than it was 60 years ago and international opportunities are now at our door, opening up countless options for sophisticated financial deal making.

Other things that are in a constant state of change can also affect our financial well-being, including:

| | | |
|---|---|---|
| Attitudes | Income | Marriages |
| Health | Debts | Environment |
| Government | Laws | Desires |
| Relationships | Goals | Emotions |

For the 52 percent of Americans who are divorced, a change in their marital status drastically changes their cash-flow situation. That's because they now have to maintain two residences, including all utilities and phone services, and they must pay out attorney's fees and face forced liquidation to split all assets between the estranged parties. How was money affected the last time you had to deal with a change in marital status, or your health, or your income level? Like everyone else, when you experienced one of these life changes, you may have felt a bit unprepared because you weren't expecting a shift in your situation. But because change can take place on a day-to-day-basis, it's something we're required to deal with continually.

***Life's only constant is change.***

The fact is, the only thing we can really count on is change itself. That's why it's so important to learn the value of Principle 6, because just as people, attitudes, taxation, and world markets can change, so do the rules that govern these things. Knowing that "the rules are always changing" will help you avoid being blindsided by change when it does occur, especially changes that can affect whether you keep or lose your money.

# The Risks of Change

When the world changes, the rules change and these alterations introduce a certain element of risk into our lives. Change brings uncertainty. When something changes, it can take a while to adapt to its new form and function and requires a bit of time to distinguish how the modification will affect a situation.

For example, say your old car is on its last leg and it's time to purchase a new one. You are used to your current financial situation that does not require making a car payment. But now you've purchased a new car. It's beautiful, but you're not quite sure yet how paying for that car is going to affect all the other debt in your life and your current spending situation. Purchasing a car isn't necessarily a huge risk but, of course, that depends. Let's say you don't choose well and end up with a lemon that requires a lot of unexpected car repairs. Or let's say that you can afford to make the car payment but you get sick and incur some medical bills that make it difficult to meet your car loan obligation. Because you have introduced change into your life by bringing the unknown (the purchase of a new car) into your financial situation, you have also introduced a certain amount of risk, which you must then deal with.

***Change forces us to take risks during that period of adjustment between the known, comfortable past and the new, uncertain future.***

Regardless of how hard you try to avoid it, change will occur and that change will bring risk with it. It is your job, therefore, to determine the degree of risk that is acceptable for you to take by keeping up with the rules and how much risk you should avoid based on the financial games you are currently playing.

Let's meet an individual who did not understand the reality of change within the stock market and took unnecessary risks that put her in jeopardy financially.

Case History

# Lori Jones:
# Taking Unnecessary Risks

Lori Jones* was an account executive for a national network marketing company. Lori had done well at the company with bonuses, commissions, and a high-paying salary. In the first two years of her career with the company, she had invested heavily in the stock market and developed a sizeable portfolio worth $500,000. Although she was doing well in her job, Lori was still battling emotionally with the death of her husband, whom she had been married to for 25 years. Because he had handled all their finances before he passed away, Lori had no idea how to really track or control her money. Without him by her side she began relying on others, including an investment broker who called her about an opportunity worth $75,000. She trusted the advice of this broker and purchased the stock right over the phone. Lori was also spending $5,700 more per month than she was making, drawing off her savings to indulge her children and do financial favors for family members. The one thing she felt proud of in her financial life was the large and impressive investment portfolio she had built. Adding the $75,000 investment to it made Lori feel empowered.

As her spending became more unmanageable, she came to Money Mastery seeking help. Her coach explained to Lori the considerable risk she was taking by owning stock in light of the market's continual ups and downs and her poor spending habits. "Lori, investments can increase, but they can also go down in value, and based on your goals and objectives, you cannot afford any losses," her coach told her. "But my broker told me the stock will go to $60 per share!!!" Lori said. Her coach then responded by saying, "Yes, but the stock market could change and you're spending more than you have each month, putting yourself in terrible risk." That was in November. By June of the following year, the value of Lori's stock had dropped to just $6,800.

In Lori's case, because she didn't want to face the changing market rules that governed her stock, she lost thousands of dollars, forcing a big change in her circumstances.

• • •

Here's another example of a client who took for granted how changing rules can impact finances. This man was a dentist who had invested close to $31,000 in mutual funds. By the time we started working with him and his wife, the value of his initial investment had dropped by $9,000. The amount of debt he had incurred over time did not allow him the luxury of losing that kind of money. When he was made aware of his short-sightedness, this man was emotionally unprepared to handle the difficulties he had brought on himself and family.

Investing in mutual funds or any other higher risk stock is not necessarily wrong, especially if you are in a position to lose a bit of money with the hopes of making more. But if you don't have the luxury of losing money, bad investments can be risky if your timing is not right because the market rules that govern those investments are constantly changing.

The following graph on the growth of mutual funds illustrates this problem.

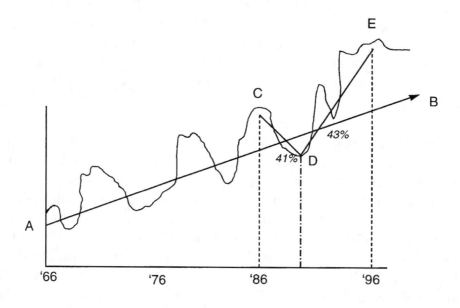

Take a look at Line A-B. This line very closely represents the stock market's success over the last 40 years. Many salespeople point this out, demonstrating that the stock market beats inflation. Line C-D shows the value of the general market when a couple we'll call Harry and Sarah invested $10,000 in mutual funds in January 1986 and then took their money out in May 1988, at which point they lost 41 percent. Why did they sell? Their daughter was diagnosed with leukemia and they needed the funds for medical bills. Line D-E shows the value of the stock market when another couple we'll call Tom and Judy invested $10,000 into the same mutual funds in February 1988 and took all their money out in May 1996, gaining 43 percent.

Two families who invested $10,000 each had results that were very far apart, even though they invested in the same time period. Mutual funds have grown in popularity over the last 25 years because of their good overall returns, and we take no issue with this apparent success. But there are rules and risks in buying mutual funds or investing in any other higher risk option. While mutual funds are represented to the buying public as a modest risk and a predictable investment, the real issue is *timing*. Circumstances can force a decision, wise or not....profitable or not. That's why it's so important to apply the Money Mastery principles we have already covered. Controlling spending, saving into emergency funds, and powering down debt as we have outlined in Principles 2, 3, and 4, all work to minimize cash-flow problems when the rules do change.

## Investing Your Way out of Debt

Another risk that people sometimes take is trying to invest their way out of debt. Many fortunes have been built on taking high risks, but far more fortunes have been lost because risks were not understood. Ask yourself this question: If I were the head of a family that made $5,000 per month, and had an emergency savings fund of $5,000 and $1,500 in an emotional fund but had nothing saved for long-term retirement, would I invest in my brother's new software start-up company? Many people have done just that, often losing every bit of money they put into the new venture and placing heavy burdens on marriages. The reason they lose their money (and sometimes their families) is because they don't control any of the variables of that investment and how those variables can change.

If you are deeply in debt or are not yet prepared for retirement, we recommend that you invest in much more conservative programs. The opportunity to make money can be found in many investment options, but knowing that you don't always control all the variables, and thus all the rules, will go a long way in helping you invest more wisely and time those investments so that you will lose the least amount of money should things change. In addition, by doing so, you will avoid losing more than just money, because bad investments can also place you in emotional risk and jeopardize your relationships with loved ones. Efficient use of money will go a long way toward protecting what money you already have as well as those emotional relationships in your life that are worth far more than anything money can buy. Efficient use of your money ensures that you will be able to safeguard your sacred family relationships and keep your emotional life intact.

# The Lack of Control That Change Can Bring

Another issue with change, in addition to the risk it introduces into our lives, is the way it can sometimes make us feel completely out of control. As we discussed in Chapter 5 and earlier in this chapter, the fact that we need to know the rules and to know how those rules are always changing can be overwhelming. It is natural in today's world to feel compelled to learn about everything that comes across our path. But this is unnecessary and definitely discouraging. The important point to remember in all this is:

***You don't have to know* everything, *but you do need to know* something.**

Here's an example of one couple who paid a high price when they became overwhelmed about learning tax laws and thus failed to learn even a few basic rules about capital gains.

Margaret and John Jacobs* wanted to sell their home, which they had originally purchased for $100,000, at its current appraised value of $600,000. They thought they could rent it out for a while if it didn't sell as long as they constantly had their home on the market. They decided not to take the time to review the capital gains laws and went ahead with their plan, renting the house for several years. Finally, the market turned around and a buyer came forward willing to pay their asking price. To the Jacobs' shock, however, their accountant told them that they would have to pay tax on the entire capital gain because they had not lived in their home for at least two of the previous five years. Because John and Margaret were not aware of the capital gains laws, their entire gain from the sale of their home was subject to tax. Not knowing the rules and how they had changed over the years, in this case, cost the Jacobs more than $100,000 in taxes!

As you can see from this example, it always costs more to be overwhelmed than it costs to learn a few things that will help avoid catastrophe. Making a commitment to begin learning at least a few things and to continue the learning process is the only way to maintain control in the face of an ever-changing world. By doing so, you will feel empowered by the confidence that even a little bit of knowledge gives you. Begin today to learn just a bit more than you knew yesterday. A good place to start is with your insurance policies, credit card contracts, and bank notifications. Read notices about changes that have been made to these documents over the previous year. One of our clients took this advice and read carefully a bank notification letter that stated that due to changes in the bank's policies, in order for her to keep her money market account, she would be required to open an accompanying checking account by a certain date or be charged fees. The bank's new policies, she felt, were inconvenient and annoying, so she took her money and invested it elsewhere.

# The Perceived "Lack of Time" to Deal With Change

We often hear our clients complain about the perceived lack of time in keeping up with how the rules are always changing. We like to point out at Money Mastery that once you understand your own emotions behind money and then put a system in place that helps track, control, and save money, the amount of time it takes to stay on top of the rules and their changes is minimal. We find that most people spend far more time worrying and stewing over finances than they will ever need to spend to get informed and stay that way. The amount of stressful energy that is directed towards financial problems is far greater than what will be required to learn how to solve those problems. Unfortunately, many people would rather spend time fretting than do anything about their situation. These same people are more comfortable swimming around in the stressful familiarity of their seemingly hopeless financial circumstances than investigating how a slight modification in their behavior could change their entire life. Those people who have the courage to break away from the binding power of their own cycle of helplessness find that they are able to quickly make changes for the better, and that they spend far less energy on money matters than they ever have before.

# Keeping Up With Changing Rules

The best advice on how to stay abreast of changing rules is simply to start! Begin today to take a more proactive approach to this principle. We're confident that with just a bit of effort to learn how rules can change, you can improve your life in ways you never thought possible. Following are some additional ideas to help you implement this principle more fully.

- *Don't be afraid of change.* We have already established that change occurs on a daily basis and that the only thing we can really count on is change itself. Consequently, there is no reason to fight it. We can be cowards, constantly worried about how a variation in our lives will affect everything, or we can face those variations head on by learning how to alter our life to meet those changes.

- *Set aside time to become informed about change.* You should plan to devote a certain amount of time each year to reviewing such things as modifications in life and medical insurance, new lending policies surrounding your loans, new bank policies, changes in tax law that may affect you personally, and changes in any other area that you think will affect your financial situation.

- *Subscribe to information sources and commit to study.* We have already noted that the time it takes to become informed and continue the process of learning is minimal compared with the time most people waste fretting and worrying over their financial situations. Subscribe to those publications and listen to news sources that will provide you with information on changes you need to know. Get in the habit of seeking out knowledge and then asking the important questions specific to your case. (See the Money Mastery Suggested Reading List found in Chapter 5.)

- *Seek professional counsel.* If after asking the important questions you are unable to find answers, it may be necessary to tap a knowledge source greater than your own. As we noted in Chapter 5, most professional advice can be secured for about $300. One way to get started is to meet once a year with a qualified financial advisor and with an insurance professional to evaluate policies, estate plans, and so on. In addition, we recommend that you meet with a qualified accountant or tax planner at least once every two years. Have him or her explain changes in tax laws that can affect your family or estate and let them suggest some tax planning strategies. Money Mastery offers coaching services that can systematically show you how to control change so it will best benefit you. (Refer to Appendix A for more information on these services.) Finally, we suggest that every couple of years, you go to a new planner or insurance agent to check out what your prior advisor has recommended. Getting another opinion is just as important when it comes to money matters as it is to your health. We strongly encourage you to look outside yourself for some of the answers by seeking qualified individuals who can best help you understand how the rules can change.

- *Develop a master plan.* We like to point out that in the absence of a plan, most people make financial decisions they cannot afford. We will discuss the importance of a master plan in more detail in Chapter 7. For now, the graphic on the right may help you see how having a goal or plan can help you stay on track and free of fear even in the face of continual change.

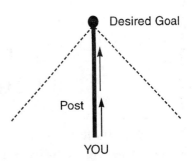

The post in this illustration represents your plan for reaching desired goals. At the top of this post is your desired goal, of say, retiring at age 65 with $900,000. You stand at the bottom of this post, intending to climb the rope that will lead you to your desired goal. By having a post (or a plan) in place, you are tethered to the desired goal at the top of the post and can climb with confidence toward it. Even as the winds of change blow you about while climbing the pole (represented by the dotted lines in the diagram extending out from the pole), you will still be tied to your desired end result because of the pole. Without a plan, we are tethered to nothing and the winds of change may blow us completely away from our desired goals altogether.

Decide today to be proactive in your approach to the rules and their constant change. Make a commitment to become wise, as the ancient Arab proverb affirms, by being one who knows that he knows all that he should to stay on the path to financial happiness. You can do it!

## Challenge #6

# Learn About Services
# That Can Keep You Informed

We challenge you this week to spend some time becoming familiar with the following three services that can keep you informed about pending tax law changes:

1. Hot Tax Tips (*www.tri.com*).
2. The "Money" section of your local newspaper (provides quick and easy resource).
3. *Wall Street Journal* (*www.wsj.com*) (consult this for details and more in-depth discussion).
4. Kiplinger Report (*www.kiplinger.com*).

You can access these through your local library or on the Internet at the Web sites listed. Find out through these services which tax law changes will have the most impact on you and your family. In addition, we further challenge you to investigate one other source that can keep you informed about important tax law changes by visiting your local library or surfing the Web for more information.

# Chapter 7

# Look at the Big Picture

Imagine for a moment that your financial situation is like a piece of art, to which you have been applying brush strokes of brilliance and detail. That detail is now beginning to take shape, creating an image of success that becomes more clear and more exciting every day. You began painting this "financial picture" the moment you applied Principle 1 by examining your emotions about money. You then applied the "brush strokes" of Principles 2, 3, and 4 by tracking your spending, saving more money, and powering down your debt. With a firm grasp of these principles, your masterpiece of financial accomplishment should really be taking shape. In Chapters 5 and 6, we encouraged you to work on the details of that masterpiece by knowing the rules and understanding how those rules are always changing.

Let's imagine further that applying all the Money Mastery principles we have covered thus far is like an artist applying very fine detail to several sections of a painting—adding veins to a hand, for instance, or light refraction to water. While that detail is important, every so often, the painter must step back and view the entire picture in order to stay focused on what he's creating and how that detail is affecting the overall image of the piece. The importance of stepping back so that you can view your entire situation leads to the next Money Mastery principle:

 ## Principle #7:
## Always look at the big picture.

Just as an artist begins to lose touch with a painting if he does not step back and look at its overall image, most people lose touch with their financial situation if they are not always "stepping back" to look at the big picture.

This map of the United States helps further illustrate why Principle 7 is so important.

Notice that a star has been placed right in the middle of the map. In order to get to the point on the map that the star represents, there are two things you must know. First, you must know where the star is. Is the star in Des Moines or in Oklahoma City? If the point on the map is neither of these two locations, then you must find where the star is located. Second, you must know where you are located in order to get to the star. If you are in Maine you will have to take a different route to get to that star than if you are in California.

Now let's analyze this illustration from your own financial situation. If you don't know how much money you spend each month, or what your real debt load is, you don't know where you are on your financial map. In addition, if you don't know how much money you need at retirement or how you are going to reach that goal, then you don't know where your star is on your financial map.

> *The two most important things you need to know are*
> *where you are and where you want to go.*

To reach your own star, or your financial goals, you must know how far away those goals are and where you are financially in relation to those goals. Everything we have been doing together up until now has been preparing you to be able to step back from your "financial picture" and see just exactly where you are. If you don't understand the emotions behind your money, you aren't ready to look at the big picture. If you don't have spending under control, you are not ready to look at the big picture. If you have not begun saving at least 1 percent of your income and started powering down your debt, you are not ready to look at the big picture. Why? Because doing these things helps you understand where you are on the map. In the beginning, as you took the challenge to get your bearings, it may have been hard to see, for example, how it can be possible to get completely out of debt in nine years or less. But if you've been successful at applying the Money Mastery principles, we are confident that it's becoming much easier to see the effects of your efforts.

The next thing you must determine is what your desired financial star is and what it will take to reach it. What is your star? Will it be early retirement at age 60? Will it include a trust fund for your kids? Will it provide for travel? As *Money* magazine writer, Denise Topolnicki, asks: "What will it be? St. Thomas in January with daiquiris at the 19th hole and a pile of dividend checks waiting for you back home? Or a part-time job at the local mall, macaroni four nights out of seven, and a stack of bills that will overwhelm your next Social Security check?"[1] Only you can decide. So many financial problems occur in people's lives because they refuse to look at the big picture, not realizing where they are now and where they want to go, ending up on the road to nowhere.

> *In the absence of long-term goals, you will make*
> *financial decisions you cannot afford.*

It's astonishing that close to 92 percent of people retiring today are totally dependent on Social Security for their monthly income,[2] and yet they have made on average more than $1.6 million over their lifetime! How is it that a person can make that kind of money and have little to show for it at age 65? The answer is simple: They don't plan to fail, they just fail to plan. This is further evidenced by the well-known U.S. Department of Health and Human Service's 1990 study. The report found that for every 100 people starting their careers, the following situation exists at age 65:

- 4 have achieved financial success.
- 25 are dead.
- 51 have annual incomes between $6,000 and $35,000.
- 20 are primarily living on Social Security and some small pension; of these, more than 60 percent are living below the poverty level.[3]

Again, we have to ask why is it that 51 percent of Americans are only receiving as little as $6,000 per year at retirement, why 20 percent are living below the poverty level after age 65, and why average age death statistics show that these people will be living below the poverty level for 28 years?! The answer is that people are not looking at the big picture in time to alter it before it gets too late.

Now let's meet a couple who had no long-term goals for the future and take a look at the emotional heartache that a lack of planning brought into their lives.

# Deena and Leon Hansen: No Map, No Plan

Case History

The Hansens* were from a rural community in the western United States and had built a loving family around their five children, whom they adored. Leon was a cabinet maker and Deena was a receptionist. They had purchased a big home that was a bit larger than they could afford, and because their children were heavily involved in athletic competitions, had also purchased a large pick-up truck to pull a fifth-wheel trailer so they could follow their kids to tournaments. Buying these expensive recreation vehicles, reasoned Deena and Leon, "would save on motel bills and meals while traveling." In addition to these vehicles, the Hansens also decided a boat would make a nice addition to their family's trips. Leon was sure that he could pay for the vehicles with the sales deals that he promised himself were always going to "come in next week." While the Hansens were a good, hardworking couple, they were constantly out of control financially. Leon owed close to $50,000 to vendors with whom he had contracted as a cabinet maker. Their home, which because of a debt consolidation was mortgaged for $220,000, appraised at only $190,000. The ultimate result was 20 years of highly charged financial frustration between Deena and Leon, and the eventual loss of their home, trailer, pick-up truck, and boat.

With these financial losses, Leon began to feel a terrible guilt as he realized that through his indebtedness he had cheated his loyal vendors because he couldn't pay them. Over the course of receiving coaching, the Hansens began to realize that they had been operating under a false premise, believing that their overspending would not catch up with them and that without any thought for the future they would still be able to retire comfortably. For years they had lived from one day to the next, spending any money that came into the family. As their coach explained Principle 7 and how the Hansens had not stepped back over the last 20 years to take a look at the big picture, Leon Hansen, a big, burly man who rarely showed emotion, began to sob. He put his head in his hands and cried uncontrollably for about 10 minutes.

"The realization of what I had done to myself and my family began to sink in, and I just couldn't deny the consequences of those decisions any longer," says Leon. "Deena sat there smiling...I think in relief, because she saw that finally I was seeing the big picture, one that she had been trying to get us to look at for years."

The Hansen's case is unfortunate and need not have happened. If they had known and understood the Money Mastery principles, paying particular attention to Principle 7, they could have avoided the absolute heartache of the situation.

•••

## Look at the Long-Term Picture

If we as Americans, living in the most affluent society in the history of humankind, are to avoid the all too typical and tragic mistakes that the Hansens made, it is imperative that we begin to look at the long-term picture.

To find out how willing you are to do this, ask yourself the following fundamental questions about your future financial goals (regardless of your current age):

1. How much money do I want to receive each month at retirement?
2. At what age do I plan to start receiving that retirement money?
3. Do I have specific plans to be able to assure I will receive this desired income?

Sometimes it can be hard to look into the future and try to predict what you will need and what you will want 20, 30, or even 40 years down the road. Because of that, most people procrastinate, never discovering where they really are today and leaving their future in hands other than their own. Looking at the big picture for our young clients seems particularly difficult. As we mentioned in Chapter 3, many individuals younger than age 40 don't want to admit that they will actually get old, assuming that youth is eternal. But stepping back to look at the big picture has nothing to do with age. It just makes good common sense, no matter how old or young you are, to have a firm grasp on where you are and where you want to go. As John Pierson states in his article "Thirty Years of Retirement," which appeared in both *Fortune* and *Money* magazines, "the sooner you start planning and saving, the sooner you start benefiting from 'the miracle of compound interest.'"[4] The longer you wait to start saving the harder it becomes. This is illustrated in the following graphic that shows, through Money Mastery's Master Plan software, the rate of saving you will need to maintain if you begin putting money away at 30 as opposed to age 50:

**Begin saving at Age 50:**

| Description | Current Amount | Annual Rate | Annual Deposit | Retirement Amount |
|---|---|---|---|---|
| | | Retirement Age: | 65 | |
| IRA | 75,000.00 | 5.00 | 2,000.00 | 199,076.74 |
| Residence | 125,000.00 | 3.00 | 0.00 | 194,745.93 |
| Savings | 6,000.00 | 4.00 | 1,800.00 | 46,848.12 |
| | | | Total: | $440,670.79 |
| | | | Percent Taxable: | 62.36 |

Amount you will have to retire on at age 65: **$440,670.79**

**Begin saving at Age 30:**

| Description | Current Amount | Annual Rate | Annual Deposit | Retirement Amount |
|---|---|---|---|---|
| | | Retirement Age: | 65 | |
| IRA | 75,000.00 | 5.00 | 2,000.00 | 594,341.76 |
| Residence | 125,000.00 | 3.00 | 0.00 | 351,732.81 |
| Savings | 6,000.00 | 4.00 | 1,800.00 | 156,250.53 |
| | | | Total: | $1,102,325.10 |
| | | | Percent Taxable: | 75.03 |

Amount you will have to retire on at age 65: **$1,102,325.10**

The difference is astonishing isn't it? When you truthfully answer the three questions we posed above, and then write down your responses, you will become instantly aware of 1) whether you even have any long-range goals, and 2) what you are doing today to accomplish those goals. You must learn to think about what kind of emotional impact the choices you make today will have on you tomorrow by asking yourself these important questions. Don't wait until you get older. Consider Leon and Deena Hansen. They thought "later" would never come and paid dearly for it when it did. Nothing stays the same, the world doesn't remain constant, and you will not always have time to say, "I'll do something tomorrow."

*Remember, there are no future decisions,*
*only decisions made today that will affect the future.*

Plan today as if tomorrow is already here because it will be upon you sooner than you think. Commit yourself to take control now!

# Look at Your Short-term Behavior in Order to See the Big Picture

While asking the tough questions about long-term retirement planning is important, it isn't the only way we need to step back to look at the big picture. We must also realize that the future depends on controlling our spending and borrowing today. Many times, the ability to be farsighted (or see the "big picture") is thwarted by our nearsighted need to spend money right now. The disease of consumerism contributes to this nearsightedness. Today's society is being devoured by the need to consume; it doesn't understand the impact of its consumption. It's easy to exchange coins for goods and services and it does not take talent or skill; even little kids can spend money. It's taking control of your money that most people find difficult. The childishness of spending money thoughtlessly and without a plan can be attributed to the respect toward money that has been lost from our society. We find that many of our clients are still acting irresponsibly about money, as if currency could be passed around like paper money from a Monopoly game.

One of the best ways to combat this irresponsible and shortsighted behavior is to become more aware of what we call "The Spending Decision." Each time a person decides to spend money they should be considering the following three fundamental elements of The Spending Decision:

1. **Utility:** Do I need or just want this item? Do I like the color, taste, size, power, dependability, performance, etc. of the item?

2. **Availability:** Do I have the money "available" to pay for the item? Do I have cash in my pocket, can I write a check, should I use my credit card, will the bank give me a loan?

3. **Affordability:** Can I "afford" the item? Does it fit into my long-range goals? What impact will this purchase have on my financial future?

Each of these decisions should be carefully considered each time you buy something. However, many people do not often give the third element any real conscious consideration. In fact, most of the time they think that because they have access to money in the form of cash, a check, or a loan, that they can afford to purchase something. Nothing could be further from the truth! The most critical question of the three you should be consciously asking yourself is whether you can afford to make the purchase. Understanding the definition of *affordability* will enhance your capacity to see the big picture like nothing else and is essential if you are going to make wise spending decisions. Affordability can only be determined based on the following two criteria:

## a) Long-Term Financial Goals

If you can achieve your personal long-term financial goals and spend money in this instance too, then you can "afford" it. Remember, in the absence of long-term financial goals, you will make financial decisions you cannot afford! For example, you might decide to buy a third car today at a cost of approximately $20,000. You have the means to purchase the car; it seems harmless enough, right? Maybe not. Without looking at the big picture and your long-term financial goals, you might not see that you truly cannot afford the extravagance of this automobile because $20,000 out of your pocket today will rob you of all the interest you would have earned at retirement had you left it in the bank. Remember the time/value of money: Purchasing the car will end up costing you $112,000 you could have had in your long-term savings for a later date when you really need it. Can you afford the car when you consider your long-term financial goals as part of the spending decision?

## b) Opportunity Cost

The second way affordability must be determined is by being aware that spending money always comes at a cost; we call this "opportunity cost." This means that you only get to spend a piece of money once. If you choose to spend a dollar in one place, you will no longer have it to spend in another. Of course you can replace that dollar, but you will still only have one dollar, whereas you could have had two.

Let's suppose that you feel compelled to stretch your financial situation so you can get into as big a home as possible. Can you afford to do so? Perhaps you can qualify for the loan, but does that mean you can really afford it? To determine that, you must weigh the opportunity cost of purchasing the house. Let's take a look at Mark and Joyce's "Get Out of Debt Report," which we first introduced in Chapter 4, to

# Get Out of Debt Report

GET OUT OF DEBT REPORT
For: Mark & Joyce

| Loan Description | Principal | Regular Payment | Power Payment | Interest Rate | Total No. Payments | Estimated Payoff Date |
|---|---|---|---|---|---|---|
| VISA | 460.00 | 55.00 | 0.00 | 18.00 | 9 | 11/23/99 |
| Medical/Dental | 2,420.00 | 215.00 | 55.00 | 12.00 | 11 | 01/23/00 |
| AT&T Credit Card | 2,236.00 | 110.00 | 270.00 | 16.50 | 14 | 04/23/00 |
| Auto | 4,866.00 | 325.00 | 380.00 | 9.50 | 15 | 05/23/00 |
| Furniture | 6,000.00 | 220.00 | 705.00 | 12.00 | 19 | 09/23/00 |
| Home | 116,032.00 | 815.00 | 925.00 | 7.50 | 103 | 09/23/07 |
| | | 1,740.00 | | | | |

| | Standard Debt Repayment- 29.5 Years | Accelerated Debt Repayment- 8.7 Years |
|---|---|---|
| Original Debt | 132,014.00 | 132,014.00 |
| Total Payments | 306,465.20 | 180,673.52 |
| Total Interest Paid | 174,451.20 | 48,659.52 |
| Savings Balance | 0.00 | 971,155.06* |

*If you save 1,740 per month for 20.7 years at 7.00%

get a better picture of what the actual opportunity cost of buying a new home might be.

You can see from this report that because they are powering down their debt, that somewhere between now and age 65 Mark and Joyce are going to have $971,155 available to them. Does that mean that they have enough money to buy a newer home twice the size of the one they are living in now? Yes, they can do whatever they want with nearly a million dollars. But, if they choose to take $300,000 out of their accumulated savings and buy a new house, that will cause their savings to shrink to less than $300,000, decreasing the amount of cash available to them at retirement. If they spend the money on the house now, will they have money later when they want to travel around the world? If they buy it now, could they be forced later to sell it at retirement because they can't afford it any longer? What will Mark and Joyce do then? Move into a tiny condo, or worse yet, in with their children?

What we have found is that most people have trouble weighing the actual opportunity cost of even the big-ticket items such as cars and houses.

Imagine how hard it is for them to weigh the opportunity cost of more consumable, disposable goods that they don't think they need to be so conscientious about. But opportunity costs are just as important to consider when determining the affordability of a less expensive item as they are when deciding whether to purchase a new car. When we understand that everything we purchase has an opportunity cost attached to it, then we can make wise spending decisions.

> *Remember, you can have anything you want,*
> *you just can't have everything you want.*

If you choose to spend money on more consumable goods rather than toward paying off a debt or accumulating wealth, you must understand the consequences of that decision because it eliminates opportunities for the future. Affordability, then, can ultimately only be defined within the context of your long-term goals and opportunity costs.

To help you more consciously consider your long-term goals, we recommend that you read *Premeditated Procrastination* by Tom Murphy. This book offers very simple strategies to help you stay with a goal. Recognize that almost everything you do will either move you toward your goal or away from it. These everyday choices are what Murphy calls "Moments of Decision." The key is to adhere to those things that move you toward the goal and eliminate those things that deter you from achieving it. For example, if you buy that sweater and slacks without consciously asking yourself whether you can actually afford them based on your long-term goals and the opportunity costs, then you are at a negative moment of decision that might possibly move you away from your goals.

> *Almost every decision you make in life has its affect on your goals.*
> *The task is to recognize that the moment to make a decision*
> *has arrived and carefully consider it.*

What is the best way to ensure conscious decision-making about your spending, future goals, and your overall big picture? Following are some strategies that might help you begin thinking about both short-term and long-term goals.

# Develop a Master Plan

A master plan is like a "snapshot" in time, representing all that your financial life is composed of today, and what its possibilities are for the future. In order to develop a master plan, you will need to combine that which you already know about spending and borrowing with some long-range planning for the future. Then, you will need to forecast what you must do today in order to achieve those future goals. Examining where you are today and what you want to do to get where you are going tomorrow is how a master plan can help you look at the big picture. We have found that our clients, once they have a master plan in place, begin to get a real sense of what their financial future looks like. In the areas where they come up short, they make plans to make up the difference. When people can see the reality of their retirement and their financial future as it's really going to be, they make serious changes!

Now let's meet some individuals who did some long-range planning and forecasting in order to develop a master plan. See how taking a snapshot in time helped bring power and financial control into their lives.

Case History

## Sherri Long: Planning for Retirement

Sherri Long* was a 45-year-old postal worker from Jacksonville, Florida. She had recently divorced and was very concerned about her big financial picture. She wanted to make sure that when she was 65, she would have enough in savings so that she could retire. We began working with Sherri using the Money Mastery Retirement Worksheet from the Master Plan software (refer to Appendix A), which is shown on the next page.

The first section of this worksheet helped Sherri identify what she thought her retirement needs would be. At the time, she was grossing $35,000 a year. She estimated that she would need about 80 percent of that to retire comfortably, which meant she would need $28,000 per year at retirement. The worksheet further helped her assess what funds would be available to her in the future. She determined that she would be getting $13,300 from Social Security annually, a $5,000 per year company pension, and $2,400 from a duplex she owned, from which she collected a monthly rental fee of $200. When all of these outside sources of income were totalled, Sherri found she would have $20,700 in annual income she could count on at retirement. This meant that she would be $7,300 short each year in order to reach her retirement goal of $28,000 annual income. With the help of the Retirement Worksheet, Sherri now realized that she must save a grand total of $161,330 by the time she reached age 65 in order to retire as she desired. Based on what she had already saved, she had to come up with $141,330. After subtracting the $1,200 a year that her

# Money Mastery

### Principle #7 - Retirement Savings Worksheet

This worksheet is designed for anyone to obtain a basic understanding of financial needs at retirement. The numbers and estimates will not be exact, but can be used as general guidelines toward retirement planning.

### *Retirement Needs*

| | | | Example | You | Spouse |
|---|---|---|---|---|---|
| 1. | Enter your current annual income. This is your gross income, before taxes and other deductions. | 1. | $35,000 | | |
| 2. | Estimate the percentage of your income that you will need at retirement. This estimate should be between 70% and 90%. Enter the percentage on line 2. | 2. | 80 % | | |
| 3. | Multiply line 1 by line 2. This is your approximate annual needs at retirement. The higher the percentage in line 2 the more comfortable you will live at retirement. | 3. | $28,000 | | |

### *Retirement Income from Outside Sources*

| | | | Example | You | Spouse |
|---|---|---|---|---|---|
| 4. | Enter the annual amount from Social Security. Use the Social Security Estimate worksheet on page 2. Enter the amount from line C. | 4. | $13,300 | | |
| 5. | Enter the annual income from company pension plans (not 401(k) or personal savings). | 5. | $5,000 | | |
| 6. | Enter other annual income (like rental income, annuity income, etc). | 6. | $2,400 | | |
| 7. | Add lines 4, 5, and 6. This is the total income received from outside sources for your retirement. | 7. | $20,700 | | |

### *Retirement Savings Goal - How Much You Will Need*

| | | | Example | You | Spouse |
|---|---|---|---|---|---|
| 8. | Subtract line 7 from line 3. This is the amount of income you will need to generate from personal savings. If this number is less than zero, you have planned very well. | 8. | $7,300 | | |
| 9. | Use the Retirement Needs Table on page 2. Enter the total amount you will need from line F. | 9. | $161,330 | | |
| 10. | Enter the amount of your current savings balances for retirement. Include my savings accounts, IRA's, 401(k) balances, etc. | 10. | $20,000 | | |
| 11. | Subtract line 10 from line 9. This is the amount of savings you will need to accumulate by the time you retire. | 11. | $141,330 | | |

### *Annual Savings Amount*

| | | | Example | You | Spouse |
|---|---|---|---|---|---|
| 12. | Use the Savings Factor table on the back to determine the savings factor for your retirement savings. Enter the factor here. | 12. | .034 | | |
| 13. | Multiply line 11 by the savings factor on line 12. This is the annual amount you will need to save in order to maintain you desired standard of living. | 13. | $4,805 | | |
| 14. | Enter the amount your employer contributes to your 401(k) annually. | 14. | $1,200 | | |
| 15. | Subtract line 14 from line 13. This is the annual amount you need to be saving. | 15. | $3,605 | | |
| 16. | Divide line 15 by twelve to determine the monthly amount. Find room in your Budget Builder for this amount. | 16. | $300 | | |

Factors in this worksheet assume an average 4% inflation rate and a 5% growth rate during retirement. It is also assumed that the participant will live to age 90, which is longer than the statistical life expectancy, and that there will be no retirement money remaining for heirs.

employer contributed to a 401(k), the Retirement Worksheet helped Sherri to see that she would need to be saving $300 per month in order to reach her retirement goals.

Sherri was very pleased with these findings, and even though she found she was quite short of the funds she would need to retire, she was excited to know she now had a plan in place and that she was in control of it. Because of Principle 2, she knew how she could save $300 per month and now felt in charge of her future, which gave her much needed peace of mind.

• • •

Case History

# Joe Barcone: Funding Retirement

Joe Barcone* was from Des Moines, Iowa. He was 49 years old when he became alarmed with how little money he would have at retirement. He had always planned on retiring at age 65, but had not put away any significant amount of money into a savings program. When his Money Mastery coach asked him to look at the big picture, he realized he was not in control of his smoking habit and the money it was costing him. As he kept track of his spending, he found that he was smoking three packs a day and it was costing him $251 per month. After looking at his situation closely he realized that if he could stop smoking and put the $251 into a savings account every month for the next 14 years, he could accumulate more than $88,000 towards retirement. This motivated Joe and he eventually quit smoking. When he applied Principle 2 and Principle 7, he was able to make a major effort toward solving a big financial problem. That problem was one that he didn't even know existed until he stepped back and took a hard look at where he really was and where he really wanted to go.

• • •

A master plan is like the post we mentioned at the end of Chapter 6.

By having a post (or a master plan) in place, you can be tethered to your desired goals. Even as the winds of change blow you about, you will still be tied to your desired end result. Without a master plan, you are tethered to nothing and the winds of change may blow you completely away from you desired goals altogether.

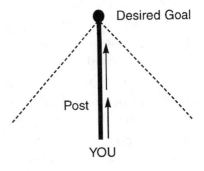

Both Sherri and Joe learned the value of developing a master plan, which is bringing more control and peace of mind into their lives than they ever thought possible. However, creating this kind of plan requires some tools, which up until now have been very limited. Most people do not own a financial calculator or know how to use one to figure the time/value of money. Knowing how to calculate the numbers needed to predict the future can be very complex when such things as interest, growth, risk, maturity, and taxation must be considered. Fortunately, there are a myriad of tools available today, including those offered by Money Mastery, which make it easy for the average consumer to develop a master plan. The Retirement Worksheet that Joe and Sherri used is just one way that Money Mastery works to make master planning easy because it gives a greater view of what will be available at retirement. This worksheet is included at the end of this chapter as part of Challenge #7. The Master Plan software is also another extremely valuable tool that includes Master Planning, Get Out of Debt reporting, Retirement Worksheets, and several other valuable features which help you play "what if" scenarios with your money using powerful financial calculating tools. (To obtain Money Mastery forecasting tools, including the Master Plan Software, refer to Appendix A for more information.)

## Become Aware of Things That Can Affect the Master Plan

In addition to developing a master plan, another way to ensure that you are able to see the "big picture" is to become aware of those things that can affect your master plan and what you may need to do to adjust it in order to stay on track.

### Changes to Social Security

Did you know that according to the Social Security Administration, by 2029 the Social Security trust fund will not have enough money to pay benefits to the wave of aging Baby Boomers? In 1951, there were 20 workers for every one person retired. Today there are 2.5 workers for every retiree. By 2015, the ratio will be 1 to 1.[5]

A *USA Today* article also states that by 2032 the entire Social Security fund will become totally insolvent.[6] Many people are baffled by this insolvency. They mistakenly think that their payroll taxes deducted for Social Security go into a personal account at the Social Security Administration, which will be paid to them as soon as they retire. This is not so. The *USA Today* article "For Boomers, Social Security Is Near Bust" explains:

"What [payroll taxes] are not spent on benefits are used to buy Treasury bonds. That means the Social Security surplus is being loaned to the federal government to cover its other expenses."[7]

In other words, your FICA taxes are not being set aside for you but are being spent in other areas of government where policies on spending are not fiscally sound. That means that with the influx of Baby Boomers making huge draws on the system, if you will be 65 in the year 2032, you may not be able to count on any Social Security income at all.

What will you do to make up for those lost funds? How will you modify your master plan to offset those losses?

If you, similar to many other Americans today, are mistakenly falling back on Social Security as your only source of retirement income, perhaps it's time to rethink things, especially in light of the changes to the system that are sure to occur. According to the Commissioner of Social Security, Kenneth S. Apfel, "Social Security can help support your family in the event of your death and pay you benefits if you become severely disabled. But it was never intended to be your *only* source of income when you retire or become disabled, or your family's only income when you die. Social Security supplements the income you have through pension plans, savings, and investments."[8] As we have already noted, it is important to know where you are and where you want to go in the future so that you can revise the master plan in case these Social Security funds are not available to you at retirement.

## Extended Life Expectancy

According to the article "Thirty Years of Retirement" by John Pierson:

*It used to be that people retired at 65 and died by 72. Seven years of retirement. Not anymore. Thanks to advances in medicine, quite a few folks will live to a ripe old 85 or 90. Instead of seven years of retirement, many Americans can now look forward to 30 years of life after work. Thirty years! These words can strike terror into the heart...or joy. Joy for those who've planned fun things to do with the last third of their time on earth and have saved enough money to pay for them. Terror for those who who haven't planned and haven't saved. As it happens, far too many people feel terror, or would feel terror if they only knew how ill-prepared they are for 30 years of retirement. Or for 20 years. Or for 10.[9]*

How prepared will you be if you should live at least 30 more years after retirement? Because of medical intervention, it is possible that you will live much longer than your money will last. You must take this extended life expectancy into consideration and adjust your master plan to help best prepare for the future.

## Deteriorating Health

Although Americans are living longer, statistics show that the last 10 years of a person's life are the most expensive because many times they are spent in a nursing home or long-term care facility. More than 60 percent of people age 65 and older will need long-term care before they die[10] because even though Americans live longer, their quality of life in the later years is not very good. Unfortunately, health is one aspect of our lives that is hard to control, especially as we age, so it's vital that you anticipate that your own health may deteriorate and take steps to plan for it. Again, John Pierson puts it best in "Thirty Years of Retirement": "By the time members of the Baby Boom generation have reached retirement, in about 2020, an average year in a nursing home will cost $160,000. Crushing expenses like that can soon destroy the best-laid retirement plans and nest eggs."[11]

Charles E. Gerrard, a financial advisor columnist, points out that we plan well for other risks and catastrophes, but we don't often think about planning for poor health in old age: "How does the risk of long-term care compare to other major risks that we insure against?"[12] asks Gerrard. Take a look at the following chart to see how he answers the question.

| Home Fire | Auto Accident | Major Medical | Long-Term Care |
|---|---|---|---|
| 1 out of 1,200 homes | 1 out of 240 automobiles | 1 out of 15 people | 1 out of 4 people |

Obviously, we can see from these figures that your risk of needing long-term care is much greater than an auto accident, for instance. Are you taking that risk seriously by making long-term insurance a part of your master planning?

## Bad Investments

As we have already outlined in previous chapters, investing money in mutual funds and other ventures comes at a risk, and we may not always be able to predict how those investments are going to pay off. Naturally, everyone makes mistakes and sometimes we may lose big on those investments. According to an article entitled, "Ten Problems That Often Hit Investors If They Lose Track of the Big Picture" by Jonathan Clements, "Investors often parcel out their dollars, without comparing the likely return from different investments. In pursuit of market-beating returns, many investors single-mindedly search for the best investments." Clements cites Pittsburgh financial planner Jonathan Kuhn in the article as saying, "They [investors] look at one mutual fund or one stock at a time, rather than looking at the whole portfolio."[13] Other investments that may not always make sense include loading up on lots of stock of the company for which you work. If the company makes it big, then the payoff can be an important part of your retirement future. But if the company goes belly-up, you will have lost those funds that could have been invested in more stable options. Being aware of the many ways you can invest wisely will help you stick to your long-range goals and keep the master plan on track.

## Disappearing Company Pension Plans

It wasn't long ago that most full-time employees could look forward to some sort of company pension at retirement. Those days are disappearing. That's because most employers can no longer afford the expense of paying retired employees a full pension with health insurance and other benefits. Today, most employers require their employees to contribute to their own retirement program through a 401(k) plan and will match any contribution to that plan up to 100 percent. If, at one time, you were counting on a company pension to fund your retirement and it has now been eliminated, you may need to revise your master plan to make up the difference. You can still make good headway towards saving for retirement by taking full advantage of 401(k) programs. Unfortunately, many people do not see the value of these programs and are not contributing to them; don't be one of them. As *Money* magazine advises: "Stop living only for today, and make a lifetime commitment to your 401(k). Fund it to the max."[14] Offset any loss of pension plans by finding out the maximum annual amount of money you can contribute to your 401(k) program. If you cannot put away the maximum amount, at least contribute enough to get the maximum matching contribution from your employer. If you are self-employed, plan to contribute the maximum amount allowed by law into your IRA or Roth IRA accounts.

Other factors you may want to consider that can affect the Master Plan include inflation, life insurance proceeds that can be taxed, estate taxes, and changes to IRA plans.

The following photo representing a river depicts why it is so important to adjust your master plan so you can always see the big picture:

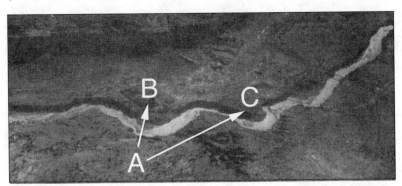

Let's say you are standing on the banks of this river at point "A." You wish to cross the river to reach a point marked "B" directly opposite of where you are standing. Although you will make efforts to cross the river by walking, swimming, or boating directly across to the other side, it is not possible to reach this point due to the river's current that pulls you slightly down river, landing you further downstream at the point marked "C." To get to the point marked "B," you will need to adjust your plan by starting up stream from the point marked "A" just a bit farther. Although it is difficult to anticipate every factor that may pull you "down stream" and affect your long-term big picture, becoming aware of at least some of these factors will help you stay in control and on track.

Most people spend more time planning a party or vacation than they do planning their lives. Don't be one of them. Take the following challenge so you can see your big picture more clearly.

## Challenge #7

# Begin to Plant the Master Plan "Post"

Stepping back from the big picture will be very eye-opening. We can promise that if you will take a serious look at the long-term picture and analyze how your short-term behavior is affecting that picture, you will take even more control of your financial life, bringing you a sense of well-being and peace of mind that you have never known before. To help you achieve that peace of mind, we challenge you this week to decide where you are on your financial map and where you want to ultimately go in the future.

1. Create a "Vision Statement" for your life. What is it that you really want to achieve overall, and what will you need financially to get there?

2. Reach out and plant the Master Plan "post" solidly into your financial ground by answering the following questions:

   a. At what age do I plan to retire?

   b. How much money do I want to receive each month at retirement?

   c. What plans do I already have in place that will help me receive my desired monthly retirement income?

3. Using the Money Mastery Retirement Worksheet on page 118, determine in what areas you fall short of your desired monthly retirement income. Consider what you may need to do to make up for any shortfalls.

# Chapter 8

# Organize Your Wealth

We invite you to begin this chapter with a moment of reflection. Think about the way you felt about your financial future before you began reading this book. Now, after learning seven of the 10 Money Mastery principles, consider your feelings today about your current financial situation and your retirement plans for the future. How have things changed? In our experience, once our clients get to this point, the synergistic nature of each of the Money Mastery principles energizes and empowers them to take further control and brings more happiness to their lives than they ever thought possible.

We are confident that you too are becoming more optimistic about your options for future financial security and happiness. With a big picture view of how everything can work together for your good when you apply each of the principles, you are now ready to embrace the next Money Mastery principle. This principle will help you see the value of arranging and coordinating all aspects of your master plan so that you can keep more of what you make, and create an optimum amount of new wealth:

 ## Principle #8: Organizing your finances enables the creation of additional wealth.

What does it mean to organize your finances in order to create more wealth? As you have gained greater control of your spending and borrowing, and have begun planning and saving for the future, you have naturally been led towards more opportunities to create wealth. As this new wealth accumulates, your overall financial picture, though perhaps better understood by you now, is also becoming more complex. Without organization, it is impossible to continue painting that picture because you will not understand how to order and control some of the complex issues that can surround wealth creation and retention within that big picture.

The image on the right of a "junk" drawer helps further illustrate why Principle 8 is so important in light of everything else you have learned thus far.

If you're like most people, you probably have a "junk" drawer in your home where you keep odds and ends. You most likely store items in this drawer because you haven't decided where an item really belongs and figuring out where to put some things is

overwhelming and time-consuming. Consequently, nothing in the drawer ever gets properly organized.

Most people have a "financial junk drawer" as well, like the one illustrated here. If you were to examine your own financial junk drawer what would it look like? Perhaps it would resemble this picture where a mishmash of important financial and legal documents have been tossed. Like the junk drawer in your home, this drawer only exists because you haven't taken the time to order and arrange your important financial documents or to sort and review them as necessary.

## Organize Your Financial Life

If you are going to continue painting that detailed masterpiece of financial brilliance, you must adopt an organizational system that will help you arrange and order your financial life. Once a system is in place, disorganization and procrastination will diminish making it much easier for you to maintain that big picture view so you can see better how to create additional wealth.

Although you have just been introduced to the idea of organizing your finances, as you have taken each of our challenges you've already begun practicing good financial organization. For example, when you begin to understand your own feelings about money (Principle 1), you are actually getting mentally organized about your financial situation. When you track your money (Principle 2), you are implementing organization in a big way! Remember Stan Harbrecht, who until he became organized through tracking, did not see the amount of money he was wasting on Big Gulps? When you spend your money into emergency, emotional, and retirement savings categories (Principle 3), you are implementing the kind of ordered financial organization that brings real peace of mind and long-term rewards. When you power down your debt (Principle 4), you are executing a very strict form of organization by prioritizing debt and working systematically to eliminate it, saving thousands of interest dollars. When you take the time to know the rules and are aware of their changes (Principles 5 and 6), you are mentally organizing the information you need to play complex financial games and come out the winner. And when you develop a Master Plan (Principle 7) and set measurable financial goals, you are practicing one of the most important forms of organization, evaluating your short-term and long-term objectives in order to create more wealth.

As you can see, organization helps us sort out complex emotional thoughts and feelings related to money. Organization helps us make good spending decisions. Organization helps us make good investment choices. Organization helps us get out of debt—quickly! Organization creates additional wealth because it helps us make the most out of the hard-earned assets we create through good long-term planning. Once you have organized every other aspect of your financial life by following each of the previous Money Mastery principles, it is vital that you continue on that path in order to take full advantage of the wealth you create through this organization. If you do not make the effort to do so, you will make decisions that will make it difficult to keep that wealth. A disorganized mind keeps people in poverty.

*Absent an organized approach,*
*you will make financial decisions you will regret.*

Eliminating financial junk drawers so that you can create more wealth is an idea that needs more attention. Most information sources today claim the secret to financial control and wealth creation lies in making more money and avoiding taxes. But at Money Mastery, we believe that fixating on a bigger income is like adding more "stuff" to the junk drawer rather than ordering and optimizing that which is already there.

Thomas J. Stanley makes a good case for this in his article, "Why You're Not As Wealthy As You Should Be." Stanley's research indicates that of all the high-income occupations in the United States, physicians are the worst at holding onto their money. "The fact that so many MDs are millionaires— by estimates printed in *Medical Economics* magazine (nearly 40 percent have a net worth of $1 million or more)—is a testament to how much doctors earn rather than how well they manage their money. Simply put, doctors could and should accumulate much more and at a much younger age but they don't."[1] Stanley also notes that after surveying people in posh neighborhoods across the country, that he discovered something odd: "Many people who live in expensive homes and drive luxury cars don't really have much wealth. They may earn a fair amount of money, but they spend it all."[2] Stanley also points out in his article that if you make $1 million a year and spend $1 million, "you're not getting wealthier, you're just living high. Wealth is what you accumulate."[3]

Accumulating wealth requires organization because if you're not organized you won't keep any of the money you make, regardless of how little or how great the amount may be. Although a higher wage certainly helps create greater opportunity to accumulate wealth and covers a multitude of mistakes, it doesn't automatically guarantee a person will be rich. It has been our experience at Money Mastery that high-wage earners are just as apt to create financial junk drawers as anyone else, becoming disorganized and unable to control some of the complex issues surrounding financial planning and estate organization. Organizing how you spend and save the money that you have already earned is the real secret to creating and retaining additional wealth.

> *Financial organization helps you learn how*
> *to get more out of the money you already make.*

Now let's meet a family that profoundly illustrates how financial disorganization and a lack of planning made it impossible to control the complex issues surrounding the disbursement of assets during an estate settlement. See how this family lost more than just money because they had no organized plan for keeping highly valued and sentimental property safe within the family circle.

Case History

# The Judds:
# Unable to Keep It All in the Family

Sam and Janice Judd* had been married for 25 years when their marriage finally broke apart. Parting as friends with four children, the Judds decided that Janice would take the house, which had been Sam's childhood home. In exchange for the home and all furnishings and other assets that Sam left Janice, Janice would continue making payments on the home until the mortgage was paid in full. The house, besides having sentimental value for the Judd children and a 70-year history in the family, sat on more than five acres of prime property. Its real estate value was very high and all during the years that Sam and Janice had been married, a nearby developer had hounded the Judds to sell the house and property. The Judds always refused, wanting to keep the house within the family and to possibly pass it on to their children later. Because Sam and Janice had not taken the time during their marriage to do any financial planning or estate organization, when they divorced, there was no plan in place to ensure that Janice would disburse of the house in due time in a way that would best suit their children. Within five years of the divorce, Janice had met a new man and remarried. Because she was anxious to get on with her new life, she was also anxious to get away from the old house where she and Sam had spent so many turbulent years together and where there were often sad and painful memories.

With a new husband and life, Janice no longer had a desire to be tied to the Judd family home in any way, even changing her desire to pass it on to her children. Janice hastily sold the house and property for almost half its market value to the same developer that had hounded her for more than 20 years.

Within four years of her new marriage, Janice became ill and passed away. Janice had no will and proceeds from the sale of the Judd family home, which were being paid out yearly, were subject to probate fees and state and federal estate taxes. In addition, half of the remaining monies from the sale of the Judd family home that did not go toward paying the estate tax were inherited by Janice's second husband. The remaining half went to the Judd children, each of whom only received $3,000, when in fact they should have received a far greater sum due to the extremely high real estate value of the home. The Judd children, while not that interested in the actual monetary inheritance from their deceased mother's assets, were somewhat bitter over the loss of the home to a powerful developer.

• • •

Of course Janice Judd did not set out to hurt her children, but because she and her first husband did not take time to plan and organize their financial and legal affairs during their divorce, their children experienced a great monetary and sentimental loss. All that regret could have been avoided with a little organization on the part of Sam and Janice Judd.

# Why Don't More People Get Organized?

Naturally, organization makes sense. But why is it that so many people fail to do it? As we have already noted, many people simply do not want to take the time to sort through the issues surrounding their assets. We have also found that people don't get organized because they simply do not know how! That's because many of the issues related to financial organization are emotional and the amount of energy and effort it will take to resolve these issues can sometimes seem overwhelming. Without an understanding of where to start the process, fear sets in, making it difficult to draw up a will, or create a trust, for instance. Attorneys have reported to us that only two in seven families have a will made out in writing, and of those, only 20 percent are current wills in the last five years.[4] But how important is a will? As illustrated through the Judd family, if you don't have a will and you pass away, your assets will go to a court for processing (probate), and there will be fees and expenses that will come out of your assets to pay for this processing.

## Mental Shivering

Without knowledge of how to start, where to turn for help, or what resources to utilize, many individuals go about handling all aspects of their lives minus any organization, creating great stress and tension. Much of this tension is due to an inability to make decisions and resolve concerns. In, *A Guide to Confident Living,* Dr. Norman Vincent Peale teaches that the main ingredient in tension is mental disorganization. "The mind refuses to make decisions about many different things and as a result always carries around numerous burdens, never really resolving any of them. The mind in this situation reacts somewhat like the body when shivering. One shivers when passing suddenly from a warm to a cold area; the body attempts to accommodate itself quickly to the sudden change in temperature. It has been estimated that as much energy is expended in a half-minute of shivering as in several hours of work. This results in depletion of vigor. In a similar way, shivering in the mind depletes its force when one fails to practice the fundamental principle of mental organization."[5]

We find that most people spend far more time worrying and stewing over financial planning and organization than necessary because they are in the process of this "mental shivering." Unfortunately, many people would rather spend time fretting than learning a few simple skills that will help them improve their situation. These same people are more comfortable with the stressful familiarity of their financial situation than investigating how a slight modification in their behavior could create an even better economic outcome for them and their families. It goes without saying that if you take the time to get your spending and borrowing under control, then work very hard to build up a sizeable nest egg, you should also take the time and effort to learn how to protect that nest egg through good financial organization.

One of our clients we'll call Bob, is an excellent example of how getting organized and implementing Principle 8 can help you protect your hard-earned nest egg. As Bob reviewed his company pension plan, he found that the company was under no obligation to make a contribution to his pension if the company made no profits. Bob hadn't paid any attention to the annual reports in the past, but he now carefully reviewed each of them and found that the contributions to his retirement plan had been very small in three years out of five. If this trend continued, Bob knew he would have a very small accumulation at retirement. He approached his employer and inquired about the small contributions. "We're sorry, but we have not been very profitable and in the future it will be unlikely that the company will contribute any more than we have this year," his boss said. Knowing this, Bob realized that he better examine all his options. In his case, he pressed for more income and got it. He then took this extra money and established his own retirement plan.

We've established the importance of getting organized, but perhaps you're thinking, "Well, I'd like to get my financial life in order, but I'm one of those people who just doesn't know how." Don't worry. Getting organized is easier than it seems and can bring tremendous rewards to your life.

# Ideas for Good Financial Organization

Getting that financial junk drawer in order doesn't have to be difficult. Besides giving it the time it deserves, following are some basic ideas that will make organizing your financial life a little easier.

### Get Mentally Organized

The first thing to consider when getting organized is your own mental state. Ask yourself if you are mentally disorganized or mentally calm. If you are a person who constantly "shivers" because you cannot make decisions about financial concerns, now is the time to learn how to organize your mind. Dr. Peale suggests an excellent way to do this:

*Get the calm selective ability to take up one thing at a time and concentrate upon it. Deal finally with it, if possible before passing to the next matter. When you organize your mind, a sense of power will come to you, and you will soon wonder at the ease with which you can handle responsibilities. Your capacity for work will increase, so will your pleasure in what you are doing. Strain and tension will subside.[6]*

As Dr. Peale notes, the best way to begin getting organized is to calm your mind first by doing one thing at a time. Trying to tackle your entire financial situation in one sitting will simply overwhelm you. Organization requires patience and steady persistence, but it does not require that everything be done at once. Getting organized is like the man on an African safari who came across a little pygmy who had just finished eating an elephant. "How on earth did you manage to do that?" the man asked the pygmy. The pygmy replied, "I didn't swallow him whole, you know. I ate him one bite at a time!"

## Know What to Keep and What to Throw Away

After you have organized your own mental processes, you should next consider how to sort through important paperwork. Some people save almost everything they come across. Others can't stand to keep anything. But not saving and organizing the right documents can cost you and your family thousands of dollars. At the same time, preserving the wrong documents ensures that you'll go through life heavily burdened by worthless material. The American Institute for Economic Research published an article entitled, "How to Avoid Financial Tangles," which gives important tidbits of wisdom on what you should keep and why:

*The problem most of us face is the avalanche of paper we must deal with each year. What to keep and for how long? What you need to ask in order to decide what to keep is: Why am I keeping this? The second question you might ask is: What would be the worst thing that would happen if I did not have this and I needed it? And finally, is it likely that someone else will be keeping this record and could I get a copy of it if I needed to? There is only one fundamental reason to keep any given document: to prove something. Some things you might need to prove to yourself. What these are is left up to personal discretion....there is, however, far less flexibility and discretion for the things that you might be called upon to prove to others. These include records of payments and receipts, especially those that substantiate the legitimacy of exemptions, deductions, or credits taken on income tax returns. One broad category of things you need to keep is composed of items that you may need to refer to in order to prepare your tax return for the year.*[7]

Once you have determined what to keep so that you are not deluged by a barrage of worthless material, you should organize important documents into a simple, yet efficient, filing system. We have found that 95 percent of our clients, when asked where they keep their automobile policy cannot accurately pinpoint where it is located in their house—95 percent! That means that most people do not have a filing system by which they can quickly and easily locate all important documents they may need at a moments notice. We suggest filing paper work using the following categories in the order they appear:

- Automobile.
- Debt.
- Home Improvements.
- Income Tax.
- Investments.
  - Taxed.
  - Tax-Free.
  - Tax-Deferred.
  - Life Insurance.
  - Capital Gains.
- Medical/Dental.
- Miscellaneous.
- Property Tax.
- Utilities.
- Warranties.
- Wills/Trusts.

## Organize Based on What's Left After Taxes

Once you have filed important documents in your home so that they can be easily located, it is important to go one step further by organizing all your financial assets into a system based on the following four criteria:

1. Organizing an investment based on its risks.
2. Organizing based on the liquidity of the asset, that is, how easily can I sell this investment?

3. Organizing based on timing, i.e., when will it be wise to sell this investment?

4. Organizing based on valuation, or in other words, based on a dollar value.

In addition to these criteria, we have found the most successful way to get organized is based on a fifth and most critical criteria:

5. Organize based on the taxation of investments.

While each individual's situation may vary according to risk, liquidity, timing, and so on, everyone's situation is universal when it comes to taxation. All people are subject to tax. Unlike the other criteria, taxation does not vary greatly depending on your individual situation. Taxation is definable and absolute. (The subject of taxation and how it affects your wealth and what you can do to tax dollars will be covered in even greater detail in Chapter 9 and particularly in Part II of this book.)

The taxes we pay are demanded of us before we do anything else. That's why we teach our clients to organize their finances around what they get to keep after paying taxes. By doing so, it becomes easier to understand what you need to do to plan because you know what's absolutely going to be left over. If you organize based on risk, for instance, you may never be quite sure what you have to work with because that risk will always vary. But taxes are sure. By organizing based on taxation, you can know either how to keep  taxes to a minimum, thus keeping more of your wealth, or know how much money you will have left after paying taxes so you can feel free to work with the balance in order to create additional wealth.

Important documents should be organized in what we call "Tax Drawers." Because there are only five ways you can be taxed, financial affairs should be organized based on the following five dimensions of taxation:

- **Drawer #1: Taxed**—savings accounts, checking accounts, reserve funds, and so on.
- **Drawer #2: Tax Free**—municipal bonds, Roth IRAs, and so on.
- **Drawer #3: Tax Deferred**—401(k)s, IRAs, and so on.

- **Drawer #4: Life Insurance**—life insurance can be taxed in a variety of ways, and most often is not taxed until the benefit is received in cash while you are living. If you die, then the income is tax-free. How you receive the money determines whether it will be taxed or not.

- **Drawer #5: Capital Gains**—real estate, mutual funds, or stocks that appreciate in value. There will be a loss or gain depending on tax rules at the time.

Organizing your financial assets into these five "Tax Drawers" will help you find a lot of extra money you didn't know you had. How is this possible?

1. It makes it easier for you to visualize your assets and in terms of what you get to keep for retirement.
2. It provides a basis for calculating and projecting the accumulation of your wealth.
3. It helps you understand the impact taxes have on your long-term savings.

The following example illustrates the importance of organizing into "Tax Drawers."

Suppose you put all your money in a 401(k) program for retirement. This money will grow because you will be able to defer paying taxes on it all those years you are working. However, when you begin withdrawing this money, 100 percent of it will be subject to income tax. If you organize your assets into five "Tax Drawers" and use a forecasting tool such as the Master Plan software you will be able to play "what if" scenarios with your money. "What if" you put this money into a tax-free municipal bond rather than a 401(k) or capital gains account? "What if" you took your money and put it into a Roth IRA, or "what if" you put it elsewhere? Of all the tools available to get and keep oneself organized financially, being able to project your debt, income, and assets over time is among the most valuable. Staying organized is a function of being able to sweep all financial elements (spending, borrowing, and saving) out to a future date and look at the results. By doing this, it is easy to play "what if" so that you can test how a financial decision made today will impact your future. Using organizational tools such as the Master Plan software can help you determine the best way to accumulate money so that you can maximize your assets. And because there are no future decisions, only decisions made today that affect the future, this knowledge allows you to make much better choices. You can make the necessary changes today and not get down the road and have to look back and say, "Oh, I wish I had known!"

Now meet Susan*, a woman whose husband could not see how his actions would affect his family over time because he did not properly organize his life insurance. Susan and her husband Bob* had set up a trust and conveyed most of their assets to it. Each would be the beneficiary of the trust if one of them died. After their deaths, the trust assets would be used for the education and support of their minor children until the children were 35, at which time they would receive their inheritance outright. When Bob completed life insurance forms at his place of employment, he named as beneficiaries "my wife and children." Bob was killed in a freak on-the-job accident soon after. Bob's company insurance totaled $600,000, and although Susan expected to inherit all of it and manage it for herself and her two teenage sons, she was shocked to find that because Bob had named "my wife *and* children" as beneficiaries, Susan was only entitled to one-third of the proceeds. Her two sons were entitled to the other two-thirds. Because they were minors, Susan had to become appointed by the court as custodian for her sons' $400,000, and manage it under strict court supervision. She was also dismayed to learn that when her sons turned 18, they would be entitled to receive their money to spend as they chose. Bob's lack of care in naming his beneficiaries left a large sum of money in the hands of his children instead of his wife.

## Take Advantage of Estate Organizing Tools

As we have already noted, creating and retaining additional wealth can be complex. Tools such as Money Mastery's Estate Organizer (refer to Appendix A for information on how to obtain it) can help organize that complexity because they're designed to help you order and store, in one place, all essential information and copies of documents you'll need to manage the important financial events in your life. At your death, your heirs will be able to easily find all the necessary documents and financial information they'll need to quickly and inexpensively settle your estate. Once you have gathered all pertinent information, you are then prepared to meet with a qualified estate planning attorney. Using an estate organizer you will have easy access to all the information you will need, assuring you of the most cost effective meeting and keeping the time you need to retain a lawyer to a minimum.

A good estate planner, like the example of the Money Mastery Estate Organizer shown on the following page, is designed to help you collect and organize everything you will need to manage your estate and all your financial documents:

---

*Estate Masters Institute*
## EstatePlanner™     INDEX

---

### Overview of EstatePlanner Sections and Contents

What happens when we don't use planning tools like the Estate Organizer? A man we'll call Frederick declined to purchase the Estate Organizer as had been recommended saying, "I've already got a great organizational system that I'm sure will help my family if I die." When he did pass away, his "great organization system" had little of the information the family really needed. His daughter, inexperienced in settling an estate, spent needless hours listing assets, getting appraisals, and updating financial information—much of which could have been expedited by proper completion of the Asset Schedule in the Estate Organizer. Was this costly? Her accountant and the estate planner estimated that the settlement costs could have been reduced by thousands of dollars had proper financial information been maintained by her father.

Because Frederick didn't feel the need to do estate planning and organization while he was still alive, his daughter was burdened with doing it later.

# David Steed:
# The Power of Organization

Case History

David Steed* is an example of one of our clients that understood the power of proper organization. As he learned about Principle 8, he began organizing all his assets according to the five "Tax Drawers" and then further arranged his important documents using the Money Mastery Estate Organizer. While organizing his various titles, deeds, and contracts, he came across his home deed and noticed it had never been legally assigned to him. The home that he lived in had been built in the 1860s and had been handed down to his family members from generation to generation. Around 1920, it was sold to someone outside the family. Later, David arranged to buy the house back and raise his own family in it, never realizing that the deed hadn't been signed over to him.

David sought legal counsel and an attorney ended up charging him a little more than $5,000 so the home could be reprocessed and recorded properly at the county seat. The man who had previously owned the house was now 92. The attorney mentioned to David as they completed the transaction that if David had not been able to accomplish the transfer before the 92-year-old man had died, it would have taken nearly five years to clear the title at an expense of well more than $15,000. Because David took the time to begin organizing his assets and estate documents, he saved himself a lot of trouble and several thousand dollars.

• • •

When we get organized, we find that emotional issues can arise and we learn many things about ourselves and our financial situations that we didn't previously know. This knowledge, while eye-opening, can also be very encouraging, building a motivating fire underneath us.

## Hold Annual Reviews

It is always a good idea to hold an annual review of important paperwork related to your vital documents and assets to be sure they are in order. Set a specific time to hold this meeting with yourself and/or your companion once each year. It may be a good idea to hold it on your birthday or at the first of the calendar year so that you don't forget it. Using an organizing system such as the Estate Organizer, begin gathering all important papers for each of the sections within the organizer. For example, one year you may want to begin by completing and/or updating the Personal and Family Information section by gathering dates, household information, medical records, and family histories. Another year you may want to concentrate on life insurance, will preparation, trusts, and so forth.

Holding annual reviews can save thousands of dollars and maximize the wealth you have already created. Take for instance, Laurel* who was reviewing the index in her Estate Organizer when she remembered her father telling her 30 years earlier that he had some stock set aside for her. She had forgotten all about it, but did some checking and found the certificates. Laurel took the certificates to a brokerage house, which determined that the stocks had a value of $45,000. Because Laurel took the time to hold an annual review, her memory about the stocks was triggered and she was able to retrieve the money from the certificates to use as a down payment on a new house.

Another client, Harold*, began reviewing all his insurance policies on his house, cars, and professional practice during an annual review. He then took the policies to his insurance agent, who pointed out that Harold no longer needed half the insurance he was carrying. Eliminating this insurance saved Harold more than $7,000 annually in premiums.

George Briggs* had tried to be careful in the way he had organized the disbursement of his assets through a well-planned will. Unfortunately, George had inadvertently disinherited his own children when he titled his assets for the children in "joint tenancy" with Joan, his second wife. When George died, Joan, being the surviving joint tenant on the assets, became the sole legal owner. It didn't matter that her late husband's will left his assets to his children; the wording of the jointly titled assets prevailed over the wording of George's will. Because Joan despised the Briggs children, she instructed her lawyer to transfer all of the newly acquired inheritance from George's assets to a living trust she had created for her own children from a previous marriage. "George's children always treated me like the evil stepmother, and I don't want them to get anything!" Joan told her lawyer. Ethically bound to be Joan's advocate, the lawyer did as she was instructed. When Joan died,

George Briggs's legacy did not get passed on to his own children. Instead, it went to the children of his second wife, leaving the Briggs family with nothing. Although Joan's lawyer felt bad about the outcome, the law was clear. Even though the Briggs children hired an attorney, they ended up empty-handed. If George Briggs had been better organized, he would have learned that the way assets are titled at death determines who inherits those assets. If he had held an annual review of his important documents, George might have caught the dangerous wording in his will and changed it in order to protect his children.

# Be Aware of Things That Can Affect Your Estate Organization

Becoming organized and staying that way not only requires a good estate organizing system, but also demands that you be aware of those things that through change, can affect your assets over time. By applying Principles 5 and 6, you can stay ahead of any changes that may affect your ability to keep and maximize wealth by becoming informed and staying that way. Following are just some of the things that can affect your estate planning and organization:

- Tax laws that affect real estate purchases.
- Newly created retirement accounts.
- Living trusts, wills, and probate.
- Capital gains tax charged when mutual funds and/or stocks are sold.
- Changes to estate tax laws.

By implementing Principle 8, you can be sure to keep more of your assets secure. We can promise that if you get organized, you will see financial rewards you never thought possible, and you will thank yourself later for having the forethought to plan ahead. And more importantly, your loved ones will be grateful to you for caring about them enough to plan for their future through solid organization. If you haven't done so already, decide today to put your financial affairs in order!

## Challenge #8

# Begin Establishing
# an Estate Organizer System

We challenge you this week to obtain an estate organizing system. We strongly recommend the Money Mastery Estate Organizer, which is a comprehensive collection of everything you will need to get fully organized. Information on how to obtain this system is in Appendix A of this book. Once you have an estate organizer, take the challenge to do the following:

1. Review financial documents that you are still unsure about and identify areas that need greater clarification. Seek professional counsel about these issues.

2. Review each of your current savings and investment programs and determine if they are taxed, tax-deferred, or tax-free.

3. Begin organizing each of your savings accounts, life insurance policies, and capital gains items into the five "Tax Drawers."

4. Project what your financial future will be like based on your goals from the Master Plan.

# Chapter 9

# Understanding Taxation

Having come this far, you should be astounded with the way your financial life is being transformed into one with the potential for great success. There is still more work to do, but you are well on your way to achieving goals that you probably thought were impossible only a few short chapters ago. By now you should be in better control, better informed, better prepared, and a whole lot more organized. By organizing your finances into the five tax drawers we outlined in Chapter 8, you're now ready to take the last few steps towards true money mastery. To do this, consider carefully the ninth Money Mastery principle.

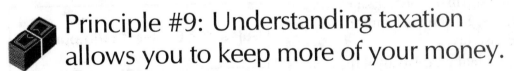

## Principle #9: Understanding taxation allows you to keep more of your money.

As we mentioned in the Introduction, along with consumerism and indebtedness, excessive taxation is a force at work in the world today that we must learn to control if we are to create or maximize any kind of wealth. It goes without saying that taxes are a huge part of our lives and have a pervasive effect on everything we do. Not only do they have an impact on how much money we keep, but they also affect what we can and cannot do with that money. Almost all Americans pay a fortune in taxes over a lifetime, but most don't fully understand the true extent of their tax bill. Consider the following illustration of this massive tax obligation.

First, we must pay income taxes, both federal and state.

The amount Americans pay here is extensive, especially when you consider that those taxes are being collected for close to 40 years.

Add FICA (Social Security), Medicare, Medicaid, and individual state income taxes. When these taxes are added to income tax, it requires the average American to work until approximately May 8th of every year for the government before they can begin earning any money they can keep for themselves.

Next, add to these taxes the burden of property tax on homes and cars, along with estate tax, and inheritance tax. When you combine these with all the other taxes, some Americans are paying as much as 55 percent of their annual income in taxes!

Don't forget the quiet taxes that slip in unnoticed: sales tax, use taxes, gasoline tax, import tax, and excise taxes.

Finally, add to all of these taxes the penalties (which are also a tax) and interest expense for late filing and excess distribution from retirement plans.

What do you get? A staggering tax bill that makes it very hard for the average American to get ahead!

| Federal/State Income Taxes |
|:---:|
| **+** |
| FICA/Medicare/Medicaid |
| **+** |
| Property Tax/Estate Tax |
| **+** |
| Sales Tax/Excise Tax/Import Tax |
| **+** |
| Penalties/Interest Expense |
| **=** |
| **Whopping Tax Fee!** |

This gigantic tax bill now exceeds what most Americans pay for food, clothing, lodging, mortgage, and transportation combined![1] Hard to believe, isn't it?

Most Americans have no idea the amount of money they are actually paying in taxes. The following quote by the 17th-century French finance minister, Jean Baptiste Colbert, very aptly sums up the subtle ways that taxes are exacted from us:

*"The art of taxation consists in so plucking the goose as to obtain the largest possible amount of feathers with the smallest amount of hissing."*

Why is it that our feathers are being plucked so extensively? Based on our work with thousands of clients, we believe it's because most people have bought into a host of dangerous tax myths that keep them perpetually yoked to a relentless tax machine.

# Tax Myths

Rather than "hissing" at government, which some preach as the answer to the tax problem, the objective of Principle 9 is to help dispel these myths and motivate you to spend the time and effort necessary to understand taxation so that you can learn how to keep the government from plucking as few of your feathers as possible.

Let's take a look at some of these tax myths.

## Myth #1: A huge tax bill is inevitable and inescapable.

This pernicious myth has evolved over the years due to the continual expansion of government, which has required more taxes from Americans to sustain its girth. As we have already mentioned, taxes have become the largest expense for most people, exceeding what they pay for food, clothing, rent or mortgage, and transportation combined. While many Americans grumble over the high cost of taxes, few seem to question what they can do about it, assuming they must pay such ridiculous sums of money. The truth of the matter is that the IRS gets away with taking far more money from you than is required by law simply because you don't know any better. This chapter and the subsequent chapters in Part II will help you learn the rules you need to know to escape an unnecessarily large tax burden.

## Myth #2: A large and complex government supported by citizen tax dollars is necessary.

Through an attitude of "entitlement," many Americans are unknowingly subjecting themselves to larger and larger tax burdens. As we have already noted, over the last 60 years, post-Depression generations have held their hands out in expectation, demanding more services and greater benefits from government than at any other time in the history of the United States. But tax-supported social programs are getting harder to fund as more Americans sag under the financial burden of such programs. Now is the time to ask yourself if you can really afford to continue believing the myth that a large and complex government is necessary, especially when it is getting increasingly more difficult to support it. Abandoning an attitude of entitlement and embracing the Money Mastery principles that promote self-reliance and self-control will go a long way toward reducing overall tax burdens.

## Myth #3: Questioning the system and trying to take the most advantage of it increases my chances of getting audited.

This is absolutely untrue. The people that believe this myth only do so because they don't know about all the "good" tax laws and are therefore living in fear of the IRS. Remaining in the dark about tax law and just paying what you think you have to pay, without learning what is really expected might seem like the "safe" path to take, but it's actually a foolish one. By applying Principle 5, you no longer need to cower in fear; knowing the rules changes everything because it puts you in control.

## Myth #4: My accountant takes care of my taxes.

As we noted in the Introduction, this is the most pernicious tax myth of all. It is also one of the worst wealth killers and makes more money for the IRS than anything else. Believing such a myth is like eating nothing but fatty fried foods, ignoring the symptoms of heart disease, and then going to your doctor and expecting him to make you well. Likewise, if you don't know the rules for good "tax health," you can't go to your accountant and expect he or she to save you thousands of dollars in taxes at the end of each year. If you don't know what to tell your accountant by December 31st, there is very little he or she can do for you. In addition, accountants will usually err on the side of conservatism with regard to deductions in order to avoid the severe IRS penalties that they will incur if they wrongfully counsel their clients. This protects their own pocketbook, but not usually yours. If you want to stop wasting money on excessive taxes, it is up to you to learn the rules and make sure your accountant is helping you take full advantage of them. If you believe that your accountant takes care of your taxes, you will end up paying more to the government than even it requires!

*Remember, your accountant is only as good as you are.*

This does not mean that we are dismissing professional advisors as many times we do need their expertise, but we can save ourselves a lot of money by knowing some of the rules ourselves and what we personally need to understand about our own situation so that our accountants can help us save every tax dollar they can.

Which of these tax myths are keeping you in a cycle of excessive taxation? If we want to keep more of the money we make and prevent as few feathers as possible from being plucked, we must see the futility of such myths and get out from underneath them.

In addition to this, if we want to keep more of the money we make, we must understand more fully how it is taxed today, tomorrow, and even after we die. To do this, let's examine each of the life phases we pass through and how our money is affected by taxes within each of these stages.

# Accumulation Stage

During this stage, a person usually works 40 or so years to provide for his own needs and the needs of his family. If you are still in this stage, you spend the majority of your time accumulating money. During this stage, you should be applying all of the previous Money Mastery principles we have covered in order to keep as much of that money as possible. If you are, we can guarantee that you are accumulating far more wealth than you ever have before because you are in control. But now it's time to take things a step further by understanding how taxation can affect how much of this accumulated money you actually get to keep. To do this, you must understand that in the accumulation stage, your money is taxed in one of two ways:

1. **The W-2 System:** This system of paying income taxes is for W-2 employees who work for an employer. Most people fall into this category. The taxes on W-2 income are easy to calculate because they are automatically withheld from a paycheck. Under this system, there are certain tax deductions that are allowed when filing the standard 1040 tax form. These deductions are provided for on IRS form "Schedule A."

2. **The Self-Employed System:** The second system for paying income tax is prescribed for the self-employed. These individuals use IRS form "Schedule C" to determine taxable income. Schedule C allows for business expenses to be deducted before taxes are figured. When a person uses Schedule C, the rules allow for many more deductions than are listed on Schedule A. After a self-employed individual uses Schedule C, they

still get to itemize their deductions on Schedule A (just like W-2 employees) before calculating their income tax.

# Schedule C: Expenses Section

| Part II | Expenses. Enter expenses for business use of your home **only** on line 30. | | | | | | |
|---|---|---|---|---|---|---|---|
| 8 | Advertising | 8 | 390.00 | 19 | Pension and profit-sharing plans | 19 | |
| 9 | Bad debts from sales or services (see instructions) | 9 | | 20 | Rent or lease (see instructions): | | |
| 10 | Car and truck expenses (see instructions) | 10 | 3,290.00 | a | Vehicles, machinery, & equipment | 20a | 210.00 |
| 11 | Commissions and fees | 11 | | b | Other business property | 20b | |
| 12 | Depletion | 12 | | 21 | Repairs and maintenance | 21 | 157.00 |
| 13 | Depreciation and section 179 expense deduction (not included in Part III) (see instructions) | 13 | | 22 | Supplies (not included in Part III) | 22 | 532.00 |
| | | | | 23 | Taxes and licenses | 23 | 1,219.00 |
| 14 | Employee benefit programs (other than on line 19) | 14 | | 24 | Travel, meals, and entertainment: | | |
| 15 | Insurance (other than health) | 15 | 260.00 | a | Travel | 24a | |
| 16 | Interest: | | | b | Meals and entertainment | | |
| a | Mortgage (paid to banks, etc.) | 16a | | c | Enter 50% of line 24b subject to limitations (see instr.) | | |
| b | Other | 16b | 200.00 | d | Subtract line 24c from line 24b | 24d | |
| 17 | Legal and professional services | 17 | | 25 | Utilities | 25 | |
| | | | | 26 | Wages (less employment credits) | 26 | 2,450.00 |
| 18 | Office expense | 18 | 422.00 | 27 | Other expenses (from line 48 on page 2) | 27 | |
| 28 | Total expenses before expenses for business use of home. Add lines 8 through 27 in columns ▶ | | | | | 28 | $9,130.00 |

Example: On Schedule A, medical expenses must exceed 7.5 percent of adjusted gross income before you can deduct these expenses. However, the self-employed are allowed to deduct 100 percent of all medical expenses if they have provided for them on line 13 of Schedule C. Many kinds of expenses that cannot be deducted on Schedule A are deductible on Schedule C.

If W-2 employees knew how to move normal expenses to Schedule C, thus making them tax deductible, they could keep more of their money. If you take advantage of the self-employed tax system, you could put an extra $2,000 to $5,000 in your pocket every year. That also applies to self-employed people who rarely take full advantage of all the business expense deductions available to them through Schedule C.

If you are not self-employed, you may be asking how it's possible to take advantage of the self-employed system. It's simple; the tax rules allow for it! The reason most W-2 employees don't use this system is because they don't know that the rules allow any person, even those who are W-2 employees, to take deductions using Schedule C.

*Don't miss out on this valuable tax saving point: All W-2 employees can make use of the powerful deductions on Schedule C.*

To the extent that you take advantage of this rule, you could be deducting anywhere from $5,000 to $19,000 in expenses. Let's take a look at some of the misconceptions that most W-2 employees have about the Schedule C system that keep them from taking full advantage of it:

## Misconception #1: I am not self-employed.

Many W-2 employees don't think they can use the Schedule C system because they incorrectly presume that they are not self-employed. What we tell our clients is that there are many hobbies and activities that could be considered a viable business venture if they would consider them as such. Here's an example of a Money Mastery client that learned how to take advantage of the self-employed tax system by examining their own lifestyle for tax saving opportunities:

# Perry and Michelle Kamboris: Mixing Love of Dogs with "Self-Employment"

Case History

Perry and Michelle Kamboris* were from a small midwestern town and liked to go boating at many different lakes and reservoirs with their two registered Husky dogs. The couple loved meeting new people and making friends from all parts of the country. After learning about Money Mastery Principle 9 and the significance of Schedule C the Kamborises immediately applied this new information to their travel lifestyle. They realized that their knowledge and interest in Huskies, along with their love of travel, could be turned into a "self-employment" business opportunity.

They arranged for a referral fee with the same person from whom they bought their dogs to begin promoting the sale of the Husky breed while on their boating trips. They then took pictures of their dogs and prepared an inexpensive advertising flyer that they placed on all windshields of the trucks at the boat docks wherever they went boating. The response was overwhelming! They not only made some money on the referral fee, but now, because they were running a small side business, they were able to deduct the veterinarian bills on their dogs, travel expenses for their boating trips, and even the food for their Huskies on Schedule C. Veterinarians' bills alone for their two dogs averaged $300 each month and the travel expenses to various lakes and reservoirs were sizable. Combining these Schedule C deductions with all their other deductions, Perry and Michelle began saving $300 on their taxes each month. By putting this saved tax money into a retirement savings plan, the Kamborises will have nearly $178,000 extra interest income in 25 years simply by forming a small business.

"We were thrilled when we actually saw the results of our actions on paper," said Perry. "We had no idea that developing our hobby with the dogs into a little part-time business venture could bring such valuable dividends. Plus we love going out on the boat and meeting new people anyway. To us it was a no-brainer!"

The Kamborises' self-employment opportunity took very little of their time to operate and brought tremendous tax savings to their family. Because they were already heavily involved in the Huskies as a hobby, it seemed only logical to them to take advantage of that interest by creating it into a viable business and then into a viable tax write-off. If you are a W-2 employee and think that you cannot be self-employed, it's time to think again.

*If you don't have a side business, it's time to start one!*

How to get that side business up and running and how to take advantage of all the tax write-offs a self-employed person is entitled to will be covered in complete detail in Part II of this book. Please be sure to refer to Part II after reading Chapters 9 and 10.

## Misconception #2: I can only deduct expenses up to the amount of income I made in my self-employed activities.

This is false. You do not have to make a profit in order to take advantage of Schedule C deductions. Most self-employed people in their first few years make little profit on their businesses, and start out with huge losses that they carry forward on their tax returns. Did you know that expenses for advertising, car and truck maintenance, commissions and fees, insurance, legal and professional services, office, equipment, supplies, travel, meals, utilities, and entertainment can all be deducted from your self-employed activities, regardless of whether you turn a profit or not? In Part II, we will show you all the airtight ways to take these business deductions using Schedule C. Using a tax diary, we'll explain how to keep accurate substantiation records that are IRS audit-proof.

## Misconception #3: I feel like I am cheating by taking deductions for simple activities I was going to pay for anyway.

This too is an incorrect assumption. The tax laws provide for these deductions, even if you were "planning to do them anyway." As was illustrated by the Kamborises, it makes no difference where the source of self-employment comes from, the tax laws provide for those deductions. Even though the Kamborises were going to travel and show their Huskies around to new friends and acquaintances anyway, they might as well have used that time and those resources to conduct a little business, make a little extra money, and thereby take advantage of available tax write-offs. The tax laws that allow for those simple activities to be deducted are available to all who will learn them. Naturally, there are certain requirements in order to consider activities as a viable business venture and to claim deductions from Schedule C. You must go through the process of setting up a business, but the law is clear about the protocol for this as well, making it possible for anyone to take advantage of it if they will only try. (Please refer to Chapter 13 in Part II for information on how to do this.)

One of our clients we'll call Karen* dried flowers as a hobby. After learning the value of Principle 9, she decided to turn this hobby into an actual business. She set up a separate bank account and obtained a business license from her city government. Today Karen makes a few sales per month, and although her business is not a large source of income for her and her husband, Karen now writes off all her flowers and drying chemicals on Schedule C. She is able to maintain her hobby while enjoying some added income and saving valuable tax dollars all at the same time.

## Misconception #4: I don't want to trigger and IRS audit.

This is another naïve comment we often hear. People incorrectly assume that if they take the deductions allowed on Schedule C and then have a big loss, that this will spur the IRS to come after them. This is wrong. As long as you know the rules and apply them fairly, there will be no problem. The way to legally and ethically pay taxes while taking advantage of tax laws for the self-employed is fully covered in Part II.

From each of these examples it is clear that these fearful misconceptions are the product of ignorance about the real tax laws and how they work. There are numerous ways to minimize the amount of feathers plucked from you during the accumulation stage if you will only take the time to learn about them. Once again, we strongly encourage you to explore the detailed treatment of these tax saving strategies in Part II.

# Conservation Stage

After a person spends 40 years earning money during the accumulation stage, he eventually begins to slow down and prepare for retirement. This retirement period is called the conservation stage. If you are no longer accumulating money, you are now using that which you have already saved as a means of support. As we mentioned in Chapter 7, because people are living longer, most individuals will need at least 20 years of retirement funds in order to live comfortably during this stage; some may even need money for as long as 30 years. But knowing how to project into the future how much your assets will be worth so you will have this 20 to 30 years of money can be difficult. Predicting how much your assets will grow, how much risk will be carried with each investment, and how inflation will affect those funds, can be hard. Not only do each of these factors influence our assets over time, but trying to predict how taxes will influence the overall worth of our retirement investments can also be tricky. Following is a common example used by industry experts to examine the value of investments.

Let's suppose you invest $10,000 for 40 years in a long-term savings plan that receives an average annual rate of return of 12 percent. At the end of 40 years you will accumulate $930,000 right? Wrong. Take a look at the following graph:

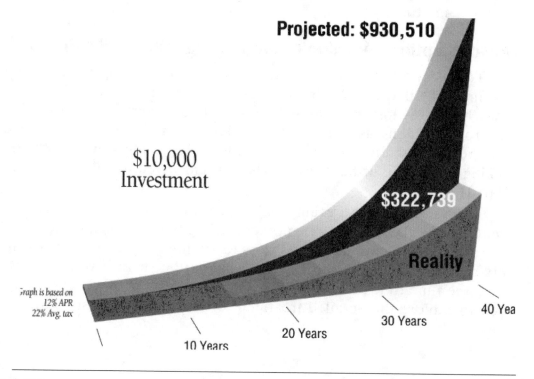

**Projected: $930,510**

$10,000
Investment

$322,739

**Reality**

Graph is based on
12% APR
22% Avg. tax

10 Years

20 Years

30 Years

40 Yea

You will notice from this diagram that if you were taxed at a 22 percent rate on that gain, year after year right out of that savings plan, the amount of money you would actually earn in 40 years is only $322,000. You will lose two-thirds of your wealth to taxes even paying in a low-end tax bracket of 22 percent. Losing $600,000 in taxes is a huge amount of money, don't you think?

When investment values are presented to you, you must consider whether the growth figures of that investment reflect the amount of taxes you will be required to pay over the life of the investment. Remember the time/value of money and how certain factors such as taxes can affect the *value* of money over *time*.

Now let's use that same $10,000 to illustrate another way that the true impact of tax obligations on "conservation" money can be hidden from plain view. Suppose that same $10,000 was deposited into a CD that paid 8 percent interest. If you received the 8 percent on $10,000 in one year, the bank would owe you $800. If your tax bracket is 25 percent, then you will pay $200 in taxes on that $800 interest the bank pays you. At the beginning of the second year, how much money will you then have in the CD? The answer should be $10,600, right? Actually, the amount is $10,800. The reason for this is because at tax time we generally do not withdraw the $200 from our CD and deposit it in our checking account to cover the check we write to the IRS for taxes. We come up with that $200 from other sources. The $800 of interest income will just stay in the CD and that $200 tax liability will be absorbed into our whole owed tax amount. In other words, what really happens is that we compound our taxes in savings, camouflaging the true tax impact.

## Assessing Your Retirement Plans

Taxes have such a subtle, yet profound effect on our money. That's why, as we mentioned in the last chapter, we encourage our clients to organize their conservation stage funds into the five tax drawers. By doing so, it becomes easier to see how taxes will affect your retirement money over time. In addition, using calculating tools like the Master Plan software can help you project how much money you will have at retirement age, the total value of all your assets at retirement, and what percent of them will be subject to some kind of taxation.

For example, without the tools to play "what if" scenarios with your money, it may be easy to get caught up in popular retirement and savings programs that may or may not help save the most tax dollars. Take 401(k) retirement programs, for instance. Most people today are very enthused about these tax-qualified deferment plans because they can be a great way to benefit from an employer's matching contribution. The argument for these plans is that when a person begins to withdraw funds at age 65, he or she will usually "be in a much lower tax bracket" than they were in during the "accumulating" years so theoretically, they should pay much less in taxes on those funds. But that may not actually be the case. Bart Croxford, a CPA writing for the *Salt Lake Tribune*, spells out what may be closer to the truth about tax-deferred plans such as 401(k)s:

> *"I have never seen anyone who promotes tax-qualified plans run the figures through retirement. They run the figures to age 65 or beyond and show how much more you can accumulate if you use a tax-qualified plan, such as an IRA or 401(k), and defer your taxes until retirement. But in savings, as in sports, it's the final score that counts, not the score at half-time or even after three quarters. The real clincher in the whole plan is the fact that with tax-qualified plans, one must pay taxes on the entire amount taken at retirement, including the growth, which accounts for the largest portion by far. Whereas on tax-free plans, one pays no taxes on the growth at all. In other words, one can be taxed either on the seed or the crop. With tax-qualified plans, one pays on the crop and on tax-free plans, one pays on the seed. One does not receive the tax deduction now but he or she receives a far greater benefit by not having to pay taxes on the amount received at retirement.[2]"*

Of course we do not automatically dismiss 401(k) and IRA accounts as a way to save for retirement, and we strongly encourage you to take advantage of matching contributions your employer may make towards a fund. However, Croxford does make an excellent point about saving valuable tax dollars:

*"You can be taxed either on the seed or the crop. Which would you prefer?"*

The only way to determine what you prefer is to organize your assets into the five tax drawers and use a forecasting tool such as the Master Plan software. By doing so, you will be able to predict more accurately exactly what kind of effect paying taxes on the seed or paying taxes on the crop will have on your various retirement plans.

As an example, take a look at the chart on page 155, which compares taxed, tax-deferred, and tax-free investments over time.

This illustration shows the value (after taxes) of your $10,000 investment over a 28-year period. If you invest that money today at 7 percent interest

$10,000
Investment
28 Years
7% Interest
25% tax rate

Value of
investment
after taxes

$41,900

Taxed
Investment

$49,866

Tax
Deferred
Investment

$66,488

Tax
Free
Investment

and just pay the taxes along the way, you would have $41,900 at retirement. If you defer the taxes and pay them at the end of 28 years, the amount you would earn is $49,866. But if you accumulated the money tax-free, the investment would be worth $66,488 in 28 years. That's a big difference.

Understanding how your money can grow and how you can cut your tax obligation in half if you invest it in tax-free savings programs such as life insurance, municipal bonds, and Roth IRAs can make a big difference during the conservation stage of your life. To gain that understanding, apply Money Mastery Principles 5, 6, and 7 so that you can become informed about various retirement plans, the rules that govern them, and which plans would be best to integrate into your big financial picture.

Joe and Miriam Price* are a good example of how investing wisely during the conservation stage can save a lot of tax dollars. The Prices were in their 50s when they decided to buy a duplex and rent it out. The experience was so good they decided to buy additional duplexes located on adjacent parcels. They took the rental cash flow from these duplexes and paid off all their debt. Over the course of a year, the value of the property on which the duplexes sat went up. Joe and Miriam decided to trade the group of parcels for one large commercial piece of land and were able to build a 42-unit rental property without going into debt for it. The new property is now appraised at $1.2 million. The Prices have created a trust, have retired, and are now living on the income. The interesting part of this story is that Joe was a "traditional" W-2 employee and decided to use the management of the properties as his home-based business in order to claim as many Schedule C tax deductions as possible. The Prices are now making a decent income off what was once their "side business," and saving taxes along the way.

# Distribution Stage

At some point, we all die. Whatever assets we have built up during the accumulation stage and the conservation stage will be distributed either by way of our own plan, or if we don't plan, according to the laws in effect at the time of our death. You've heard of the statement, "You can't take it with you." Well, either you spend your money before you die, or it will be spent by others after you pass away during this distribution stage. All states have laws specifically treating how to distribute money and assets of a person who passes away. The reason for this is because only two out of seven individuals have preplanned how they want to distribute their wealth after their death.[3]

As we noted in the last chapter, without a Master Plan and good estate organization, your money will be handled in a way far different from that which might be the most beneficial to your surviving loved ones. Remember the Judds we profiled in Chapter 8, who made no provision for the sale of the family home, and lost it to a powerful developer? Without tax planning and estate organization, following are only some of the ways that money and assets can be devoured by the state.

| **Probate Fees:** | If you have not planned well by preparing a will before death, every bit of your money and any property or accumulated assets will be subject to probate fees and court processing costs. These can eat into your assets considerably. |
| --- | --- |
| **Appraisal Fees:** | These are charged to appraise your property and to assess taxes at death. |
| **Legal Fees:** | These may be charged to determine actual owners and to contest wills, etc. |
| **Forced Sales:** | If taxes are owing at your death, the IRS will often force the sale of property at a reduced price in order to exact the taxes. |
| **Federal Estate Tax:** | Can be as high as 55 percent. |
| **State Inheritance Tax:** | Can climb as high as 11 percent depending on the state in which you reside. |

The last two items in this list, federal estate tax and state inheritance tax, consume the largest amount of your wealth at the time of your death if you have not planned a way to protect your assets from taxation. When we do not plan for the disbursement of our money during the distribution stage, it will be subject to far more taxes than are necessary. Unfortunately, this stage is where most people lose the majority of their money.

Warren Burger, former chief justice of the Supreme Court, is a perfect example of what can happen to your assets during the distribution stage if you do not plan to protect them from estate and inheritance taxes. Because he had only prepared a simple will, which lacked adequate detail, his $1.8 million estate was subject to thousands of dollars in unnecessary taxes. According to the online court and legal reporting cable network, *Court TV*, "the former chief justice of the Supreme Court left behind a self-written, 176-word will. He gave his entire estate to his two children. But he failed to give any power to his executors and made no provisions for estate taxes."[4]

### LAST WILL AND TESTAMENT OF WARREN E. BURGER

I hereby make and declare the following to be my last will and testament.

1. My executors will first pay all claims against my estate;
2. The remainder of my estate will be distributed as follows: one-third to my daughter, Margaret Elizabeth Burger Rose and two-thirds to my son, Wade A. Burger;
3. I designate and appoint as executors of this will, Wade A. Burger and J. Michael Luttig.

IN WITNESS WHEREOF, I have hereunto set my hand to this my Last Will and Testament this 9th day of June, 1994.

/s/Warren E. Burger

We hereby certify that in our presence on the date written above WARREN E. BURGER signed the foregoing instrument and declared it to be his Last Will and Testament and that at this request in his presence and in the presence of each other we have signed our names below as witnesses.

/s/Nathaniel E. Brady residing at 120 F St., NW, Washington, DC
/s/Alice M. Khu residing at 3041 Meeting St., Falls Church, VA

• • •

Burger's lack of planning cost his heirs almost $600,000 in probate costs and estate taxes. The sad part is that almost the entire $600,000 could have been saved if Burger had prepared a simple trust and done some estate planning. On page 158 is an estimate of savings if a Revocable Living Trust would have been prepared by Burger as compared to what his heirs actually received.

Even a chief justice of the Supreme Court, who should have known and understood the tax laws, did not prepare his estate to be properly distributed. He failed to implement Principle 8 by getting properly organized, and

|  | Estimated Cost of Burger Estate | With a Revocable Living Trust | With Trust & Additional Estate Planning |
|---|---|---|---|
| Estimated Value of the Estate | $1,800,000 | $1,800,000 | $1,800,000 |
| Estimated Federal Estate Tax (33%) | $396,000 | $198,000 | $0 |
| Estimated Virginia Estate Tax | $78,000 | $39,000 | $0 |
| Estimated Probate Costs (7%) | $126,000 | $0 | $0 |
| Estimated Value After Costs | $1,200,000 | $1,563,000 | $1,800,000 |

then completely missed the boat on Principle 9, which consequently made his heirs victim to the very system that he was sworn to uphold. It ended up costing them $600,000!

You can see from the above chart that you can protect virtually 100 percent of your wealth during the distribution stage if you will take the time to understand the tax laws governing estate disbursement and take action to protect those assets through living trusts, wills, and so forth.

# Paul Van Ekert: Lack of Planning

Case History

Here's another example of what can happen if you don't take Principle 9 seriously: Paul Van Ekert* was a 57-year-old ranche [10] om Utah. In preparation for retirement, Paul decided to meet with an insurance planner to determine what he would owe in estate tax upon his death. The planner explained to Paul that his total risk would be $222,000 and that if he purchased a life insurance policy, would be covered by the policy at his death. He was advised by a new practicing attorney in the area to hold off on the coverage until the policy could be further examined, so Paul declined the coverage and sent the insurance planner on his way. About nine months later he died suddenly without having taken care of the life insurance. His two boys, who had ranched with him and helped Paul successfully run the business, were forced to sell the ranch to cover outstanding debts and to meet the IRS's tax requirement that the $222,000 in estate taxes be paid within nine months of Paul's death. This forced a hasty sale of the ranch at a greatly reduced price to a neighbor who came forward as a buyer of the property. The loss to Paul's family was tremendous, both financially and emotionally. In less than a year the boys lost not only their means of support, but the legacy that Paul had wanted to pass onto his sons. Today, the two boys are working as hired hands for the new owner of the ranch. If Paul had taken the life insurance policy, his two sons would have kept the family ranch going and had a wonderful inheritance to pass on to their own children.

• • •

Now let's summarize how much you can save in taxes if you take the time to understand and apply Principle 9:

- **Accumulation Stage:** Taking advantage of the Schedule C tax system and looking for viable ways to write off business, travel, and other expenses can generally save you a minimum of $2,000 per year in taxes.

- **Conservation Stage:** By organizing properly, using the right forecasting tools, and investing wisely, you will be able to cut taxes on the growth of your investments up to 50 percent.

- **Distribution Stage:** By organizing your estate, preparing wills, protecting assets through living trusts and other tax sheltered programs, you will be able to eliminate almost all inheritance and estate taxes in most cases, and at the very least pay only a fraction of the costs.

Although taxes can be the source of much fear and frustration, they need no longer tear through the fabric of your financial life and weaken your accumulated wealth. Besides the value of getting your spending and borrowing under control using Principles 1, 2, 3, and 4, knowing the rules about taxation (Principle 5), keeping on top of the changes (Principle 6), and getting organized so you can see exactly how you will be taxed (Principles 7 and 8) all go a long way towards grasping the power of Principle 9. If you're still paying more taxes today than you need to now is the time to change. Commit today to make Principle 9 a part of your life!

Because understanding taxation is such an important part of Money Mastery, we have devoted not only this chapter, but six additional chapters in Part II of this book to this important topic. Part II, "Tax Strategies," will help you understand in even greater detail how to take advantage of all the "good" tax laws. We strongly encourage you to explore, through Part II's step-by-step approach, how to legally pay the least amount of taxes possible. It's easier than you think to get this important part of your financial life under control. "Tax Strategies" makes it easy. Stop cheating yourself out of thousands of tax deduction dollars. After discovering the power of Money Mastery Principle #10 found in Chapter 10, turn to Part II and learn the secrets that will change the way you pay taxes forever!

# Challenge #9

# Examining Your Tax Liability

**Acceleration Stage:** If you are a W-2 employee, consider what hobby or activity you are currently engaging in that could possibly be turned into a small business venture. Come up with two ways you can take advantage of the tax deductions allowed on Schedule C. (We have included a copy of the business write-off section of Schedule C below as a reference; in addition, please refer to Part II for more information.) If you are already self-employed, study carefully Part II of this book on tax strategies.

**Conservation Stage:** Examine each of your long-term investment and retirement savings programs and use a forecasting tool like the Master Plan software to decide which ones may need to be converted to a stronger tax saving plan.

**Distribution Stage:** Review the ways in which your property and money will be distributed at the time of your death and determine whether you need to convert any of these assets into a tax sheltered program.

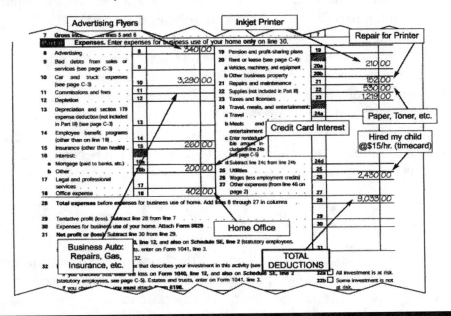

# Chapter 10

# Put Your Money in Motion

We begin this chapter by introducing a principle, that in our experience, will have the biggest impact on your financial well-being over all the other principles combined:

 ## Principle #10: Money in motion creates more money.

How does money in motion produce additional wealth? This is possible only when each of the other nine principles are applied to your financial situation, coming together like a crescendo behind Principle 10. The application of all the principles builds momentum and creates opportunities to put your money to work in a variety of ways. Applying each of the 10 principles at the same time has exponential power to transform your life, creating a multiplier effect. Systematically building from one Money Mastery principle to the next and applying each principle on top of the other is like multiplying two times two times two times two: The end result is much greater than if those numbers are simply added together. That's because each principle builds on the power and potency of the one that came before.

$$2 \times 2 \times 2 \times 2 = 16$$

On the other hand, applying some of the principles part of the time is much like adding two plus two plus two plus two. You will see some results, but the overall effectiveness will be much less potent.

# 2 + 2 + 2 + 2 = 8

When you apply all of the principles all of the time by controlling your spending, eliminating debt, planning for the future, and reducing your taxes, you are in a position to put your money to work for you so that it can do more than one thing at the same time, creating opportunities to maximize your wealth to its fullest; this is what Principle 10's "money in motion" is all about.

*The basic concept behind Principle 10 is learning how to get your dollar to do more than one thing at the same time.*

So how can money be put in motion to create more money? Let's take a look at banks as a prime example of Principle 10. Suppose you deposit $1,000 in a bank. The bank pays you, in turn, 4 percent interest on that amount. What does the bank then do with that $1,000? Under the rules of the banking system, it can go to the Federal Reserve and get an additional amount to go with it, $10,000 for example. It now has $11,000 it can lend out at a much higher rate of interest than it pays you. Of course this is a simplified example of a very complex system, but it gives you an idea of how money in motion creates more money. Banks follow the very strict federal regulations that govern the banking industry, along with their own operating protocols to get your dollars to do more than one thing for them at a time. Take a closer look at how banks put money in motion, continually turning your money over and over to make a profit.

If the bank lends out your money as part of a car loan and gets 10 percent interest on the loan, it will make 6 percent profit (after paying you 4 percent interest ) on that car loan, right? Now when the car dealer gets the loan proceeds, he puts that money into his bank. While the car dealer lets the money sit until needed, that bank loans his money out on a home construction loan at a rate of 9 percent. Then, the contractor for that construction job puts the

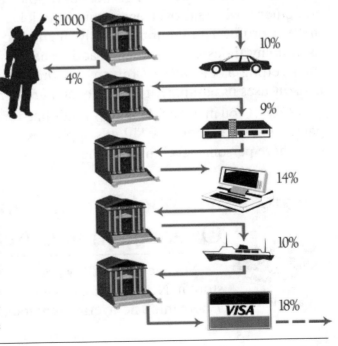

money in his bank and before he makes payroll or buys lumber, his bank has already loaned that money for a computer at 14 percent. When the computer dealer puts the loan proceeds into the bank, the bank turns around and loans it out on a boat for 10 percent. The boat dealer then deposits that money in his bank, and that bank loans it out on a Visa card at 18 percent.

From this example you can see that $1,000 will typically multiply within the banking system eight to 10 times; often this will occur very quickly, within hours or days. The banks benefit every time that money turns over, no matter what the rate—18, 6, 10, 8, and even 4 percent. If you add up all the turns on that original $1,000 in a year, the banking system will have earned between 38 to 42 percent while you only earn 4. Who's winning this game? The point is, that if like the bank, you can get your money to do more than one thing at a time, you can look forward to both safety for your money and higher rates of return. This idea is worth repeating:

> *If you can get your money to turn over, or in other words,*
> *do more than one thing at the same time, you can make*
> *a constant and higher rate of return on that money.*

In the prior bank example, we showed how these institutions literally turn money over and over again. In this next example, we'll demonstrate how more than just money can be put in motion to build more income and wealth. Take for instance a large public company that sells shares of stock. Let's say this company builds roads and bridges and takes the money from the sold shares to buy road-graders and other machinery. It then uses this equipment over and over again on many jobs, "turning" it many times to make a profit. The equipment only needed to be purchased once, but is used many times over to create additional wealth. This company, rather than getting a set "rate of return" on their money like its share holders, actually uses its equipment to turn over a greater and more continual profit.

"Okay," you might be thinking, "that's fine for banks and large public companies, but what about me?" Let's apply this concept of "money in motion" on a more personal level through the following account of one of our clients.

Case History

# Michael Perez: Turning Product Over Again and Again

Michael Perez* owned and operated a small grocery store in New Mexico. His gross profit margin on all sales was 7 percent. The average number of days it took Michael to turn his entire inventory of groceries was 21 days. Assuming he had $100,000 in merchandise on the shelf, he made close to $7,000 every three weeks. When Michael learned from his Money Mastery coach the value of Principle 10, he took inventory with a new purpose and decided to research how fast each item in his store turned over. His study revealed that Cheerios in the cereal section turned over three to four cases a day, and if he could keep that shelf stocked completely for the entire year, gross sales on Cheerios alone would total $57,000. The Cheerios were being ordered and stocked by an untrained employee who left the shelf bare at least half of the day every day. When people wanted to buy Cheerios and constantly found an empty shelf, they began to shop somewhere else. Michael knew he would have to make changes in the cereal aisle.

A product that wasn't turning over quickly was hot chocolate mix because the warm weather in New Mexico discouraged its sale. For an entire year, the store only sold one case at a profit of about $28. By using Principle 2, Michael was able to track his inventory of hot chocolate more closely and determined that it was no longer profitable to carry it. Once he had a firm understanding of which products made him a profit and which were liabilities, he made necessary changes in advertising and inventory control so he could turn his entire inventory over every seven days applying Principle 10. This meant that every week (not just every three weeks) he was making 7 percent on his inventory, thus tripling his previous profits. And he was able to do this without paying more taxes, increasing his utility usage, or subjecting himself to any additional overhead cost required to maintain the store.

"The wonderful part of understanding Principle 10 is that I was able to triple my profitability without any additional money out of my pocket and without taking any additional risk," said Michael. "Basically I just became more aware of my ability to turn a profit and revised some of the processes in my store so that my money began working overtime for me. Up until I made those changes, my money really wasn't working very hard at all because I hadn't put any momentum behind it."

## A Simple Idea

Although the idea of making your money do more than one thing at a time is actually quite simple, and one of the easiest and risk-free ways of generating additional wealth, it is rarely understood. In our experience, it is very difficult for people to change the way they think, especially when most are still living paycheck to paycheck. Their first tendency is to spend any extra money on consumable goods rather than thinking about how it could be turned over to make a profit. This mind-set prevents these people from ever having any money with which they can experience the incredible power of Principle 10.

In our coaching, we spend considerable time with clients teaching them how to examine where and how they should be spending their money by asking them to look at what will get them the best return. It is vital that people resist spending all their extra money on consumable and depreciating assets so that they can keep the momentum of their money going. We discourage borrowing too much money for homes, cars, and consumer goods because this forces the borrower to pay three times the value of something, making it extremely difficult to set any additional money in motion. Can you see how not applying each of the other nine Money Mastery principles makes it extremely difficult to make Principle 10 work for you? Following is an example that perfectly illustrates this point.

## Mark and Stacey Kleinman: Applying Principle 10

Case History

Mark and Stacey Kleinman* were spending more than they brought in each month. In addition, they were so in debt that it took nearly half of their income just to pay their loan obligations. They had no idea how to create an additional side business in order to take advantage of Schedule C tax write-offs. This couple was also very disorganized and had no estate planning or wills prepared. Needless to say, it was very difficult for their coach to explain the concept of Principle 10 to Mark and Stacey.

Fortunately, the Kleinmans saw the value of applying the other Money Mastery principles. First, they reviewed their spending habits for the previous 12 months and were shocked to see that they were upside down, spending $300 a month more than they had. They cut their spending and started tracking their money using Principle 2 and immediately found they could save $71 a month on their auto insurance. They stopped eating out so often and saved another $120 per month. Mark and Stacey continued this process until they found the entire $300 they were overspending each month. They began to discuss their finances with each other on a weekly basis and their conversations went from blaming to quiet decision-making. They got in control of their emotions and eventually in control of their spending.

The second financial improvement the Kleinmans made was to start contributing to their company's 401(k) plan. They could do this because once they got their spending under control, they found some additional money they could then contribute to Mark's employee-matching program, which they had never utilized before. They calculated that their monthly contribution to the plan would grow to $234,600 at retirement. Using Principle 3, the Kleinmans began setting money aside for this program.

Using Principle 4, the Kleinmans began powering down their debts. Mark and Stacey figured that they could pay off all of their debts within seven years and save more than $180,000 in interest expense. Money they were using to pay off debt could then be saved and used to create an additional $560,000 for their future. Applying Principles 5 and 6, Mark and Stacey got better informed about laws governing their retirement plans and how taxes would affect their money. Stacey began a small flower-arranging business based on a 10-year hobby and began saving $2,300 a year in taxes through implementing Principle 9.

Once the Kleinmans got in control of all the other areas of their financial lives, they were finally prepared to take full advantage of Principle 10 by closely examining their assets, investments, and equipment to make sure these resources were creating money for them rather than just sitting idle. They determined that buying a truck to help Stacey make her deliveries was a depreciating cost that would not bring any additional value to the business. They then decided to lease a truck, and spend the money they would have used to purchase the vehicle on appreciating assets, which in their case was more floral arranging supplies and equipment. By applying the nine other Money Mastery principles to their lives, Stacey and Mark now understand how to make their money work for them.

• • •

Similar to Stacey and Mark, you too are ready to take full advantage of Principle 10 because you have learned how to apply each of the other nine principles. As we continue to explore ways that you can set your money in motion so that it can do more than one thing for you at a time, we invite you to consider the wisdom of the following Chinese proverb:

*"When the student is ready, the teacher shall appear."*

Having come this far, we know that you are ready; we know that you are prepared. The teacher, Principle 10, is now before you. There are incredible opportunities to create more money all around you. The options are endless! Although there is no formula for making Principle 10 a success in your life, there are lots of options and we strongly encourage you to consider each of them. We will assist you in this effort by showcasing a number of ways that money, product, equipment, time, talent, real estate, or any number of resources can be utilized to create additional wealth.

# Ideas: Turning a Profit Again and Again From a Single Notion

How many times have you had an idea pop in your head that you thought was an absolute stroke of brilliance? Have you ever considered that some of these ideas could be set in motion to create additional wealth? Wendy Potts* did. As a dental hygienist, she spent countless hours pouring molds of people's teeth and mouths. As she poured these molds, she thought about Principle 10, and decided it might be a fun idea to use plaster to make molds of a baby's hands and feet. She then had the idea of preparing a keepsake kit called "Precious Impressions" that she could sell to parents that would allow them to make plaster molds of their children's hands and feet. In the beginning she sold more than 40 of these kits a month. In time, retailers such as Wal-Mart and Shopko began signing distribution agreements with her to sell her kits in their stores. Sales took off, and Wendy was asked to appear on QVC, where she sold more than $129,000 worth of product in less than eight minutes. Needless to say, Wendy no longer works as a dental hygienist and the "little idea" that she had one day while pouring molds in the dentist's office has begun turning a profit for her in a way she could never have imagined. This one idea, which she had in one single moment, is now producing untold wealth for her over and over again, demonstrating the power of Principle 10 in a very exciting way.

# Rent: Making Money from Existing Property

Charging someone to live or work within a space is an obvious way that people can make a profit from an existing asset. As part of applying Principle 10, Joylyn and Steve Ashcraft* were advised by their Money Mastery coach to finish the basement of an office building they owned. Steve said he didn't have the money, but the coach told the Ashcrafts to sublease the space to someone who did have the money to finish the basement. Joylyn and Steve thought this was an excellent idea and were surprised that they hadn't thought of it themselves. The Ashcrafts then found a tenant who was willing to improve the basement by putting in floors, plumbing, window wells, and stairs if the Ashcrafts would give him a $2 credit towards his lease every month for every $1 he spent making improvements.

The amount of money that the tenant spent making improvement carried him for a full three years before he ever had to make a rent payment to the Ashcrafts. The tenant really enjoyed the arrangement because he didn't have to pay rent for more than 36 months. The Ashcrafts were pleased because they didn't have to spend any money for the desired improvements to the basement and were still able to benefit because the property value of the office building went up. Just after the three-year mark, Joylyn and Steve began receiving $380 a month in rent from the tenant, which they are now saving as part of their retirement fund. The building is now worth $74,000 more than it was because the basement has been improved; it also brings in cash flow to the Ashcrafts because they can collect rent on it. All this was possible for Steve and Joylyn without costing them an extra dime. In this case, the Ashcrafts used their real estate property to get their money to do more than one thing at a time.

# Skill: Getting Your Talent to Reward You Again and Again

We all have skills we use on a daily basis either to make us money or to entertain and delight others. But when was the last time you examined all your talents to determine which ones could be used to turn a profit for you? Maria Carlisle* certainly hadn't considered carefully her options when it came to her writing skills until her coach explained how she could make Principle 10 work for her. As a freelance writer, Maria charged an hourly wage for her advertising and marketing services. She was paid a good rate for each of these projects, but once they were completed, she never saw an additional penny generated from her work.

As she began a project for one of her clients as a ghost writer for a book, she began to realize that once this large project was complete, she would never see any more benefit from the countless hours she was spending researching and writing the book. Maria began to wonder how she could turn her writing skill from a talent that only made her money once to something that made her money again and again. She concluded that she needed to structure her next book-writing project so that she could retain royalties each time the book was sold. She did, and today she is receiving a 5- percent royalty fee on a book she co-authored. Instead of just getting an hourly one time return on her invested time and skill, Maria is now getting her work to pay her over and over again. What's more, she is not required to pay any FICA (Social Security) tax on the royalty proceeds. Using her skills as a means to a turn a profit, Maria is not only making an hourly wage for her work, but is getting her skill to do more than one thing for her at a time.

# Leasing: Turning Need into a Continual Source of Profit

Many small businesses today have a need for certain kinds of office and computer equipment only on a sporadic basis, making it hard to justify the cost of purchasing that equipment if it sits idle half the year. That need was something Garner Shim* knew he could use to turn a profit. Garner had a brilliant mechanical mind. From childhood, he had loved tinkering with machinery, taking things apart and putting them back together again just to see how they worked. Everyone who knew Garner knew he could fix just about anything. Over time, as the computer craze swept the country, Garner began troubleshooting and fixing hardware problems for his friends and co-workers. His own interest in computers led him to buy and sell computer equipment on a regular basis and he became very savvy at this trading process. He would purchase equipment such as monitors and hard drives for as little as $10 from people who claimed that the items were "broken." Garner was experienced enough to know these items probably just needed a few minor repairs and was able to immediately fix them.

Over time, he collected enough of this repaired equipment at a fraction of its actual value to fill an entire room in his basement. He then began leasing the equipment to some of his friends who owned small businesses. These small businesses would bring in temporary help for a week or two to complete a pressing project and would lease Garner's equipment just long enough to get the project done. With time, Garner was running a profitable leasing business in addition to his regular job, making anywhere from $100 to $250 a day on various computer equipment he loaned out. He was able to do this with very little investment on his part, and with a minimal amount of upkeep on the equipment. As new computer products came on the market, Garner would replace his outdated equipment by shopping for deals from people who claimed their equipment was broken. In this way, Garner turned his skill and acquired property into a viable means to turn a profit again and again.

# Real Estate: Buying Trust Deeds to Generate Additional Wealth

As people apply each of the Money Mastery principles, in time they find themselves in control of their financial situation, with no debt and a surplus of funds they can use to make additional money. Guy Walters* was just such a person. Guy had no debt and a fairly good chunk of money to work with, but really had no idea what do with it. He was advised by his Money Mastery coach to buy trust deeds with the money as a way to turn a profit. He did this by purchasing the deed of bankrupt properties from banks at approximately $.18 on the dollar.

At one point, he became interested in a defaulted triplex with a price tag of $140,000. Its actual appraised value was $170,000, but Guy offered the bank $50,000 to get the property off its hands. At first the bank balked at his offer, but knew that maintaining the property until it could be sold at a price closer to its actual value would not be cost-effective. It did not want to be hassled with trying to find tenants and keeping up the grounds so it sold the trust deed to Guy. Then, he found suitable renters for each of the apartments and began renting each for $850 a month, generating over $30,000 in one year. Using this profit, he made improvements on the property and turned around and sold it for $180,000. You can see from Guy's case that the original $50,000 eventually made him an additional $130,000, which he used to buy additional defaulted trust deeds to continue the process. Using his investment in real estate, Guy is applying Principle 10 in order to create additional wealth.

# Knowledge: Generating Money Over and Over by Applying an Educational Background

Sue and Derek Cassel* both had degrees in biology, Sue having received her master's degree in that field. They were both employees for the state where they lived. One managed industrial chemical dumping, and the other was responsible to monitor the water fowl along the Missouri River. The Cassels had grown to love the Missouri River and wanted to live near by it. They were able to secure an option to purchase a piece of land within the flood zone, but didn't know how to approach a lender to get enough money to be able to build a home on the site. Their dream was to create their own "farm over the water."

While discussing these problems with their coach, the Cassels were advised to apply Principle 7 by stepping back to look at their long-term big picture. Once they did this, they decided to verify the property's value so they could qualify for a loan by planting ginseng in the two to three feet of standing water found on the property. From their biology background, they knew that the property possessed the ideal conditions needed to grow ginseng. It would take 10 years to harvest a good crop, but Sue and Derek knew it could become very profitable for them. Once the ginseng started to produce, they could harvest the crop for more than 50 years. They estimated that they could have a net profit of about $20,000 per year after the initial 10 years of maturation occurred. In addition to the ginseng crop, this property had a large standing forest of straight hardwood trees. These too could be harvested and sold to produce a net profit of approximately $20,000 per year.

To make their dream of creating a "farm over the water" come true, the Cassels tracked all their expenses using Principle 2 and were able to put together enough money to pay for a commercial appraisal. This appraisal verified the property's ability to produce an income of $40,000 a year. A local credit union then loaned Sue and Derek the money to build a new home on stilts with a big patio that extended out to their ginseng crop. They were also able to pour a gravel road to their home and build a bridge over a large canal. Using all the Money Mastery principles, and especially by applying Principle 10 through their biology knowledge, Sue and Derek will be able to retire in 13 years at the age of 53. Money from the ginseng and the hardwood lumber will generate far more money for them than if they were employed.

# Technology: Creating "Multiple Impressions" from a Single Web Site

It goes without saying that the high-tech advancements that have been made in the last 20 years have been phenomenal. Wonders such as the Internet have opened up a world of opportunity for small business that were previously reserved for large international corporations with big budgets. Nathan Warnas*, a real estate agent, is a perfect example of how taking advantage of this technology can turn a profit again and again.

Prior to the broad adoption of the Internet, Nathan would spend countless hours preparing marketing fliers, letters, and other materials to help him sell a single residential property listing. He then decided that he could automate his processes by creating a Web site on which he could place several property listings and their individual amenities and benefits. By doing so, he eliminated the need to mail to each individual prospect a sales letter and flier announcing the available properties. Instead, he began marketing his site through Internet search engines and through linking his page to other co-op sites that helped him drive additional traffic to his Web page. This increased his exposure in the market. Taking advantage of the World

Wide Web, Nathan is now able to compete with larger real estate firms because he gets some of the same kinds of exposure in the market as these big, multimillion-dollar companies, without having to individually cold call each prospect. The Web makes it possible for him to prospect more than one person at the same time, reducing his out-of-pocket marketing expenses and decreasing the time and resources required to locate potential buyers. This has allowed Nathan to use his energy to locate additional properties he can list on his Web site, increasing his sales figures 50 percent and helping him turn a profit quicker and more often than he did before.

# Continually Create Wealth

While these examples are not a comprehensive listing of all the ways Principle 10 can be applied to your life, we are confident that they have helped generate some new and different thinking in you. What skill, talent, property, equipment, money, or knowledge do you have which could be used to create a "machine" that is continually working for you? Many people, rather than think in terms of using these existing resources to create more wealth, continue to fall back on the idea that they need to have a better job or invest in risky stock opportunities in order to create additional wealth. Many of our Money Mastery clients are able to generate 10 to 20 percent more money per month just by turning a profit using what they already have available to them. In addition, they do this without the risk that other investments can bring to the game.

> *Remember, when you apply Principle 10, you are not working to make money, you are putting your money (or resources) to work for you!*

Applying Principle 10 is like putting work clothes on your money and sending it out as a hired hand to make you more cash. And the best thing about it is that this money works for you day and night, seven days a week, 365 days a year.

Each of the "Money in Motion" examples we have highlighted above not only demonstrate the power of Principle 10, but also the importance of applying each of the other nine principles at the same time. It is not enough to apply Principles 2, 3, and 4 by getting spending and borrowing under control. And it isn't enough to casually apply Principle 7, for example, or Principle 9 here and there in an effort to maximize the money that comes available to us as we implement the other principles. It isn't enough to assume that all is well because we seem to be doing some things so much better than we used to financially.

Being content with applying only part of the principles, part of the time is like owning a beautiful ocean island where time is spent on the beach with good food, sun, and the sound of the waves crashing on the shore. Things may seem fine, the surroundings are pleasant, and you appear to have everything under control. Would you ever want to leave such a situation? If you thought all was well, then probably not. You're comfortable where you are and making the effort to get out of your beach chair and do something different doesn't seem worth it. But, what if at some point a geologist showed up in his stinky fishing boat and informed you that according to his calculations, your beautiful island is sitting on top of a volcano and is going to blow within three days to two weeks. To prove his point, he takes you to a part of the island where a fissure in the ground is spewing steam. Will you stay there and take your chances that all will remain well, or will you get on his stinky boat, the only boat within hundreds of miles, and leave? The answer is obvious.

Without the knowledge, consciousness, awareness, and wisdom that each of the Money Master principles can bring to a person's life when applied systematically, you will not have the motivation to make change when it is necessary. You will be satisfied with what you know and not realize there is so much more! Absent a system such as Money Mastery, a person will never see how to change, and consequently will never realize any real momentum or power behind their cash flow. A systematic approach, like that which Money Mastery offers, brings all the principles together and makes it possible, as we have already noted, to multiply the effect of your actions over and over again to create additional wealth.

*You add motion to your money when you add all the principles to your life.*

In order to keep that money in motion, it is vital that you not take for granted any of the principles. Following are just some of the ways that people sabotage their best efforts at applying all 10 principles all of the time:

1. Consume every bit of their income on depreciating items.
2. Have no reserve accounts when an emergency takes place or the market takes a down-turn.
3. Don't know the rules when they sign a contract, thereby roping themselves into a costly mistake.
4. Pay three times what they need to in tax expense.
5. Lack the discipline to use extra money to pay off debt, instead using it for impulse purchases.
6. Don't organize themselves to streamline the processes that will affect taxes, retirement, assets, and property.

7. Lack vision for the future by failing to step back and look at the big picture.

8. Sit on their money and resources rather than making these work for them.

We're confident that you have begun to strip from your life these saboteurs. By now you are successfully controlling your spending using Principles 1, 2, and 3. You are eliminating your debt by applying Principle 4. And you are maximizing your assets using Principles 5, 6, 7, 8, and 9. Now you are ready to implement a total money management system by applying Principle 10. This principle has the ability to exponentially build wealth for you at a rate you never dreamed possible.

Again, we encourage you to examine all the possibilities for wealth creation that are available to you. The whole world is waiting and ready to be explored. Take the time today to look carefully at yourself, your mindset, your resources, and your attitude. If you will, we can promise that you will open yourself to a bright and prosperous future!

---

## Challenge #10

# Get Your Dollar to Do More than One Thing at the Same Time

This week we challenge you to:

1. Ponder what talent, skill, idea, knowledge, property, equipment, or source of money can be put in motion in order to create more money.

2. Pick one of these available resources and determine a method by which you will use it to generate additional income.

Because understanding taxation is such an important part of money mastery, we have devoted an additional six chapters in Part II of this book to this important topic. Part II, "Tax Strategies," will help you understand in even greater detail, the power of Money Mastery Principle 9: Understanding Taxation Enables You To Retain More of Your Money. Part II will also help you to take advantage of all the "good" tax laws available to you.

We strongly encourage you to explore, through Part II's step-by-step approach, how to legally pay the least amount of taxes possible. It's easier than you think to get this important part of your financial life under control. Turn to Part II and learn the secrets that will change the way you pay taxes forever!

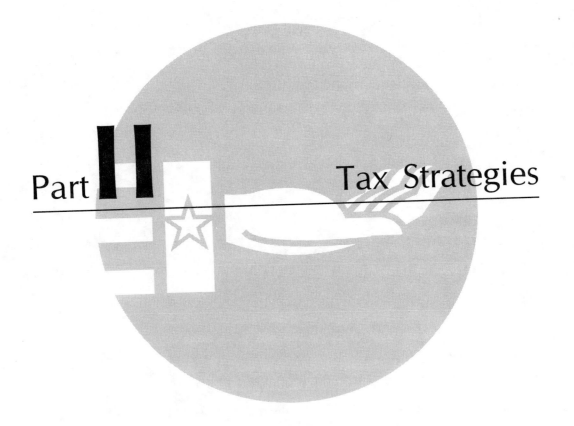

Part **II**                    Tax Strategies

# Chapter 11

# Why You Should Start a Home-Based Business

Having turned to Part II of this book, we're confident that you have grasped the importance of Money Mastery Principle 9, and are interested in learning more deeply about the subject of taxation and how it can dramatically impact the amount of money you make and keep. In this part of the book, we will discuss in greater detail some of the concepts we introduced in Chapter 9, explaining the rules that govern how your money will be taxed and giving you practical applications that will help you take advantage of those rules. As you have already learned through Principle 5, knowing the rules brings power and control into your financial life like nothing else can, and when combined with the information found in this section, will help you save anywhere from $2,000 to $10,000 in tax deductions every year.

It goes without saying that taxes are a huge part of our lives and have a pervasive effect on everything we do. Almost all Americans pay a fortune in taxes over a lifetime, but most don't fully understand the true extent of their tax bill. In fact, a recent study found that the average American pays almost 40 percent of their salary in federal, state, and local taxes alone.[1]

Part of what keeps us enslaved to this huge tax burden is that, as a nation, we have become entrenched in a "W-2" mentality, where we believe that the only way to make a living is to be subject to an employer and have a set percentage of taxes extracted from our paycheck. But working within this W-2 system isn't helping most people get ahead. Today, many households need two or even three incomes just to survive. Sadly, even more than one spouse working outside the home does not produce any major positive effect on most people's bank accounts.

Jane Bryant Quinn's article in *Woman's Day*,[2] which we profiled in Chapter 2, illustrates this point quite well. If you remember, Quinn assumed in her article that the husband in this family was earning $40,000 per year, and his wife, Lori*, wasn't working. Every month, the family was short on funds, so this prompted Lori to get an administrative job for an annual salary of $15,000. When Quinn examined the economics of working for this extra income, the results were startling! Remember that after all the non tax-deductible expenses that Lori incurred due to her new job, she ended up taking home a paltry $1,156 a year from her annual $15,000 salary! She could have netted that entire $15,000 had she earned it in a home-based business, an increase of almost 13 times her take-home pay as a nine-to-five employee. Notice that Lori would not be spending dramatically any more money than she would already be spending operating a home-based business. She would still be eating out, going on trips, and driving her car the same as if she were a W-2 employee. But by having a home-based business, many of these expenses would be tax deductible.

# Home-Based Businesses Make "Cents"

There are several reasons why more people are favoring home-based business over traditional W-2 employment. First of all, there's no commute (unless you have a really big home!), and there's no boss, no employees (or very few), and no corporate politics to put up with. Did you know that there are currently an estimated 30 million people working from their homes? This number is expected to more than triple to 97 million by the year 2015 and to keep on growing.[3] Working from home has become and will continue to be one of the greatest mass movements in the United States.

Here's why a home-based business makes so much "cents":

- As we noted in Chapter 9, using Schedule C (when filing 1040 tax forms) and the tax laws for home-based business, you can deduct all kinds of expenses that are not allowed on Schedule A. With proper documentation, you can write off your house, spouse, and even your children (by hiring them), business vacations, cars, and food with colleagues (more details to come in Chapters 13, 14, and 15).

- You can set up a pension retirement plan that makes any government plan seem paltry by comparison.

- You can glean more tax deductions, which is similar to having Congress subsidize you while you are growing your home-based business.

- If your business produces a tax loss in the first year or so, you can use that tax loss against any other form of income you have.

It can be used against wages earned as a W-2 employee, dividends, pensions, or interest income.[4] You can also use the loss against your spouse's earning if you file a joint return.[5]

- If the tax loss exceeds all your income for the current year, no problem. You can carry back the loss two years and get a refund from the IRS for up to the last two years of income taxes paid, or you can carry the loss over 20 years. That's right, you can offset up to 20 years of income.[6]

As we noted in Chapter 9, it is imperative that you take advantage of all the tax laws that will save you the most money during the accumulation stage by thinking outside of the W-2 box. This idea is so important that it is the basis of our first tax saving strategy:

# Tax Strategy #1: If you don't have a home-based business, start one!

If everyone in the United States employed full-time as a W-2 worker would start a part-time or full-time business and follow the tax deduction strategies outlined, in the next several chapters, each person could reduce his or her taxes anywhere from $2,000 to $10,000 each year.

When our clients begin to understand the power a home-based business has for earning extra money and saving tax dollars, they are usually very excited about the prospect. They are also more than just a little nervous about launching out into new territory. We often hear people express both excitement and fear in the same breath.

- "I've always wanted to work for myself, but I've never seen a way that I could actually do it."
- "We've talked about starting our own business a number of times and I've always wondered when we would have the time to launch such a venture. We both work more than 50 hours a week."
- "It seems like it would be very rewarding, but also very risky...besides, I'm not an entrepreneur."

Have you ever had any of these kinds of conversations with yourself? We often hear objections like the following from people who are afraid to launch a home-based business.

## I already work myself into the ground.
## When would I have time to launch a business?

This is a common concern that many people express because they lack the proper perspective about what it means to really launch a home-based business. They falsely assume that people who succeed at working for themselves don't have a regular W-2 job. Actually, most people who start a successful venture are able to do so while still working for someone else. These people are successful because they don't take the prospect of striking out on their own too seriously. And because it is not their only source of revenue, they don't make too many bad decisions due to financial stress. Successful home-based business people realize that the amount of time they spend on their business doesn't matter, the size of their business doesn't matter, and their profitability doesn't matter. What matters is the intent behind a home-based business: to make a little more money each month and save tax dollars. They determine for themselves how much time and energy they want to devote to the venture.

What we have also found is that as a person works a side business, it becomes so successful and so much more viable as a means of support that people usually end up walking completely away from their W-2 job. Now whether this happens for you or not, it doesn't matter. The important thing is to have the proper perspective about what it really means to "start a home-based business." If you think that this prospect has to be difficult, time-consuming, or exhausting, perhaps it's time to think again. It's a lot easier than most people think!

Michelle Kapos* decided to change her perspective about launching her own business when she realized that she wasn't completely happy with her job as a teacher at a public elementary school. She was, however, very happy with her efforts selling Mary Kay cosmetics and spent every Saturday conducting seminars, teaching classes, and giving facials. Each weekend, Michelle sold more than $500 worth of cosmetics, $200 of which she kept as gross profit. Michelle decided she needed to consider her Mary Kay business as a viable home-based venture and use it to save more tax dollars. Using Schedule C, Michelle now deducts her car expenses for travel to and from consultations as well as entertainment and food expenses while she is hosting prospective clients in her home. She saves $1,000 in taxes each year working only 16 hours extra every month on the weekends. She plans to retire from teaching at age 31 and become a full-time Mary Kay consultant. For now, she uses her Saturdays to make extra money and save tax dollars.

## I'm not an entrepreneur.
## What can I possibly do for my home-based business?

This is the most common objection we hear. Unfortunately, many people view themselves as simply a "nine-to-fiver," with no idea of what they could do to make extra money in a side business.

Our response to this objection is that you don't have to have the ambition of Bill Gates to become a successful business owner. All you need is a little imagination.

The biggest obstacle to forming a home-based venture that we see is a lack of vision. Without this vision it can be almost impossible to remove ourselves from the predictable and "safe" haven of our W-2 jobs. We will go on indefinitely, perhaps, stuck in the ruts of a path that affords no other choice besides collecting a paycheck from someone else. Imagination is so important. As Einstein once said:

*"Imagination is more important than knowledge."*

It has been our intent to infuse you with this imagination and vision for the future by introducing you to the 10 Money Mastery principles we explained in the first part of this book. With an understanding of those principles, especially Principle 7, "Always look at the big picture," you should now have a clear view of all that your financial life should be today and tomorrow. Having committed to changing your life by accepting this principle and all the others, you should now be ready to take action by building a home-based business. It will be one of the best steps you can take toward eliminating ruts of predictable behavior, behavior that keeps you in a cycle that prevents financial growth, encourages tax waste, and does little to mitigate economic risk.

With a little imagination, you will begin to see just how many ways there are for you to make extra money in a side business. As we noted in Chapter 9, we tell our clients that there are many hobbies and activities that could be considered a viable business venture if they would be considered as such.

Remember Perry and Michelle Kamboris we profiled in Chapter 9? They realized that their knowledge and interest in their Husky dogs, along with their love of travel, could be turned into a business opportunity that could save them thousands of dollars in taxes each year. Because they were already heavily involved in the Huskies as a hobby, it seemed only logical to them to take advantage of that interest by turning it into a legitimate home-based business and a viable tax write-off.

Hobbies and interests that our clients have transformed into home-based businesses include teaching adult community education classes, selling real estate, leasing property and rental units, cutting hair, selling cosmetics, selling household cleaners, and teaching piano or other lessons. These are only a few of the ideas that can be turned into a side business venture. There are literally hundreds of opportunities if you will take the time to explore them.

What do you like to do in your spare time? What products do you like to use that you would be more than happy to sell to others? What hobbies could you turn into a viable home-based business? Let your imagination run wild. The possibilities for financial growth and happiness are endless when you step outside the W-2 box.

### Okay, I'm sold on the idea. But can I really succeed?

Many people are thrilled with the prospect of being more than just a W-2 employee, but they are also afraid of the risks. We like to point out that research consistently shows that the majority of home-based businesses are successful. In fact, according to the Small Business Administration, the average home-based business succeeds in its first year and achieves an average income of $40,000 per year with many earning much more, and this is not even counting all the tax benefits that you can earn once you are in business.[7]

# The Risks of Not Starting a Home-Based Business

Although launching a home-based business can seem like a gamble, the risks of remaining strictly a W-2 employee may actually be worse. How much of an economic and emotional impact did your last layoff have in your life? If you've ever lost a job you know how totally exposed and vulnerable it can make you feel.

The following is a good example of the way in which W-2 employment fully exposes a person to economic hazards.

Suppose Sally and Roger purchase a three-bedroom house to rent to a single family. They use the rental proceeds to pay for the mortgage on the house, but then the renter decides to move after six months. Until Sally and Roger can find another renter, they are 100 percent responsible for the payment of the mortgage.

*Sally and Roger's exposure is now 100 percent.*

Renting a single-unit dwelling, just as Sally and Roger do, is similar to being a W-2 employee. If you lose your job, your economic exposure is going to be 100 percent.

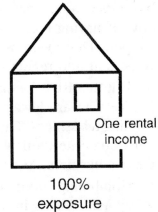

One rental income

100% exposure

But, let's say that Sally and Roger, instead of buying a single-unit dwelling, purchase a multiple-unit building that has 10 apartments. If one renter decides to move, Sally and Roger can still count on the other nine rent checks to help cover their mortgage payment, mitigating their risk from 100 percent to only 10 percent .

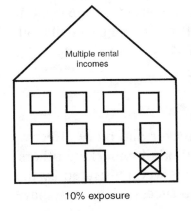

Multiple rental incomes

10% exposure

Having a home-based business is much like renting out multiple units within an apartment building; it helps mitigate your risk should you ever lose your W-2 job because it provides a means of income on which you can fall back. In addition, the emotional cost of losing a job is also mitigated. That's because you are not emotionally invested in just one thing. With a home-based business you can spread out your emotional risk across other income bearing interests. That way, if anything happens to your job, you can feel more confident and know that you have worth, even if your employer doesn't think you do. Finally, there are some good tax laws that accrue to you when you have a home-based business that can subsidize you while you are building up this business. These good tax laws do not apply to those people who are solely W-2 employees.

## Success or failure? Only you can decide.

Success or failure in a home-based business is rarely determined by the business itself, but rather by the business owner. Once you have put your imagination to work and caught the vision of what you'd like to do, you must keep in mind two things that will determine whether that new venture will succeed:

### Action and Knowledge.

These two things are the reason why one person will succeed and another will fail at the exact same business. As we have already noted, a successful business can only get started by taking action. Some people want the benefits of having their own business, but they don't do anything to make it happen. Those who make a business work are constantly taking action in a consistent and regular manner.

But that isn't the only thing that will ensure success. There are plenty of people who are always working, always taking action, but may still fail at running a business. That's because they aren't taking the *right* actions. They must combine their work efforts with the correct knowledge in order to make a business work.

Combining action and knowledge together is like drilling for oil. If you set up a drilling rig in your backyard, it's going to fail at producing oil unless your backyard is in Texas or Alaska! Not only must you set up the rig, but you also have to know the right place to set it up if you're going to strike oil.

How can you ensure that you take the right actions and know the right things so that your home-based business will succeed?

## Learn to duplicate the success of others.

Duplicating the strategy of others is much quicker and more effective than going to the school of hard knocks. This method of mimicking others' successes is also known as "modeling." Modeling is well illustrated by the way the McDonalds Corporation blazed a trail to success that many have since followed.

In the early 1950's, McDonalds and other start-up companies discovered that through franchising, they could grow many times faster than other firms that followed a conventional business model. For example, a company, instead of investing millions of dollars to build new stores, could let independent franchisers do it for them. It seemed like a great idea, but at first it wasn't successful on a consistent basis, so the media constantly criticized it. News articles featured destitute families who had lost their life savings through franchising schemes. Virtually every state attorney general in the United States condemned the new marketing method; some Congressmen even tried to outlaw franchising entirely. Over the years, however, Ray Kroc and his management team at McDonald's developed a turnkey franchise business team that made it possible for franchised McDonald's restaurants to succeed. This newfound success turned public perception of franchising around. Today, virtually every franchise business model, to some extent, is based on the business system created by McDonald's. Franchising has become one of the most respected ways of doing business in the world and literally thousands of franchises are available for almost any business that you can imagine.

Akin to franchising are multi-level marketing (MLM) companies. MLM opportunities abound and can be a great way to break into a home-based business. That's because the model for working within an MLM is already stamped out with a specific pattern to follow. Reputable MLM companies include quality products or services, solid management personnel, and years of proven success. The step-by-step approach that MLM's can offer is a good way to break into business for yourself if you're a bit nervous about the prospect.

There are countless opportunities to enjoy tax deductions you never even knew existed if you'll take the time to explore your options. Add to those tax savings the satisfaction of being your own boss, controlling your own schedule, and determining how much money you want to make, and you can't afford not to start a home-based business.

If you already have a business going, make sure you are enjoying the many financial advantages to which your smart choice entitles you by learning how to deduct as many taxes as possible through the information found in this part of the book. The tax advantage alone can, in many instances, make a home-based business the single best financial move you will ever make.

You will find many wealth-building tax tips contained in this book that are based on the actual experience of thousands of clients we have coached throughout the years. We encourage you to read on as we explain the details you will need to know to make your home-based business a tax success. In the meantime, get on the road to launching your own business opportunity by taking the following challenge.

## Challenge #11

# Determine Which Hobby or Interest Could Be Turned into a Viable Home-based Business

1.  This week, examine closely your daily activities, your hobbies, your interests, and where you most love spending you time. Is there something you do in your "spare time" that could be turned into a business venture? What about a particular skill you possess that others rely upon and for which you could begin charging a fee? Brainstorm any and all ideas and then write them down. Discuss them with your spouse and children. Roll these ideas off your friends and neighbors. Imagine yourself doing the activity on a daily basis. Consider the logistics of how and where you would conduct the business. Settle on one or two ideas that you are serious about exploring. Check out individuals or companies that are already doing a similar type of business and see how they are doing. Are they making money or "starving on the vine"?

2.  If you are already running your own business, this week we challenge you to throw out all your biases about tax planning and read on about how you can get all the deductions to which you are legally and ethically entitled. Remember Principle 5, "Know the rules," and Principle 6, "The rules are always changing," and don't assume that your accountant knows everything about saving you valuable tax dollars. Remember, your accountant is only as good as you are.

By launching a home-based business and using the tax strategies outlined in this book, you will become more financially stable and make your life a whole lot less "taxing"!

# Chapter 12

# To Incorporate or Not

Taking action. Remember, it's one of two things a person must do if he or she expects to be successful at a home-based business venture. Now that you have taken that action by determining what kind of business on which you wish to embark, the next step is to make sure you have the proper knowledge you will need to start that venture off on the right track.

## Tax Strategy #2: Consider how to best legally structure your new business venture.

The information in this chapter, while certainly not comprehensive, outlines five basic ways a business can be legally structured and will help you determine whether you should incorporate your new home-based business or not. This knowledge will aid you, before you become entrenched in the every day effort of running your business, determine how to best take advantage of tax benefits. This information will also help you learn how to limit your liabilities as a business owner.

There are no hard and fast rules as to what is the best way to structure a business, and naturally, the decision will be based on your individual circumstances. But keep in mind, there are certain rules that regulate the way business may be conducted in the United States, and as Money Mastery Principle 5 teaches, you must know these rules!

# Sole Proprietorship

A sole proprietorship is a business entity that is not incorporated and allows a person running that business to be taxed personally. Without question, this is the simplest way to structure your business. Here's why a sole proprietorship may be right for you:

## Advantages

- Requires no federal or state unemployment taxes.
- No "double taxation" meaning that only the owner is taxed and not the business itself.
- No shareholder or board meetings to hold.
- No federal tax ID number to obtain from the IRS unless you have employees. That means you can use your own Social Security number for tax filing.
- No special tax filing forms required other than Schedule C with your 1040 form.

Sole proprietorships also have the advantage of being the best entity to use if any losses are incurred. If you have losses in your business, which is usually the case in the first year or two, these losses can be used against any form of income on your tax return such as wages, interest, dividends, pensions, rents, etc.[1] For example, Mike earns $50,000 in a regular W-2 job. If he starts a home-based business that generates a tax loss of $10,000, he only pays federal and state income tax on $40,000 of his regular W-2 salary if he is structured as a sole proprietorship.

In addition, if the losses you incur exceed your income, you can carry back all business losses two years, or carry forward business losses 20 years and offset the next 20 years of income.[2]

Moreover, sole proprietorships allow some fringe benefits such as:

- A 60 percent deduction for medical insurance premiums for the owner and his or her family when the owner pays the premiums directly out of his or her bank account. This can be increased to 100 percent by hiring a spouse as we will profile in Chapter 16.
- Business owner gets to keep all the profits.
- No expenses for incorporating.
- Simple structure so there's less paperwork and tax filing forms.
- Lower cost to maintain business.
- Flexible; passing on ownership is fairly easy.

- Easy to promote business in some ways because clients and customers personally know the owner of business and can expect his or her personal touch.

With all these advantages, you would think that a sole proprietorship is the best way to structure a home-based business. There are some drawbacks, however, that can be rather substantial:

## Disadvantages

The biggest drawback to a sole proprietorship is that as a business owner, you are personally liable for everything that happens within the business. A sole proprietorship does not protect the individual owner against liabilities, and although much of this risk can be mitigated with business risk or personal liability insurance, we believe that any business that has substantial potential for liability should not be a sole proprietorship. Your decision should be based on how much exposure you want to take on personally.

*Tip: If you have any employees, you will have substantial liability because all employers are liable for the acts and conduct of their employees. Thus, if you have any employees, you should not be a sole proprietor.*

# Penbrook Stevens: Freelance Writer

Case History

On the day that Penbrook Stevens* was laid off her public relations job for the third time in 10 years, she decided it was time to strike out on her own as a freelance writer. Because of the nature of her work, she wasn't too worried about limiting her liability and wanted to keep things simple so she conducted her business as a sole proprietor. This allowed her to take a percentage of her apartment rent as a tax deduction for office space. It also let her deduct car, utilities, phone, and many other expenses related to her business. She was also able to write off 60 percent of her medical insurance premiums, which were substantial because she was self-employed and could not obtain group coverage.

Penbrook, however, did pay more than her fair share in Social Security taxes. Because she was single, FICA taxes accounted for a large percentage of her tax burden each year. While she enjoyed the simplicity of a sole proprietorship, she also knew that incorporation might save her thousands of dollars in Social Security tax. Today, Penbrook is weighing each method for structuring a business and determining if remaining structured as a sole proprietorship is the best option for her. In fact, because of the high Social

Security taxes she is paying, she may prefer to structure her business as a Sub S Corporation, which will be discussed later in this chapter.

# Partnerships

A partnership is defined as a legal entity that involves two or more people who share profits in a venture. This structure is a little more complex than a sole proprietorship but is still less complicated and formal than incorporation. Paperwork for a partnership must be filed with your state government.

## Advantages

- Requires no separate tax at the partnership level, meaning both partners are taxed individually as sole proprietors (the tax is determined based on ownership levels).
- All income and losses pass through to the partners as if they earned them individually (thus a partnership is called a "pass-through" entity).
- Unlike sole proprietorships, losses are limited to the sum of the cash or property basis you contributed to the partnership and all loans that you guaranteed or made to the partnership.
- Different skills and abilities of each partner allows diversity and strong support for the entity.
- Partnerships can take advantage of almost all of the same tax benefits as that of a sole proprietor.

## Disadvantages

- A partnership requires the filing of a separate partnership tax return.
- Because this business structure involves more people than a sole proprietorship, salaries are usually paid to either the partners or staff or both, so a federal tax ID number is required.
- Subject to federal and state employment tax on salaries.
- The biggest disadvantage to a partnership is that you are unlimitedly liable for partnership debts and for the acts of your partner. In fact, this liability can be such a major problem that we do not regularly recommend that our clients form a partnership with another individual (with the exception, perhaps, of husband and wife) to start their home-based business.

Case History

# John Caldwell and Nathan Hamblin: Property Management Partnership

John Caldwell* and Nathan Hamblin* are a good example of a business partnership. The two men had complementary skills and desired to work as a business team, forming a property management company called ITC Properties. Through this company, John and Nathan bought real estate, improved these properties, and then rented or sold them. The partnership required that both John and Nathan be responsible individually for the property mortgages. But forming a partnership where they bought and sold property allowed the two men to save valuable tax dollars through deductions for real estate business. As a partnership, all income and property that came into the partnership was passed to both John and Nathan as if they had earned them individually, plus each had a different set of skills that helped them run the business. For example, John was skilled at showing and selling the properties, while Nathan had experience in accounting and bookkeeping. Each contributed to the business in their own way.

The partnership also had some disadvantages, because it required them to file a separate tax return, which was time consuming. In addition, each of their salaries was subject to federal and state employment tax. They also had to deal with the inherent liability that comes with a partnership, each agreeing to be responsible for the acts of the other partner, putting themselves at some risk.

•••

# Regular "C" Corporation

Corporations are legal entities that require filing with state government. They are separate entities that require their own tax return to be filed with the IRS (IRS form 1120). A "C" corporation is taxed separately on all monies that are not paid out in expenses, bonuses, or salaries. Corporations are very formal beasts. In fact, based on the complexity and formalities involved, corporations can be very unwieldy, so you should carefully consider each of the pros and cons of incorporating before making a move.

## Advantages

- The biggest advantage is that corporations limit liabilities. If you maintain the formalities, your liabilities are generally limited to the assets of the corporation with the exception of malpractice suits. (In malpractice, the owners may be unconditionally liable regardless of the way the business is structured.)

- Can deduct 100 percent of health insurance premiums and 100 percent of any disability insurance premium, which are both tax-free benefits to employees.

- Can accumulate (with planning) $50,000 per year for future business needs and have this amount taxed at the 15 percent rate. If you are in a 40 percent tax bracket, this represents a substantial 25 percent savings. We should note here that this is a major overlooked advantage of being a regular corporation. If you want to accumulate substantial working capital, this allows you to keep up to $50,000 per year and have it taxed to the corporation at the 15 percent tax bracket.

- Can have many different classes of public or private stock, which adds value to the company and is great for estate planning and raising capital.

*Tip: Because liability protection is so important in making the decision of whether to incorporate, we almost always recommend some form of corporation or LLC (limited liability company) if you employ workers. If you have employees, you MUST limit your liability through the legal protection allowed by incorporation laws. For example, if you are incorporated and one of your employees accidentally burns your restaurant to the ground through a grease fire, you will not be responsible to pay for the loss of the building personally unless you have assumed or guaranteed any indebtedness. Responsibility for the building is transferred to the business entity itself if you are incorporated.*

## Disadvantages

- If funds are paid out again in dividends, you could be "double taxed" on these dividends, meaning that the funds would be taxed first through the business entity, and then taxed to you as a dividend. In fact, based on the complexity and formalities involved, double taxation is the biggest headache of incorporating. We should note however, that this headache can be somewhat alleviated with proper year-end tax planning with your accountant.

- Must hold yearly stockholder meetings, even if you are the only stockholder, and yearly board of director meetings.

- Must have a separate business bank account; if you do not take this step and co-mingle your personal funds with business funds, you will automatically forfeit your legal protection against liability.

(While it is advisable for all business entities, including sole proprietorships, to set up separate business bank accounts and distinguish between all business and personal funds, corporations are legally bound to do so.)

- Must obtain a federal tax ID number from both the IRS and the state.
- Some states impose strict taxes on corporations. For example, California requires that a corporation pay what the state's normal tax rate would be or $800, whichever is higher. Thus, if your corporation is located in, or does business in California and incurs a loss, you will wind up paying the state $800!
- If planning has been done poorly or incorrectly, the corporation will be subject to potentially nasty surprises such as having to pay taxes on accumulated earnings (also called "future income").
- Can be very expensive and costly to file taxes because of the amount of paperwork required.

*Cautionary Note: If you are a "personal service corporation," you will be taxed on any money left in the corporation at the end of the year at a flat 35 percent rate. A personal service corporation is a regular "C" corporation whose principal activity is the performance of personal services by its employee-owners. They also involve certain occupations such as law, medicine, accounting, architecture, veterinary, dental, etc. If you are in these fields, you should consider very carefully whether to structure your business as a "C" corporation or, at the very least, conduct annual year-end tax planning in order to insure that most of the profits are removed from the corporation in the form of salaries or bonuses.*

*Tip: Because we find that most business owners don't keep up with the required formalities and don't perform the required year-end tax planning necessary to avoid double taxation, we rarely recommend structuring your home-based business as a regular "C" corporation. This should only be set up with careful advice from your lawyer and/or accountant.*

# "S" Corporations

This type of corporation is a hybrid mix of sole proprietorships and regular "C" corporations. Here's why you may want to consider forming your business as an "S" corporation:

## Advantages

- One of the biggest advantages to an "S" corporation is that it can help you eliminate some of your Social Security taxes. For example, let's say Sam earns net after expenses $70,000 as a sole proprietor. He pays income tax on the $70,000 and pays 15.3 percent in Social Security taxes on that $70,000. This amounts to $10,600 alone![3] However, if he forms an S corporation and pays himself a reasonable salary of $35,000 a year and receives the rest in the form of a dividend, because dividends are not subject to Social Security tax, Sam will only pay Social Security on the salary and not on the remaining $35,000 dividend. He saves 15.3 percent on $35,000, which represents a $5,355 yearly savings! This method of saving Social Security taxes is not possible with any other business structure.

- All income and losses flow through to the owners (just like a partnership), thus eliminating most of the double taxation problem.

- Limits liability just like a regular "C" corporation, so if you will have employees, this is a good choice.

- Stockholders are taxed on the earnings of the corporation based on their ownership so you can split off income into lower tax brackets. For example, if there is only one owner of the corporation, and the business brings in $100,000 annually, that owner will be taxed at the 50 percent tax bracket. But say the owner gives part ownership to each of his three children and his wife. Now there are five stockholders, each receiving a fifth of the $100,000 dividend or $20,000 each. His 17-year-old son can now be taxed on his share of the dividends at a much lower tax bracket because of his age.

- Allows taxes to be filed using IRS form K-1, which reduces Schedule C into a much more generalized statement of business dealings, lessening tax exposure.

## Disadvantages

- No more than 75 individual stockholders are allowed.

- There are no provisions for several classes of stock as in a "C" corporation, thus greatly limiting estate planning and opportunities to raise capital. In addition, these private shares cannot be sold and the company cannot go public in order for shares to be bought and sold on the stock market.

- Subject to the same formalities as a regular corporation, meaning shareholder meetings must be held, even if there's only one individual, with the same paperwork and meeting hassles.
- Must formally document all business activities for tax purposes.
- You cannot create a self-insured medical plan like you can with certain sole proprietorships and a regular "C" corporation. This kind of plan allows regular corporations to deduct 100 percent of health and disability insurance premiums; sole proprietors can also take this 100 percent deduction if they hire their spouse in the business (to be covered in detail in Chapter 16). An "S" corporation is allowed only 60 percent deductions for health insurance premiums.

One final disadvantage we must note is that both "S" corporations and partnerships are allowed to deduct any losses up to the limit of the cash or property basis that was contributed to the stock or partnership. However, with partnerships, any debt that is guaranteed is added to a cash or property basis. This is *not* true with an "S" corporation. You cannot guarantee debt; you can only contribute property or money.

Case History

## Greg and Betty Wallace: An "S" Corporation

While working as W-2 employees, Greg and Betty Wallace* decided to form a leasing and venture capital services company by structuring it as an "S" corporation. This allowed the husband and wife team to limit their personal liability while also reducing their Social Security taxes. In fact, the Wallaces were able to reduce their FICA tax by 50 percent. In addition, they took advantage of lower taxes by splitting off income from the business through paying dividends to their children, who were part owners of the company. The Wallaces did have to hold quarterly and annual stockholder meetings and keep meticulous minutes, but the somewhat formal structure of their business, while not as complex as a "C" corporation, provided them with liability protection they could not get through a partnership or sole proprietorship. For Greg and Betty, an "S" corporation was the best way to structure their business, especially with the tremendous savings in Social Security.

• • •

# Limited Liability Companies (LLC)

This is the newest method of structuring a business and is a fairly recent innovation. An LLC is like a sole proprietorship, however it provides the same protection from liabilities as that of a "C" or "S" corporation. In fact, this structure allows you to elect to be treated as a corporation without having to deal with the formalities of such.

If there is only one owner, you can file and be taxed as a sole proprietor. If there are two or more owners, you will be taxed as a partnership.

## Advantages

- Limits liability just like a regular corporation.
- Does not require the formal meetings and documentation of a "C" or "S" corporation.
- Tax filing and other paperwork is simple and inexpensive.
- Can claim all the same tax advantages of sole proprietors and partnerships.
- Don't have to hold shareholder meetings or keep meeting notes.

## Disadvantages

- Does not provide a FICA tax break like an "S" corporation does (except in the case of hiring a spouse or children...then their salary is not subject to FICA taxes if they are under age 18).
- Fairly recent entity, so some states are still working out the laws that govern an LLC.

# Jackson Montgomery: Setting Up a Side Business

Case History

Jackson Montgomery* began Small Business Development, LLC as a means to help people learn how to set up a viable home-based business. As an accountant and financial expert, Jackson felt he could assist people in learning some of the tricks to setting up a successful side-business venture. By structuring his own company as an LLC, Jackson mitigated his own liability and also made certain tax-saving benefits available through his wife and children. He hired his wife and paid her a salary for helping with the business. In addition, he also made each of his children a 1 percent owner in the business and paid them a regular dividend, which helped cover their expenses. None of this dividend was subject to FICA tax because they were under 18 years of age. Through an LLC, Jackson can pay his kids a FICA tax-free dividend as a part owner and help offset family expenses.

One final thought on multiple ownerships within partnerships, LLCs, or corporations. What happens if you and one other owner in your business do not get along? Bad relationships have resulted in some of the most expensive and protracted legal battles around. This kind of business contention is worse than a divorce. Thus, take the following advice:

If you incorporate or structure your business as an LLC and have multiple owners, always set up a buy-sell agreement at the launch of your business. This will eliminate a lot of problems and you will bless yourself for it later. Think of "buy-sell" arrangements as a sort of business prenuptial agreement.

As we have already noted, the way you start up your business can protect you from liabilities and save you thousands of tax dollars depending on your personal circumstances. While we have outlined the basics with regards to each of these entities, it is imperative that you take the time to learn more of the rules behind each of these business structures so that you can choose the one that is right for you.

*Note: We strongly recommend that you seek out the professional help of your accountant or attorney in order to sort out the issues with each of the five business entities we have outlined in this chapter.*

## Challenge #12

# Determine How You Will Legally Structure Your New Home-Based Business

This week we challenge you to take the time necessary to learn more about each of the ways you can legally structure your business. To do this, we recommend the following:

1.  Search the Web for more information on corporations, sole proprietorships, partnerships, and LLCs.
2.  Refer to your local library for more specific information.
3.  Contact your state's division of corporations and commercial code.
4.  Seek the advice of professionals such as accountants and lawyers. Keep in mind that just because these people are professional, does not mean they are infallible. It is your responsibility to know as many rules as possible. Learn enough so that when you do seek out their advice, you'll know whether it's sound or not. Remember Principles 5 and 6.

(Refer to the Appendix of this book for more information on business structure.)

Once you have investigated each business entity, determine which structure is right for you. Then read on. The following chapters will help you learn what you need to know to set up your home office so that you can take advantage of as many tax saving strategies as possible.

# Chapter 13

# You're in Business... So Act Like It!

**D**o things right the first time.

Such advice is sound, especially when it comes to setting up a new home-based business. In Chapter 12, we outlined how to start things off on the right foot by selecting the best way to legally structure your new venture. Now you are ready to begin "setting up shop," and it will be imperative that you do that right the first time, too. In this chapter, we outline some very important rules that will help you conduct your new venture—rules that will help you see that if you're going to be in business, you must act like it!

As we have already emphasized in Chapters 11 and 12, running a home-based business is the best way to take advantage of all the tax deductions available to you during the accumulation stage. Why? If your business produces a loss, you can generally deduct that loss against any form of income you have such as interest, dividends, rents, retirement income, and wages. In fact, you can even use those losses against your spouse's income, if you file jointly. These are only some of the wonderful tax-saving aspects of being in a home-based business.

Naturally, the IRS knows about all these wonderful benefits. And that's why it doesn't want you to take advantage of the home-based business strategy. It doesn't want you to learn the rules of the tax game to the extent that you can play it on an even playing field. It doesn't want you to know about all the "good" tax codes that allow you to take deductions for your home office, entertainment, food, and other business expenses. It wants you to remain in the dark. Because if it can't keep you in the dark, it knows you'll save valuable tax dollars that could be coming into the federal coffers instead.

It should come as no surprise then, that it is very much in the interest of the IRS to declare that you are playing at being in business, and not actually running one. The IRS, and Congress of course, are looking for ways to declare that what you do for your home-based business is a hobby and not a viable means to make a profit. If the IRS can demonstrate to its satisfaction (and the courts', if it should get that far), that you are only engaged in a hobby (or simply "monkeying around"), then no home-based business losses can be taken by you.[1] That's worth repeating:

*Activities that are deemed hobbies, or not engaged in for profit, do not qualify for business losses or for deductions above the income from the hobby.*

That means if you only make $200 in a year from your home-based hobby, your deduction will be limited to $200. Even worse, there is no carryover of those excess deductions; you just lose them if they are declared to be a hobby by the IRS.[2]

Thus, reclassifying your activities as a hobby, rather than a business, is the IRS's favorite weapon. Therefore, it is vital that you apply the following tax strategy.

# Tax Strategy #3: Run your business like a business, not like a hobby.

Fortunately, Congress has given all taxpayers a way to be absolutely sure that their activities will be treated like business operations, and not like a hobby. If your activity shows a profit for three or more consecutive years out of five, it will be presumed by the IRS that you are engaged in a viable business.[3]

*Note: For those business owners engaged in breeding or racing activities such as horse racing, dog racing, dog breeding, car racing, dog and horse training, and so on, then that activity should show a profit two out of seven years.[4]*

But what if you don't show a profit for three years out of the five, or if your first years are a loss? As long as you are running your venture like a real business endeavor and not as a hobby, the law cannot pronounce limits on your losses, even if the IRS tries to declare your business a hobby without waiting the three years for you to establish an operating history.[5]

That's why it's so important that you know the rules about how to run your business like a real business. There are numerous standards that the courts use to ascertain whether you are actually running a business, and helping you understand them is what this chapter is all about.

# The Rules of the Game

## Rule #1: Show business intent.

You must show that you entered your business activity with the intent to make a profit. As we have already noted, it doesn't have to be a big profit; it can actually be quite small, but it does have to be some kind of profit. A majority of court cases on this subject indicate that you are required to have an honest profit objective when you undertake the venture. Thus, if you have a sincere purpose in the venture, including eventually reaping an over-all profit, it will be assumed that you have a profit motive.

*Tip: Document your intent by sending a letter to your sponsor (for MLM networking opportunities) stating why you are entering into the business, and emphasizing your desire to make a long-term profit or career out of the home-based business. Another way to document business intent is through creating a business plan (more information on this later in the chapter).*

## Rule #2: Be businesslike.

Conduct your business in a businesslike fashion. Such advice may sound very simple, but it's probably the single most important factor in the IRS's determination of your intent. Is the manner in which you conduct your activity in accord with good business practices? Regardless of whether you make a profit, the IRS essentially wants to see you running your business as if you are serious about it.

What steps should you take to run your activity in a businesslike fashion?

**1. Keep accurate and complete tax records.** This is very important. In fact, you really have no choice but to do so if you're going to be in business for yourself. This will help your accountant so that he or she can aid you saving the most tax dollars and so that you can audit-proof your business activities. It is our goal to help you see that keeping sound supporting documentation is the best way to keep the IRS off your back, *and* to help you save more tax dollars than you ever imagined. To do this, you must create new tax habits that will help you keep accurate records.

These new tax habits are not unlike those you created when you first began learning the 10 Money Mastery principles. Therefore, keeping a detailed, accurate tax diary should not be very hard for you to do, especially now that you have embraced Money Mastery Principle 2. Using this principle, you have

---

## More Reasons Why Documentation Is So Important

- All the numbers included in your tax return are your responsibility. You create the numbers, not your accountant. You are required to have adequate support for your tax return. When you sign your return, you attest to its accuracy under penalty of perjury. And the only way to be sure this information is accurate is to keep good records.

- The IRS states in its official publications that you must maintain records that support accurate tax returns. Also, these records must be made at or near the time of the expense so that you will be sure to have accurate recall. Such records must be permanent and complete. Failure to meet the adequate documentation standards of the Internal Revenue Code can result in disallowance of your deductions.[6]

- Documentation is also important because the IRS thinks you might cheat on your taxes, and accordingly you are assumed guilty until you prove yourself innocent. The burden of support is on you. IRS examiners are not required to help you keep records. You have total responsibility for proving your deductions.

- Finally, accurate records are important because failure to keep them results in very stiff penalties if you are audited.

---

made a habit of keeping track of how you spend money. Using this same principle, we encourage you to keep a tax diary so that you can track how your business is conducted and how your day is spent while running that business.

**2. Create a separate bank account for your business.** A number of recent cases have indicated that the courts expect you to keep separate books and bank accounts for your business.[7] Don't co-mingle your personal funds with your business accounts, not even if you are a sole proprietor. Be sure to set up a separate bank account for your home-based business.[8]

**3. Be sure to control your own money.** Do not transfer the authority to sign checks over to family members, for instance, or other employees. Sign your own checks. Use purchase order systems where applicable.

## Rule #3: Create a business plan.

It is very important that you take this step.[9] Most courts have looked favorably on taxpayers who had a business plan showing projected income and expenses for their activities. The key, obviously, is that you want to show on your plan when you expect to start producing an overall business profit. You don't want that plan to show a profit 10 years down the road, with a loss every year subsequent to that. You want to demonstrate to the

---

# What Is the Best Way to Keep Accurate Records?

**a. Keep an accurate and complete tax diary.** This diary, which can be your appointment book or daily planner, is the focal point of your documentation system. The smaller your business, the more important this diary becomes.

Your daily tax diary should include:

- All of your appointments.
- Where and when you travel.
- Where you go by automobile.
- Where and when you entertain business contacts.

While documentation is important, some people resist it because they assume it will be too time consuming. But this stubborn resistance is just as shortsighted as refusing to track spending. The amount of time it takes to record necessary daily activities in your tax diary will be well worth the extra 10 or 12 seconds it takes to do so. Not only that, tracking your daily activities in this way will be just as emotionally revealing as tracking your money has been. Doing so will make you very aware of your daily habits, how you spend your time, and what you value. A good system can help you document your daily activities. (Refer to the Appendix for information on tax diary products.) Don't cheat yourself out of these deductions or the peace of mind that comes from good documentation. **Record your activities every day using a tax diary!**

**b. Keep permanent records.** These include prior years' tax returns, stock purchases and sales, equipment purchases, etc. Generally, you want to keep any record that relates to more than one tax year. If you purchase property, your permanent files should include the purchase documents, closing statements, deeds, and other expenses related to the purchase.

**c. Keep business records.** These include time sheets for part-time help, receipts, invoices, cancelled checks, and other evidence that you do business on a regular basis.

---

IRS that you expect to make a profit as quickly as possible. The numbers should have some reasonable basis in reality as well. In other words, you should have a rationale supporting each number, that is, an expert informed you about the number, or you referenced it through other substantiating material. You should document how you estimated each of your figures.

If your business requires inventories, obviously you should have enough inventory on hand to meet your profit objectives. Not every business will have inventory, but if you do, you should be aware of this when creating your business plan.

Business plans should generally project your business profitability from five to 10 years; 10 years is safer. The business plan should include not only a projection of income and expenses, but also your plans for marketing the business. A marketing plan will answer this one simple question: What do I intend to do to make money? (For more information on resources for creating a business plan, consult your local bookstore, or search the Web.)

## Rule #4: Remember that your own statements may testify against you.

In determining whether you are involved in business activities or just a hobby, the IRS listens to what you say. In fact, they are very happy to listen to your statements and then use your own words against you.[10]

Suppose you say to someone, "Well, I'm only in this business to escape taxes." Or, "I just want someplace to dump some expenses." Or, "I'm only in this to get a discount on some decent golf clubs." If the IRS gets wind of statements like these it will claim, and rightly so, that you are not in a home-based business to make a profit and you will not be treated as a business entity. One couple we know that distributed Amway products wasn't aware of how their statements could be used against them. In tax court, the IRS attorney asked them if they would continue business even if they never made a profit, to which the couple answered yes. This showed the judge that these people were in their "business" more for social reasons than to make a profit. He disallowed all losses for this couple's Amway business. Again, we can't emphasize enough that you must watch what you say! Your own words will be used against you in a court of law.

## Rule #5: Run your business the way similar profitable businesses are run.

You should try to show that your activity is being carried on in a similar manner to other profitable business ventures.[11] If you conduct your activity the way other successful people in the same business do, you will be able to argue vigorously that you are conducting your activity like a business with the expectation of making money. If you want to be a millionaire, hang around millionaires, or as they say:

*"If you want to fly like an eagle, don't hang around with turkeys."*

In addition, if you follow the path of a coach, mentor, or other financial expert, your chance of becoming successful is further enhanced. Adopt marketing efforts similar to those that are successful.[12] Remember our discussion about successful modeling that we outlined in Chapter 11?

---

Following are ways that you can run your business like other profitable ventures:

1. *Advertise Your Business.* Keep copies of the advertising flyers, promotional pieces, and press releases you use to promote your business.

2. *Create Business Cards.* Your business cards should indicate in what type of business you are engaged, your address, and telephone number.

3. *Maintain a Business Telephone Listing.*

4. *Use Promotional Materials.* Keep copies of brochures, press releases, etc.

5. *Use a Variety of Marketing Strategies.*[13] Don't just put one ad in one paper. Also, if you are in a multi-level operation, don't just listen to what your upline tells you to do if you are not making money. Consult with people such as financial coaches or entrepreneurs that have been successful at marketing a business.

---

## Rule #6: Understand that your prior business experience can help or hurt you.

If you have no prior business experience in a particular line of work, the IRS may decide that you are taking a big chance, and therefore find it questionable that you ever had a profit motive.[14]

The courts have long held that this strike against you can be overcome by making sure that you extensively study your line of business. Investigate the business you are going into before you launch it.[15] Do a feasibility study; see how profitable the type of business you want to launch can be. Listen to training tapes, take seminars, attend training meetings. You can never get enough training, and it will serve to improve your bottom line at the same time it helps to satisfy the IRS that you are really taking the business seriously. Document all your training, lectures, and outside reading using your daily tax diary. This is very important. Every time you receive training or go to a seminar, document it.

Thoroughly investigate your business venture before jumping into it:

- Get a credit report on the sponsoring company (for network marketing).
- Check out the competition to see what they are doing.
- See how much money other distributors or business owners are making in the same business.
- If you can, review some financial reports related to your industry or business venture.

The more thorough your investigation, the better the chance that the IRS is going to believe you are in business to do business.

## Rule #7: Devote regular time to your business.

Although you don't have to devote your full time and attention to a side business, it is very important that you devote some time in a regular manner to your activity. Businesses are conducted in a regular and systematic manner; hobbies are not.

Nobody says that a home-based business must be a full-time duty, but the more time and effort you put in it, the better. At least one case on record has shown that an average of as little as one hour per day was substantial enough to prove a profit motive.[16] One hour a day, four to five days a week is better than putting in eight hours every two weeks.[17]

Now you might be asking how the IRS would know whether you actually put in one hour every day. How do they know you are actually seeing people in your business and visiting prospects and doing marketing? They look at your tax diary, that's how. A good diary is irreplaceable because it can go a long way toward proving that you are running a business, not engaging in a hobby.

## Rule #8: Keep a history of income, losses, and steps you have taken to improve the bottom line.

Maintaining this kind of history is a very important step. In any business, expenses can certainly exceed income.[18] Businesses do have losses, and the hobby loss provisions aren't based on the assumption that no decent businessperson ever had a loss. However, real businesspeople do everything necessary (and legal) to turn those losses into profits.[19]

You should watch out for expenses that are unreasonable. Expenses should be in proportion to your income. For example, a case involving an Amway distributor showed that his accounting fees alone had exceeded his entire gross income from his business. Because of this, the court held that the distributor's activities constituted a hobby.[20] Marketing expenses are an exception to the principle of proportionality because they can be very costly in the early stages of a company's existence.

This concept of using excessive and unreasonable expenses as a way of assessing the lack of a business profit motive has been applied to a lot of cases. For example, a person who has a travel business and tries to deduct all her family trips, despite very little gross income, is going to have a tough time proving that these trips had a profit motive. This is especially true if each trip cost more than the gross income of the business venture itself!

Your main objective should be to show that you are really trying to make a profit or turn your losses around. You want to show that you do have a reason for spending a large sum of money in one area. The best way to do this is to document, document, document! Document all marketing activities and all reasons for trips, noting the business intent and the necessity for taking the trip in order to make money.

*Note: Recent IRS cases indicate that there needs to be some gross income in order to be considered a business. If you are in a business that shows no gross income at all, the IRS is likely to see this as evidence that you are not in business and that you are conducting a hobby instead.*

## Rule #9: Keep in mind that income from other sources can affect an IRS ruling.

The IRS also looks at the amount of income you have from other sources.[21] This may not seem fair; if you make $200,000 and you go into a side business, you are more suspect than someone making $20,000, but that's the way it is. The greater your income from other sources, the less likely the loss from your other activity will be deemed a loss. This situation, however, does not mean all is lost. There are a lot of people who make hundreds of thousands of dollars and still claim losses from their side businesses. But certainly this situation requires that you dot your i's and cross your t's more carefully.

## Rule #10: Be more alert if you are involved in inherently "suspicious" activities.

There are certain activities that seem to be inherently more suspicious to the IRS.[22] These are business ventures that may have more potential for significant personal pleasure. Following are some examples:

- Antique Collecting.
- Stamp Collecting.
- Travel and Tourism.
- Writing.
- Ministerial Duties.
- Music Recording and Production.
- Raising Show Horses.
- Training and Showing Dogs.
- Automobile Racing.

If you are involved in one of these activities, you need to pay close attention to all the other rules we have outlined in this chapter.

While the rules that determine whether you are running a business or doing a hobby may make starting a home-based business seem like a lot of work, we can assure you that learning these rules will make running your business a lot easier, and will bring peace of mind. It will also prepare you to take full advantage of the tax savings we will explain in upcoming chapters. Only by committing yourself to get organized as Money Mastery Principle 8 teaches, will you ever be ready to launch into a home-based business that will run smoothly and efficiently for you, even in the early stages. As you form new "tax habits" it will become easier and more automatic to do the things we have discussed in this chapter. Plan to start your new business venture on the right foot by doing things right the first time.

## Challenge #13

# Review the "Business vs. Hobby Checklist" and Obtain a Good Tax Diary

1. This week, review the following checklist to ensure that your venture will be conducted as a business and not a hobby:

- ✔ Try to have a profit in at least three out of five consecutive years, or two out of seven years if you are involved in animal breeding or racing, or automobile racing.
- ✔ Document your intent to make a profit; a business plan or a letter to your sponsoring company (if you are in networking marketing) will do.
- ✔ Document all business activities using a tax diary or daily planner.
- ✔ Keep business and financial records separate from your personal finances.
- ✔ Open a separate bank account for your business.
- ✔ If your business requires inventory, make sure you have enough to justify your business plan goals.
- ✔ Use advertising, business telephone listings, and marketing materials as appropriate for your business, and change your advertising and marketing strategies form year-to-year if you are not making money.
- ✔ Investigate your business activity before entering it; document that investigation.
- ✔ Obtain training continually; seek out expert advice; document these efforts.
- ✔ Work your business regularly and document your activities daily.

✔ Keep a history of your business and show how you took steps to improve your bottom line.

2. This week, be sure to obtain a good tax diary or other method or recording your daily activities. (Refer to the Appendix for information about various tax diary products.)

# Chapter 14

# Your Home Office: A Tax Saving Resource

**K**now the rules. We have emphasized again and again how important it is to heed this advice. So many people suffer when they take for granted the power of this Money Mastery principle. It can be applied in so many areas of our lives to bring peace, control, and stability. And when it comes to taxation, it's especially critical that the rules of the tax game are known and understood. In Chapter 13, we outlined some very important rules that will help distinguish your new home-based venture as a business, and not simply a hobby. You are now ready to learn some rules about the way to physically set up an office so you can be sure to run your business in a way that will ensure you the most tax savings.

Without question, a home office is one of the single biggest resources for tax deductions to which you have access. Unfortunately, many people don't understand the wealth of tax savings they can get from a home office because they have heard a few myths about the limitations placed on a home office. These need clearing up:

## Myth #1: I can't claim a home office deduction because my house isn't zoned commercially.

The truth is the IRS does not care at all about the zoning laws in your area. You can live in a commercial, rural, residential, or agricultural zone and it won't make a bit of difference to the IRS.

## Myth #2: I can't claim a home office because I don't have a back entrance in my home.

The fact is that the IRS is not concerned about how many entrances you have in your house.

## Myth #3: My accountant said that the home office deduction isn't worth the trouble.

Here's what the numbers say, and these numbers are based on a $200,000 home: The value of an office in such a home is about $2,500 a year in cash, which if invested at 6 percent, makes the actual value of a home office (over a five-year period) worth almost $15,000 every five years! In our opinion, paying yourself $15,000 every five years because you operate your business in your home sounds pretty worth the trouble. Don't you think?

## Myth #4: My accountant says that the home office deduction is limited to my income so if I don't make enough profit in my business, it isn't worth taking it.

This is partly true. Your home office deduction is, indeed, limited to the net income from your business after taking all your other business deductions. Consequently, if you are not working your business, or if you are not making any kind of substantial income, you do not get an immediate benefit.

However, no "immediate benefit" is not the same as no benefit at all. If your deduction exceeds your net income from your business, you can carry it over into future income years indefinitely. So, as you make more money, you can offset those nice increases in income with carry-over deductions.

As you can see, a home office can be a very legitimate tax deduction.

 # Tax Strategy #4: If you are eligible for a home office tax deduction, take it!

Here's how to assess whether you can apply Tax Strategy #4:

The law states that a home office deduction is available only to the extent that a portion of the dwelling unit* is used exclusively and on a regular basis.[1] That means that your home office must be:

---

*A separate structure, not attached to the dwelling unit, also qualifies if it is used in connection with your trade or business. This means if you convert your garage or another outbuilding for use as a workshop, for example, it could qualify for the home office deduction. Other examples include a florist's greenhouse or an artist's studio.

1.  Your principal place of business; and/or
2.  The place of business where you meet and greet customers, patients, or clients in the normal course of your business; and/or
3.  Used for a second business you have; and/or
4.  Used to display sample products or as storage space for inventory.

In addition, if you are using an office in your home to do work as a regular W-2 employee, then the home office deduction is allowed only if the exclusive use of the office is for the convenience of your employer.[2] Thus, your employer must require you to take work home, and not provide you with an office at work.

Let's examine each of the criteria we have outlined above in more detail:

## Criteria #1: Principal Place of Business.

What constitutes a principal place of business? A famous case called the "Doc Solomon" decision explains.[3] Dr. Solomon was an anesthesiologist. He worked in three different hospitals in Fairfax, Virginia for 30 to 35 hours a week. In his condominium, he converted one of his bedrooms into an office where he worked another 10 to 15 hours a week. He did his billing and medical logs from home, read X-ray film from home, and, more interestingly, he had no other office. The hospitals for which he worked would not provide him one.

Naturally, Dr. Solomon felt justified in claiming the home office deduction on his tax returns. His argument was, "My home has to be my principal place of business because I don't have another office." Dr. Solomon was audited and the IRS took him to court because they disagreed with his reasoning. A tax court heard the case and said, "Dr. Solomon, you are right." The IRS didn't like that answer so they took the case to an appellate court. The appellate court said, "Dr. Solomon, you are right." Of course, the IRS didn't like that either, so they went all the way to the Supreme Court. And as you know, that's always where the buck stops. The Supreme Court said: "Dr Solomon, you are wrong. We have two tests we use to determine whether a home property is a principal place of business for a home office."

*Test #1*: "Where do you do your most important functions?" To that, Dr. Solomon's response was, "My most important function is done at home. That is where I do my billing."

"No," said the Supreme Court, "that is not your most important function, Dr. Solomon. You are a doctor of anesthesiology, so your most important function is done where you deliver your anesthesia—in a hospital. You don't do that out of your home. Now lets look at another way to qualify using test number two."

*Test #2*: "Do you use your home office for more than 50 percent of your at-work time? Take the total amount of hours you work in a week, Dr. Solomon," said the Supreme Court, "and divide by two. Does that yield more than 50 percent of your hours physically spent in your home?"

In Dr. Solomon's case, he spent 15 hours a week at home and 35 hours a week in the hospital, so he obviously didn't qualify. He was not entitled to the home office deduction under either rationale.

You will be happy to know, however, that there is now an exception to the "Doc Solomon" decision, especially as it applies to test #1. Remember Money Mastery Principle 6, "The Rules Are Always Changing"? Due to tremendous complaints about the effect of this case on small business, Congress passed a special exception that took effect in 1999. This exception provides two new rules that help small businesses escape the clutches of the Solomon decision:[4]

- *New Rule #1:* Your office at home is used to conduct the administrative or management activities of your business.
- *New Rule #2:* There is no other office where you conduct substantial and administrative activities for your business.

That means, in terms of Test #1, the new rules allow that your primary function does not necessarily have to take place in your home office as long as your office at home is used to conduct the administrative or management activities of your business and you have no other office where you can conduct such activities. Thus, if you keep your logs, do your paperwork, listen to sales tapes, make business calls, create business materials, etc., out of a set place in your home, you will be legally eligible for the home office deduction.

But what about Test #2? Do the new laws Congress passed help overcome the difficulties of this test? Well, not directly, but the way this test is worded can be a bit misleading. Note that what Test #2 is actually saying is "do you perform any significant services in another office?" If you don't, you qualify for the exception. Let's look at some examples:

- John and Mary have W-2 jobs, but they also have a part-time network marketing business. They have no other office for this business. They do all paperwork and greet all clients in their home. Their home qualifies as a principal place of business under either the Soloman ruling or the exception.

- David and Cari are real estate agents. Although their broker provides them an office, they rarely use it other than to drop off contracts and attend sales meetings. All calls, mailings, and real estate research is done at home. Their home qualifies as a principal office because they don't perform significant services out of the other office.

If you keep good records, and work the 50 percent required time in your home in order to operate your side business, you will have no problem taking the home office tax deduction. Moreover, even if you don't meet the 50 percent test, if you meet the exception to Soloman, that is, you conduct your significant administrative activities for your business at home and don't have another office where you can conduct those activities, then your home constitutes a "principal office" for purposes of the home office deduction.

## Criteria #2: Meet-and-Greet Test.

If you don't use your home office 50 percent of the time for your home-based business, and don't meet the exception to the Soloman decision, you can still qualify for the home office deduction. An exception allows you to claim the deduction when you use your home office as a place where you meet and greet your clients (customers, patients, distributors, and so on) as a regular and ongoing part of your business.[5] Such use must be substantial and integral to conducting your business.[6]

During an audit, the IRS will look very closely at your actual physical meeting with clientele or customers. Telephone contacts do not count, no matter how lengthy or how frequent.[7] Meeting and dealing with clients in your home office is what counts. Now-and-then meetings do not qualify.[8] The law requires that:

- Meetings occur in a planned way.
- Such meetings are ordinary (or regular).
- Such meetings are an essential part of the way you carry on your business.

Be sure to keep track of all your hours for these meetings. Every time you work, you should note in your tax diary what you are doing. When you see clients, you should note this in your diary.

## Criteria #3: Home Office Deduction for a Second Business.

You might be able to qualify for a home office deduction in yet another way. If you happen to have a second side business, you can claim a home office deduction for that as well. The deduction does not have to relate to your primary business.

### Criteria #4: Display or Inventory Storage.

If you use space in your home to display or store products that you sell on a wholesale or retail basis, you can add the square footage of this space to the space you claim for the home office deduction. One of the requirements, however, is that your residence be the sole fixed location for your business.[9] Our recommendation, in order to help you meet this criteria, is to take photographs of the location in your home where you store inventory or display product samples. This is vital. By doing so, the IRS will have proof that you are using the space in this manner and cannot question you.

# Substantiating Your Home Office Deduction

If you can meet any of the above four criteria you will have no problem proving that you use your home to conduct business and can take the home office deduction. Once you decide to take it, you should be aware of a few rules that can help you substantiate your claim.

### Exclusive Use

You must use a room, or portion of a room, exclusively and regularly in one of several business functions in order to take a home office deduction. When the IRS says "exclusively," it is not kidding. This means that no personal or other non-qualifying work activities may occur in your home office area. If you watch TV in the designated home office area, unless it's solely for videotape training purposes, remove the television.[10] Remove those cookbooks you like from the shelves in your home office work space, and remove the games and other family fun activities out of the area.

To qualify for the home office deduction, you don't have to use an entire room as your workspace. If you want to use part of a room for business, you can do that. However, there should be some physical separation of the business area from the personal area.[11] If you keep your desk, chair, and filing cabinet in your living room, for instance (which is the way many home-based businesses start out), then the square footage those items occupy qualifies for the home office; the rest of the room's square footage does not. You are not allowed to co-mingle your business and personal furniture. We often hear people wondering if the IRS will really send someone over to their house to see if they are using an exclusive portion of a room for business. Yes, it will. Fortunately, if it plans to send anyone by your house, it will give between four and 12 weeks advance notice. Even with a notice, however, the IRS still manages to nail the unsuspecting taxpayer.

Here's an example of just how sneaky IRS agents can be. When Sandy was working as an attorney with the IRS, one of his agent colleagues audited a person claiming the home office deduction. Everything appeared to be in order in this taxpayer's home office. But then the agent ran a directory of the taxpayer's hard drive and discovered a game called "King's Quest" on it. Naturally, a person can have games loaded on their office computer; he just can't play them in his home office. The problem was that the taxpayer played the game and then saved it onto his hard drive in the same year that he was claiming the home office deduction. Even though he may have played the game only once during the year, by keeping the computer in the area he claimed for his home office, this taxpayer lost his deduction.

In another instance involving an audit, an IRS agent visited the home of the taxpayer and noticed a sofa bed in the home office area. Of course it was perfectly acceptable for this taxpayer to have a sofa bed in his office, as long as nobody slept on it! The IRS agent knew what would happen if he just flat out asked the taxpayer if anybody ever slept on the sofa bed; of course his answer would be no! Instead, after completing the audit, the agent sat on the sofa and said, "Gee, you know, I'm thinking of buying something like this for my parents to use when they come to visit me. My dad has a bad back. Do you have any experience with this? About somebody who might have hurt his back?" Obviously, the taxpayer was taken off guard and said, "Yeah, my brother and dad come to visit me and they don't have any problem. My mom doesn't have any problem." The agent then nailed him because he now had proof that the individual used the sofa bed in his home office for personal reasons and disallowed the deduction.

So how can you absolutely, with confidence, prove a home office deduction? Follow these tips and you will be totally secure:

1. **Photograph Your Office.** A photo can be a very important piece of documentation. Take pictures of the bookshelves, the file cabinets, the desk, and the general workspace. Make sure you have all your personal items out of the area before you do so. You don't want the IRS to see "Crossword Puzzle Secrets" in the photograph. Date the photos, but don't send them to the IRS. Simply hold onto them in case you ever do get audited. They will come in very handy. Photographs establish exclusivity.

2. **Prepare a Floor Plan.** Keep blueprints of your home to prove the amount of space occupied by the home office. If blueprints

are not available, make a drawing of your home showing the relationship of the home office's square footage to the total square footage of the home.

This graphic shows a typical house floor plan indicating the space occupied by a home office:

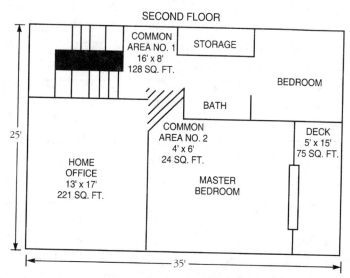

SECOND FLOOR

COMMON AREA NO. 1
16' x 8'
128 SQ. FT.

STORAGE

BEDROOM

BATH

COMMON AREA NO. 2
4' x 6'
24 SQ. FT.

DECK
5' x 15'
75 SQ. FT.

25'

HOME OFFICE
13' x 17'
221 SQ. FT.

MASTER BEDROOM

35'

Using a floor plan with the actual square footage of your home such as this one, you can easily calculate how much square footage you can deduct for a home office. You can also maximize this space using different computing methods. (For more information on these maximizing methods, refer to Appendix D.)

3. **Prominently Display Home Office Address**. Put your address and telephone number on business cards and stationery.[12] The IRS takes the position that if people don't know you're alive and kicking somewhere, you can't take a home office deduction.

4. **Use a Guest Log**. If you physically meet and greet clients at home on a regular basis, you can absolutely prove your home office exists using a guest log. Every time clients come to your home, have them write down their name, address, and occupation.

5. **Document Use of Your Office in Your Tax Diary**. This is where a tax diary can pay for itself a hundredfold. Use your tax diary to record what activities you performed in your home office such as, "studied for my network business from 8 a.m. to 9 a.m.," or "made calls from 9 a.m. to 12 p.m., HO (home office)." This work activity log in your diary does not need to be an elaborate

document; simply keep some notes about what you did during the day. If you ever get audited, you may have to answer questions about work or phone calls or training sessions that occurred two or three years prior.

When you make long distance calls, are you required to write down every person's name that you call in your tax diary? Generally not. But you should log it somewhere as a business-related call. During an audit, the IRS would ask, "Is this particular activity business or personal?" If you have not kept a log of your daily business activities, how will you ever know? You can look at your phone bill from three years previous and not be able to discern what calls were made for business and what were made for pleasure. Don't forget, the IRS, if it audits you, will not be doing so the same year you make those calls.

Remember, keep a good tax diary and organize all records.

## Furnishings and Equipment

A home office deduction relates only to the real estate and utilities for the office, and not for the furnishings and equipment used in it. However, such furniture and equipment can be depreciated. The rule is: Furniture, whether you qualify for a home office deduction or not, is depreciable only to the extent that you use it for business.[13]

For example, say you work at home and you use a desk 80 percent of the time for business. Even though you don't claim a home office, 80 percent of that desk becomes depreciable. If you sit on chairs, use desk lamps, computer equipment, file cabinets or bookshelves, these can also be depreciated if they are used to conduct business.

How do you depreciate furniture and equipment so you can deduct it? First, you must keep good tax records, as we have already emphasized. By doing so you can determine, within a 90-day period, what percentage of your time is spent in business and personal use and then use that time to help figure what percentage of the desk, chair, carpeting, lighting, equipment, etc., that you can depreciate. Second, determine the depreciation amount allowed for the item. This amount is the lower amount of the original cost, or today's market value.[14] So let's say you have an antique desk you bought three years ago. It cost you $500 and today it's worth $550. The amount you can write off for that desk is the lower of the two figures.

This depreciation rule assumes you work your business regularly, emphasizing once again how important it is to give your business, even if it's part-time, consistent efforts.[15]

What qualifies as a write-off for a home office? Anything you use in business other than an automobile. Examples include:

- Photocopy machines.
- Computers.
- Printers.
- Fax machines.
- Office furnishings including rugs, lighting, desks, chairs, and bookcases.

If you choose to depreciate such items, then you have to keep the item in your business for seven years or you must recapture some of that depreciation.

For example, a person buys a rug and a photocopier for their home-based business for a total of $4,200. That person can either depreciate that amount over seven years or they can elect to write off the entire amount in the year they purchased the items. Writing off the entire cost in the year it is purchased is usually the best course, but again, that deduction is limited to the income from the home-based business. If you don't have a lot of income, you will have to carry over the deduction. If you work your business as hard as you should, you will have the advantage of more income, and more income brings more tax benefits such as we have just outlined.

As of 2001, you can elect to expense up to $21,000 worth of business equipment per year.[16] What happens if you want to purchase more than $21,000 worth of equipment and furnishings in a year? Anything you purchase over that amount must be depreciated instead. Let's say you buy $30,000 worth of equipment for your business. You can elect to write off $21,000 of it and the remaining $9,000 you can depreciate. You can also choose to wait. You can buy only $21,000 worth of equipment in the current year, and in January of the next year, buy the additional $9,000 worth of items that you need. In this way, you can elect to write off $21,000 in the current year, and $9,000 as part of next year's purchases, avoiding any depreciation. Waiting may be a better way of saving tax dollars than purchasing all $30,000 worth of equipment in one year.

Be sure to consult with your accountant about all the rules for depreciating furnishings and equipment for your home office.

# Other Things to Consider about the Home Office Deduction

If you are eligible for a home office deduction, you have to claim it. You cannot simply decide not to deduct it if you do meet the eligibility requirements we have outlined above. Why is this? If the IRS discovers that you are eligible, they will insist that you have to reduce the basis of your home by the amount of depreciation allowable anyway, so you might as well take it.[17]

If you rent, you must take the claim by deducting a portion of your rent as it equates to the square footage of the home office. For example, if you pay $750 per month in rent on a 1,000 square-foot apartment, and your home office occupies 250 square feet of that space, you can deduct one-fourth of your rent (or $187.50 per month; $2,250 per year) for your home office.

Another thing to consider is that the home office deduction is limited to the net income from the business activity you conduct at home.[18] Consequently, if you have any expenses above and beyond the net income, you will not be able to deduct those home office expenses. That doesn't mean you shouldn't take the home office deduction because any expenses disallowed solely because they exceed your business income can be carried forward until you have sufficient income from your business conducted from home.[19]

## Challenge #14

# Determine Whether You Can Take the Home Office Deduction

This week, review the four criteria for claiming a home office as outlined in this chapter to determine if you meet any of them, then be sure to do the following:

1.  Determine the exact amount of square footage your home office area will occupy in your home. Use blueprints or floor plans as necessary.

2.  Be sure to keep the office free of personal belongings. If you have already established a work area, remove such things as TVs, computer games, personal books, board games, etc.

3.  Take photographs of your office area and date them.

4.  Purchase a guest log book if you plan to regularly meet clients in your home.

5.  Have business cards and letterhead printed with your address and business phone on them.

6.  Begin to log your personal and business time so that you can determine your "business percentage" time for the purpose of depreciating furnishings and equipment.

# Chapter 15

# Deducting Meals, Entertainment, Car, and Travel With Confidence

By now you're beginning to see that if you want to get serious about reducing your tax bill, you must know the rules! Knowing the rules is empowering and helps build self-confidence. As you learn each additional tax strategy, you are becoming better informed about the way the tax system really works and what you can do to best take advantage of it. It should be clear at this point that you can't be meek about reducing your tax burden. Those who sit back and accept what is put before them regarding their tax obligations will end up paying far more than is actually required by law.

*It may be true that "the meek shall inherit the earth," but in today's world, the meek are also more likely to overpay their taxes!*

If you want to get serious about reducing excessive taxation, you must be assertive in learning and applying the guidelines outlined in this book. By now, you should have now decided upon and launched a new business venture, legally structured it in a way most appropriate for your circumstances, and set up your business and home office work space so that you can confidently claim as many tax deductions as possible.

Now it's time to get even bolder. In this chapter we will help you learn how to write off business activities you engage in on a regular basis—and we'll teach you to do this with confidence.

# Tax Strategy #5: Put extra cash in your pocket by properly deducting meals and entertainment, car expenses, and any kind of travel.

Unfortunately, this tax strategy is one that many people miss out on because they aren't aware of all the opportunities of which they can take advantage. We have so many clients, who, after learning about the power of this tax-saving strategy, realize that they've lost thousands of dollars in tax deductions over the years because they didn't fully understand it. That's because they had never learned what you're about to learn anywhere else, and their accountant certainly never sat down and explained it to them.

Before we begin, we should note upfront that the whole topic of expense deductions is a touchy one with Congress and the IRS. But with a good tax diary and our advice about the importance of documentation ringing in your ears, you're armed and ready to keep the IRS off your back forever. If you follow the recommendations made in this chapter, you can audit-proof yourself 100 percent while taking full advantage of the "good laws" designed to give a tax break to the self-employed. Guaranteed!

# Deducting Meals and Entertainment

One of the most important activities that home-based businesspeople engage in is meeting potential customers or clients for lunch, or taking them out for an evening of entertainment as a means to secure more business. Why not take full advantage of the tax write-offs allowed by law for such things?

Following are the questions we are asked most frequently regarding this tax deduction:

- What are the substantiation requirements for my meal deductions?
- If I buy someone else's meal, what can I deduct?
- Can I deduct a meal expense if I'm not present at the meal?
- When can I deduct my spouse's (or significant other's) meal costs?
- If I go "Dutch treat" with someone, can I deduct anything?

Let's address each of these questions beginning with how meal deductions can be substantiated.

## The Five Substantiation Requirements:[1]

1.  The cost of the meal.
2.  The date you ate the meal.
3.  Where the meal was eaten.
4.  For what purpose was the meal eaten (that is, why did you take the person out to eat)?
5.  With whom was the meal consumed (that is, what is their business relationship to you)?

Every time you entertain, you should be in the habit of writing down these five requirements in your tax diary: cost, date, location, purpose, and business relationship. If you keep track of these elements "in a timely fashion" (another IRS rule we will discuss in this chapter), you will never have to worry about taking this deduction again. We should note, however, that if you don't track them, no matter what other support you may have for your meal expense, it will not be allowed as a deduction.

Let's consider each of these substantiation requirements:

### Cost

As always, we recommend you record this item in your tax diary, spending booklet, or planner on a daily basis; this is what the IRS means by "timely basis." You cannot come back later and hope to remember how much the item cost. You must do it on the day the event occurred. (Refer to Appendix A for more information on TRS Tax Diaries, and Money Mastery Spending Booklets.)

*Note: If the cost of the meal was not more than $75, you do not need to keep any documentary evidence such as a receipt, a voucher, or a credit card charge copy.[2]*

### Date

Record the date when the meal took place. If you keep track in a tax diary or daily planner, the date on the diary page is adequate support.

### Description

Give the nature of the meal you are claiming and the location where it took place. Some people assume this means they must describe the meal they ate—"hog jowl and grits"—but this is not so. The name of the eating establishment is sufficient. If the meal is over $75 and you need to keep a receipt, naturally it will include this information as well.

## Business Purpose

Of the five elements, this is the most important. You must record why you took someone out to eat. Be specific.[3] Note in your diary that you talked about skin care needs, for example, or legal or tax reduction needs or whatever activity fits the business you are in. Be brief, but be specific. Perhaps you discussed referrals with the person you took to lunch, or maybe the opportunity to launch a new venture. If you record such purposes as "good will" or "prospect," don't expect it to be accepted because it isn't specific enough. If you simply write down the word "customer," it is not specific enough.

Consider the following examples of specific business purpose documentation:

- Pre-qualified buyer.
- Pre-qualified seller.
- Talked about inviting Charlie to the business ("recruiting discussion").
- Asked for referrals ("referral discussion").
- Talked about nutritional needs.
- Talked about skin care needs.
- Talked about weight loss needs.
- Talked about legal needs.

## Business Relationship

Record the name of the person you took out to eat and their occupation in your tax diary. Naturally, the IRS will not call these people to verify that they ate lunch with you, but it does want to know who they are and what their business is in relation to you.

The illustration on page 229 from a typical tax diary is a good example of how each of the five substantiation requirements should be recorded.

Notice how simple it is, yet specific where it needs to be. The date (not referenced in this graphic) appears at the top of the diary page, and each of the other four elements are properly recorded, including the cost of valet service. Keeping track of such expenses in a tax diary will provide the trigger you need to record these elements within 24 hours of the meal. How does the IRS know if you record it in a "timely fashion"? It asks you. That's why

| ENTERTAINMENT | | | | | | |
|---|---|---|---|---|---|---|
| WHO? | S. JONES | | | | | |
| WHERE? | PALM | | | | | |
| WHY? | OBTAIN REFFERALS | | | | | |
| BREAKFAST | | HOME | | OTHER | | |
| LUNCH | 20 00 | GOLF/ETC. | | COATS & VALET | 4 00 | |
| DINNER | | COCKTAILS | | | | |
| TOTAL | —— | TOTAL | —— | TOTAL | 24 00 | |

*(ACTIVITY 1)*

you must get into the habit of recording these items each and every time you entertain clients. If you leave out any one of the five, your deductions will be disallowed and you will be hit with a 75 percent civil fraud penalty[4] should you ever be audited. There's no kidding around here.

Following is a personal example in Sandy Botkin's own words about the value of recording these five elements in a good tax diary:

> *On the eve of going to work for the IRS, I was a tax shelter syndicator with $11,000 of entertainment expenditures. All new employees of the IRS must be audited. The IRS agent assigned to audit me looked at my records, and saw that I followed the five substantiating requirements throughout my diary. I was allowed every single dime of that $11,000 entertainment claim— every single dime. Moreover, the whole entertainment audit only took four minutes because my documentation was so good!*

From this you can see how important it is to document everything. The key is to have a triggering mechanism that prompts you to make daily notations in your diary. A good tax organizer will help you keep receipts in a neat and orderly fashion and help you remember to write down the details of the meeting that the receipt documents.

## But I don't have time to record all that stuff...

This is a complaint we sometimes here, much like the one we hear about tracking the spending of money. As we noted in Chapter 2, many people believe they don't have the time for keeping records. This idea has, and will continue to cost such people loads of money. In the same light, this attitude also robs people of valuable tax dollars as well because, without keeping track on a daily basis of their activities, they cannot boldly and confidently deduct every expense to which they are entitled.

How long does it actually take to write down each of the five substantiating elements? No longer than 10 seconds for each entry. That means that it should take you no more than about 10 minutes per week to potentially save thousands of dollars in taxes. If you were to save at least $10,000 annually putting in a maximum of 500 minutes per year by properly documenting your deductions, this would produce tax-free earnings of $20 per minute or a tax-free $1,200 per hour!

> **On a per-minute basis, nothing is more cost-effective**
> **than keeping the right records for the IRS.**

It's your choice. You can give 30, 40, or even 50 percent of what you earn to the government in overly inflated tax payments, or you can take the time to document your activities and save yourself thousands of dollars. It's up to you. Make your life easier starting today by choosing some method by which you will be prompted to write down your business expenses every day.

## The Rules Governing How Much of a Meal You Can Actually Deduct

Any meal that you purchase for someone else is deductible by 50 percent for your cost and 50 percent of your guest's cost,[5] including the tip. What about drinks? These too are 50 percent deductible. Now doesn't that sound great?! Isn't it wonderful to know how good tax laws are when you know how to take advantage of them?

What else do you need to be aware of when taking this 50 percent meal deduction?

1. You must talk business during the meal in order to claim the deduction.

2. You cannot take the same people out on a too frequent basis, (for example, every day). Once per week with the same people is the most the IRS will accept.

3. The meal has to take place in surroundings conducive to a business discussion.[6] In order for a location to have "conducive surroundings," it must meet two tests:

   - *Test #1:* There is a long, hard surface between you and your business associate where you can get a contract signed. For example, you could meet in a bar, where there are at least three hard surfaces where you could sign a contract: a table, a bar stool, or the floor.

- *Test #2:* There is no floorshow. This means no tailgate parties, orchestra, or any other distracting events.[7]

What do you need to do in these dinner and lunch meetings to be sure you are actually conducting business?

Usually when a prospect or client meets you for dinner, he or she will ask, "How's business?" Your reply should always be: "Business is unbelievable, but I never have enough customers [prospects, referrals, etc.]." By making such a statement, you have discussed business. By saying you "never have enough . . ." you are also seeking more business from the person with whom you are having dinner. After the meal, you should document this discussion in your tax diary. By doing so, you will never have to worry about an IRS audit again.

## Rules for Deducting Spouse (or Significant Other) Meal Costs

Sometimes people ask: "My spouse works with me in my business; can I ever take her out alone to eat and talk about business? And if I do, shouldn't I be allowed to deduct her meal costs, just as I would with any other business client?" The answer to this question is absolutely not. You can never take your spouse alone to dinner and write it off because the IRS has a rule known as the "closely connected" spouse rule.[8] A rule called the "closely connected significant friend" also exists. The IRS is a big, romantic teddy bear at heart; it believes that if you go out to dinner with your spouse or significant other, you will have far too many other warm and cozy things to talk about to ever get around to talking about business!

Is there any way that you can ever take your spouse out to dinner and deduct the expense? Yes...whenever you are entertaining another couple, you may bring your spouse.[9] Bringing a spouse or friend along allows them to entertain the spouse or friend of the contact with whom you wish to conduct business, making it easier for you to have a one-on-one conversation with that contact.

## Rules for Deducting Dutch-Treat Meals

What if you go out with your client and the two of you split the bill? This falls under what the IRS calls the "Dutch-treat" rule. Both you and your client will be permitted to take a deduction. Here's how it works:

You and your client (we'll call him George), split the bill for lunch and your share is $24 (it was a nice lunch). Under the Dutch-treat rule, you must subtract your average cost of eating a meal at home (refer to Appendix F for the formula for calculating this average at-home meal cost), which in this case we'll say is $4, from the cost of the business lunch you had with George.[10] The difference is $20. The amount you can write off is 50 percent of that, or $10. Now $10 may not seem like much to you, but if you do this twice a week, for instance, that's $20; if you do it 50 weeks a year, the amount you can deduct adds up to $1,000 per year. Many home-based business owners miss out on some valuable tax savings because they do not know that taking a percentage of your Dutch-treat meal is allowable.

There are some internal policies at the IRS related to this rule of which you need to be aware that are not documented anywhere else:

You are limited to two Dutch-treat lunches in a week, or a total of 100 Dutch-treat lunches in a year. However, you are also allowed 100 Dutch-treat breakfasts, and 100 Dutch-treat dinners. In the course of a year, you could write off a percentage of 300 Dutch-treat meals, literally "eating" away your taxes!

## Other Meal Deduction Rules to Consider:

### What If You're Not Present at the Meal?

People often ask if they can deduct a meal that they buy for someone else when the are not physically present at the lunch or dinner gathering. You might say to one of your prospects, "Here's a gift certificate to this restaurant," or "Try this great little place I discovered and send me the bill." Marketing professionals may spend hundreds of dollars a year treating others to such meals. Unfortunately, not one penny of it is deductible if you are not physically present during the meal.[11] It is specifically provided in the Internal Revenue Code that gifts of entertainment for food are not allowed when you are not present.[12] This is considered cheating by the IRS and auditors will get you for it. Actually, in this case, the IRS's position is quite reasonable. That's because it allows business deductions for meals assuming that business will be discussed during the course of those meals.

Rather than giving away gift certificates, you should be giving away certificates for entertainment that do not include a meal, such as theater seats, baseball and football games, concert tickets, and so on. This will save you the most tax money. That's because these types of entertainment expenses can be deducted up to 50 percent and you do not have to be present in order to take advantage of the write-off.[13] You could also treat such donations as business gifts and take a 100 percent deduction for them as long as they don't exceed $25. Congress has provided this alternative treatment for entertainment tickets by giving you a choice of treating the gift as entertainment or as a business gift.[14] Someone who gives away a ballet ticket or theater ticket to a potential client can deduct 50 percent of the cost of the ticket so long as they record in their tax diary the reason for giving the client the ticket. Be sure to record the name of the donee, the date of the gift, and a notation about the reason for giving it, such as "referrals."

## Business Club Dues and Lunches

Dues for such clubs and civic organizations are almost fully deductible.[15] You may also deduct dues paid to professional societies.[16] Trade association dues are deductible if the association's purpose is to further the business interest of its members.[17] Thus dues paid to the "HomeBusiness Alliance," for instance, would be deductible.

Business lunches held at a specific business organization are 50 percent deductible. Note that meals incurred and paid for while talking business at the club are also deductible but may fall under the "Dutch-treat" rule in this case. We should add that country club and health club dues are not deductible.[18] At one point, these dues were permissible, but today, under the guise of "tax simplification," Congress has eliminated them.

## Sales Seminars and Presentations at Home

Based on a tax court memorandum decision,[19] and also a private letter ruling, all food and refreshments served to prospects at home during a sales seminar or sales presentation are 100 percent deductible! Isn't that great? You must, as we have said before, document your activities on the day of the sales presentation.

Okay, now that we have spelled out all the exciting deductions for meals and the rules governing how those deductions can be taken, let's move on to entertainment deductions.

# Rules for Deducting Entertainment

*Entertainment* is a four-syllable word that is often used in place of a simple one-syllable word: *fun*. We think you're going to like what we're about to explain about how to deduct entertainment expenses for your business, or in other words, all your fun. What this means is that if you go to the theater, play a round of golf, or go to a football game, you can deduct some of the cost of that activity, making what you do twice as much fun!

Based on IRS regulation, you may deduct up to 50 percent of your fun if you talk business in a business setting.[20] Of course the IRS will never believe that you talked business while you were watching *Hamlet*[21] or while you played a round of golf. So if you want to write off the golf game or the play, or any kind of fun, the rule according to the IRS is:

You must talk business either preceding the fun or following the fun at any time during the same 24-hour day as the "fun" occurred.[22] Suppose you are going to a football game with Jack, a potential customer, and you are buying his ticket. As you drive to the football game (preferably in Jack's car), you talk about his real estate needs, and then you go to the game. Does this meet the IRS requirement for talking business within the same 24-hour period? You bet. Now why do we suggest having Jack drive to the game? Because the IRS does not allow you to deduct mileage for entertainment, so Jack might as well pay for that!

Here's another example: Let's say you call Janet and talk about some of the latest skin care products available. Then, three hours later, you pick up Janet and go to a movie. Is that talking business within the same 24-hour period? Absolutely! Suppose you go out to lunch with Mike and talk business over lunch. Then you say, "You know, it is such a wonderful day, what do you say we go play golf?" And Mike says, "Show me how to play and I'll play!" Is that talking business within the same 24-hour period? Of course.

Like anything else related to taxes, however, it is your burden to prove that you actually did talk business in the same 24-hour day as you had fun. That's why a good tax organizing system and tax diary are so important. In the illustration below, you can see an ideally documented diary day:

| ACTIVITY 2 | | | | | |
|---|---|---|---|---|---|
| WHO? | J&S ROCK | | | | |
| WHERE? | PALM AND KENNEDY CENTER | | | | |
| WHY? | JOHNSON REFFERAL AT DINNER FOLLOWED BY THEATRE | | | | |
| BREAKFAST | | HOME | | OTHER | |
| LUNCH | | GOLF/ETC. | | THEATRE | 120 00 |
| DINNER | 235 00 | COCKTAILS | 15 00 | PARK, ETC | 11 00 |
| TOTAL | | TOTAL | | TOTAL | 381 00 |

Notice how this particular type of tax diary triggers you to document each substantiating factor required by law including the cost, date, location, purpose, and business relationship? In this example, you can see that $381 has been totaled for food and theater tickets. The three most important words in the whole English language are noted on this example. Now most people think the three most important words are "I love you." Those are good words, but as far as the IRS is concerned, the three words that matter most and which appear on this example are: "followed by theater." By documenting the fun that came after the business meeting, this taxpayer will be able to deduct a portion of his entertainment expense.

## What About Season Tickets...Can I Write Them Off?

The answer is yes, you can write off 50 percent of the cost of your season tickets for such things as theater, ballet, sporting events, and opera because the IRS says every event stands by itself.[23] Suppose you talk to your friend, Debbie about your vitamin supplement products, and then you take Debbie to the ballet using one of your season tickets. If you properly document the meeting and the entertainment following that business discussion, then you can deduct 50 percent of the cost of your ticket and her ticket.

*Note: You can only deduct the face value of the ticket. Scalpers' profits are not deductible.*[24]

## What About Business Gifts, and When Can I Deduct Them?

Everybody gives business gifts. If you ever give a birthday gift to a prospect or that prospect's children, or wedding gifts, anniversary gifts, or baby shower presents, then you can deduct 100 percent of the cost of that gift.[25] That's the good news. The bad news is that the limit you can spend on the gift you wish to write off at 100 percent is $25 per person per year; husband and wife are treated as one person.[26] There is one exception to the $25 limit. If you give a person tickets to one of your season ticket events, then this gift is 50 percent deductible, regardless of its cost.

This $25 limit on gifts only applies to individuals. If you buy a gift for a business, where there is no single person designated to receive or benefit from that gift, then there is no limit to the amount you can spend and write off at 100 percent.[27] For example, if you are giving a gift of candy or flowers to an IBM manufacturing plant, for instance, and you don't designate a specific individual in your gift card, that gift will be 100 percent deductible, no matter how much you spend on it.

# Taking Advantage of the #1
# Overlooked Business Entertainment Deduction

Most people don't know that they can take, as a business dedication, home entertainment if done properly. Here's how it works:

You invite a couple of your friends (that is, prospects, customers, clients, referrals) over for a small dinner party at your home. What's usually the first thing that friends and neighbors ask a person engaged in running a home-based business? "How's business?" And of course, you should say, "Business is unbelievable, but I never have enough contacts [referrals, prospects, etc.]." Even if the party lasts four hours and you never talk business again, that 10 second conversation entitles you to write off 50 percent of the cost of that party! That's right, 50 percent. No time requirement exists that forces you to spend a certain amount of time discussing business; however, the rule is you must document what you did discuss. In addition, if you spend less than $75 to serve a light dinner to a couple of guests, then you do not need a receipt for your food and beverage.

If you hold large dinner parties at your home, talking business to all 20 of your guests on an individual basis could become quite tiresome. There is a better way to meet the IRS's requirement.[28] The following case study of a woman named Sharon Ladd* shows you how.

## Sharon Ladd: Hosting a Tax-Deductible Party

Case History

On her eighth anniversary of being in business for herself, Sharon sent out a letter to all her prospects in Houston saying that she planned to celebrate the anniversary. She invited these people to her house for a party. "I am celebrating eight years in the home-based direct sales marketing business, please come to my anniversary party," she said in the letter. Using such wording established a business intent for the party, meeting the IRS requirement that she talk business. At the party, where she hosted more than 20 people, Sharon didn't once talk business with any of her guests. Instead, she served a giant, Texas-sized buffet and above each food platter, she displayed photographs of what she did in her home-based business. Sharon also included products, testimonials, and prices, which as people took the food, they could not help but notice. She had her husband take pictures of everyone looking at the displays as they took their food. Doing so proved without doubt that Sharon was holding a business party where business was being discussed.

How could anyone argue that Sharon had not held a business party? Of course Sharon was subtly doing business by inviting guests to a celebration party for her business and by exposing them to the products and services she sold. But the nice thing about this style of doing it was that she didn't have to talk to each individual person at the party about her business, and she didn't have to hit any of her guests over the head with a strong sales pitch. Sharon spent more than $300 for that party. Was she required by the IRS to get a referral from the event? No. In fact she could have spent $3,000 and not received one referral. The IRS doesn't presume that it's the taxpayer's fault when a party is a "failure." It just accepts that not all marketing works!

## Exceptions to the Entertainment Deduction Rules

If you employ non-relatives in your business venture, there are exceptions of which you need to be aware. Consult with your accountant on these exceptions.

# Maximize Your Business Automobile Deductions

Anyone who operates a home-based venture knows that their car is one of the most vital tools they use to help run their business. It's also one that can cause potential tax problems if you are not aware of the laws surrounding it. Without question, claims for automobile expenses are the most frequently audited—the number one deduction that the IRS checks out. But, if you know what you're doing, your car can put thousands of saved tax dollars in your pocket.

Let's begin by explaining the two ways in which the IRS allows you to figure your car expenses:

1. "Actual" method.
2. "IRS" method.

The "Actual" method is just what it sounds like—you total up every penny you spend for your car including repairs, maintenance, gas, oil, windshield wiper fluid, insurance, wash and wax jobs, and so on. The sum is your actual expense.

The "IRS" method can be used in lieu of all that figuring. Instead, this method gives a mileage allowance whereby you figure the automobile deductions you can take. In 2001, that allowance was 34.5 cents per business mile, which includes 15 cents in depreciation, with no limit to how many miles you can travel in a year.[29] Naturally, this allowance can change from year to year depending on inflation, so keep this in mind.

How do you decide which of the two methods will work best for you?

Suppose in 2001 you put 20,000 business miles on your 4-year-old car that cost you $12,000; you could then claim 34.5 cents a mile times your 20,000 business miles; your deduction would equal $6,900. Not bad. For the owner of an average-priced vehicle, the IRS method may offer the most tax savings. The bottom line in determining whether to use the actual or IRS method depends on the value of the car—the cheaper the car, the better the IRS method. That's because the more expensive the car, the less value the 34.5 cents per mile will have. The IRS tends to allow 4 cents less than what it actually takes to operate a typical mid-size car (according to the American Automobile Association [AAA][30]). If you own a Mercedes, Porsche, Jaguar, Audi, Lexus, Cadillac, or large sports utility vehicle such as a Chevrolet Suburban or Ford Explorer, you should probably use the actual method. That's because these cars cost more to run and maintain, so the low 34.5 cent mileage allowance really isn't going to provide much of a tax savings.

## Figuring Deductible "Business Miles"

Regardless of which method you use, IRS or actual, you will still need to keep track of all your "business miles." The IRS says that whenever you go from your home to a "temporary business stop," or in other words, to a place that you don't go regularly, all that mileage is considered "business mileage."[31] Examples of a temporary business stop include:

- A prospect's home or place of business.
- A downline distributor if you are in a network marketing business.
- A presentation you are giving.
- To deliver a distributor's kit or deliver a product.
- A seminar.
- To visit an accountant or lawyer.
- To pick up supplies.
- Taking a prospect to lunch.
- Anywhere you don't go regularly, or don't go every day.

The IRS breaks down these temporary business stops into four types of trips:

- **Type 1: Home is your principal office.** All temporary business stops from your home constitute business mileage.[32] Thus, going from home to the bank (for business purposes), customer, meeting, seminar, or client would constitute business mileage.
- **Type 2: Your home is not your principal office, but you travel outside of the geographic area of your normal work.** In this case, all round-trip mileage would constitute business.[33] For example, Sheridan normally lives and works in Salt Lake City. If she has a meeting in Provo, a city 45 miles south of Salt Lake, she may deduct all round-trip mileage to Provo because she traveled outside of her normal geographic work area.

- **Type 3: Your home is not your principal office, but you are on a temporary job assignment that is expected to last less than one year.** Should you be temporarily assigned to a new job site or office where the job or the engagement is expected to last less then one year, you may deduct all round trip mileage.[34] The key to taking this mileage as a business expense is that you expect to be there less than one year. If your engagement takes longer than that, all mileage incurred after the one-year period would constitute non-deductible personal commuting.[35]

- **Type 4: Your home is not your principal office and you make some business stops outside your normal business location.** This is where most of the confusion arises, and this is where the law becomes murky. It is our understanding that the IRS would mandate that your first "business stop" would be deemed personal and your last business stop back home would be deemed personal. All stops in between would be for business. Can the mileage between those stops be counted (other than the first and last stop) as business mileage? Yes. Those miles are counted as business whether you traveled one block away from your home or office or 100 blocks. You can see from this that working your business regularly will increase the chances that you will need to make a temporary business stop and you can then deduct those miles for business.

Example: Marc makes some business stops on the way to his office. He sees some clients and makes some presentations. His first stop would be deemed personal and all other stops on the way to the office, including his mileage from the last stop to the office, would constitute business mileage.

*Tip: If your home is not your principal place of business, arrange your first business stop and your last temporary business stop as close to your home as possible so you can take the most mileage for all those stops in between. And try to avoid just driving straight from home to your office—work your business on the way by making those necessary business stops and write off most of the mileage as business!*

The flow chart on page 240 summarizes these temporary business stops.

How does the IRS know that you went to a temporary business stop on your way to your office or on the way home? Simple: The auditor looks in your tax diary. If you do not have a downtown office, your diary is very critical. That's because you have to show that you are really spending at least a few hours per week working out of your home. Then, every time you go to a business stop, you can count that mileage as business. But you must document this!

Now, if you try to tell the IRS that you had zero commuting miles 365 days out of the year, don't plan on the auditor buying it. The IRS will not believe that you don't ever commute, even if you work out of your home office. It reasons that you more than likely will make some personal stops such as taking the kids to dance lessons or stopping in at the store for groceries. For this reason, you should show at least one day a week of commuting or some personal stops within your week.

**Flow Chart of Business Mileage**

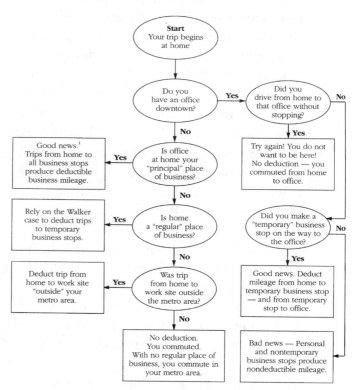

1. Home business owners should be able to deduct all trips from home to any business stop.
Rev. Rul. 90-23, 1990-11 I.R.B. 4.
Rev. Rul. 90-23, 1990-11 I.R.B. 4.

## Properly Documenting Business Miles

To document business miles, you must have a good tax diary or tax organizer, as we have already stressed repeatedly. Second, you must be able to answer through that log or diary the following five questions:

- **Question #1: Do you have objective evidence of your automobile mileage?** If you can say yes, you will be allowed all the deductions you want. If you say yes, but really don't have a log, the IRS can hit you with a 75 percent civil fraud penalty. Be aware of how important it is to document mileage properly.

- **Question #2: Is your evidence in writing?** As far as the IRS is concerned, putting it in writing proves the pudding. Keeping it on a hard disc such as a Personal Digital Assistant (PDA) would not be good enough unless you print it out.

- **Question #3: What is your total mileage for the car for the year?** How can you know what this figure is? By placing the beginning and ending year's odometer readings in your diary, for each car you use for business.

- **Question #4: What is your business mileage for each car?** Your diary or log must include this information if you want to tame the IRS's not-so-benevolent interest in you should you be audited.

- **Question #5: What is your commuting mileage?** Remember, commuting is going to your office, if you have an office away from your home. If you work part-time in a home-based business, then whenever you go from your home to your primary job, that is commuting. You must account for your "other personal miles" as well. These miles are anything but commuting and include such things as the grocery store, cleaners, church or synagogue, driving kids around, and so on.

The third thing you must do to properly document business miles is to write down your mileage at the time you incur it, or close to the time. If you use the "actual" method for claiming expenses, you must keep receipts for everything.[36] If you use the IRS method, you will not need to keep gas receipts, but you will still need to keep a mileage log so you can multiply the miles driven for business by the current car allowance.

## Methods for Keeping a Car Log

### Perfect Daily Log

With this method, you keep track of your mileage every day, and for every stop, for the entire year. For example, if your home is not your principle place of business, your log might read: "to office, 5 miles, personal; to Kelley's office, 14 miles, business; to lunch with Wilson, 21 miles, business; to the printer, 14 miles, business; back to my office, 11 miles, business; home, 5 miles, personal." This type of daily log is called a "perfect one-day log." People who can manage this kind of nitpicking precision every day all year long deserve a round of applause and a few sessions of therapy to relieve them of their obsessive-compulsive natures!

### 90-Day Rule

This method works just about as well as the daily log, but you only have to keep track of your mileage, both business and personal, every day for 90 consecutive days.[37] Pick any three months to track, but be warned: This method only works if you are regularly working your business. If you are the type that only works six months a year, it obviously won't work. That's because this rule assumes you have the same number of appointments each and every month and put about the same number of hours from week to week, month to month in your business (with the exception of vacations and holidays). Once again, regularly working your business can have its advantages. In this case, it relieves you of the burden of keeping records every single day.

## One-Week-A-Month Method

Using this method, you can calculate your average mileage much as you would using the 90-day method. Simply keep track of one week in January, for instance, one week in February, one week in March, and so forth until you have tallied mileage for one week out of every month of the year.[38]

## The No-Hassle Approach

There is an easier method yet. We call it the "No-Hassle Approach." With this method, you keep track of your personal and commuting mileage only. Before traveling anywhere, note your beginning odometer reading, then keep track of your personal and commuting mileage. Let's say it's three miles from your home to your office. Note this figure in your tax diary, then write down all your business stops and include information about the stop. You will not need to note the mileage for these trips. When you return home, note your ending odometer reading and subtract your personal mileage from that figure. This number is the business mileage you can deduct. For example, let's say that in three months, you drove 8,000 miles, of which 2,000 were personal and commuting miles. The remaining 6,000 are business miles and can be written off.

If you fail to keep consistent records using one of these four methods, theoretically, the IRS will not allow you to guess or use an improper method referred to as the "finger-in-the-wind approach." Saying, "I used my car 60 percent for business," won't work unless you have the tax diary supporting this. The key is to keep track of all your appointments. If you do, you can use those as a basis for calculating your business miles. If you just guess, the IRS will disallow every dime of deduction and hit you with a nondeductible 75 percent civil fraud penalty. Remember, it is imperative that you keep good records.

## Use Two Cars for Business to Increase Tax Deductions

If you have more than one car, you can deduct more than 100 percent of your automobile expense (provided you have the right documentation).[39]

This can be done by swapping some of the miles around for each car by using them both for business. For example, an individual who used his car for 22,000 business miles out of 24,000 total miles would have used the car 92 percent of the mileage for business purposes. This person, whose spouse also had a car, could increase the deduction for expenses from 92 percent to 141 percent simply by putting some of those 22,000 business miles on the other car. Instead of writing off 92 percent for Car 1, he only writes off 90 percent, *but*, by putting a few thousand business miles on Car 2, he is able to write off an additional 51 percent for Car 2. In this case, it provided the taxpayer with $2,085 in extra tax deductions.

*Cautionary Note: If you are using two cars in the same business, you may have to keep track of your mileage using the Perfect Daily Log approach. The reason for this is that you are not using the same car equally throughout the year, so the three month or 90-day method will not be accurate enough.*

## Depreciate Your Car Using the Fastest Rates to Maximize Annual Deductions

You can maximize annual automobile deductions by depreciating your car. If you use the IRS method of calculating car expenses, 15 cents is built into the 34.5 cents per mile allowance (in 2001) for depreciation. Thus, on all business miles driven, you are allowed 15 cents per mile for depreciation. So if you put 20,000 miles on your car for business, you can multiply 15 cents by 20,000, which gives you $3,000, whereby you can reduce your basis for gain or loss.

There are three basic depreciation methods for business automobiles:

1.  Accelerated depreciation: This allows you more deductions upfront in the first couple of years.
2.  Straight-line method: This allows you to take a set amount of depreciation each year.
3.  Luxury limits: Today's tax law further complicates matters by placing "luxury car" limits on depreciation.[40]

We recommend consulting with your accountant for details on these methods and for information on special depreciating rules for heavy vehicles weighing more than 6,000 pounds. For more information on how to deduct the cost of expensive cars, refer to Appendix E.

## Should You Lease or Buy a New Car?

Many home-based business owners have begun to lease their business automobiles as a means to save money on car expenses. But does leasing offer you any real tax saving advantages over purchasing a brand new car? Not really. It can, however, offer some other serious cash-flow advantages over buying a new car that make it worth considering.

## Advantages

- You can deduct a percentage of the lease payment as it relates to the number of business miles driven.[41]

- Sales tax is paid as you make the lease payment, spreading it out over the duration of the lease; you are not required to pay a huge lump sum in sales tax that you would have to pay if purchasing a new car. This improves cash flow for your business.

- Eliminates the worry associated with car repairs and reliability issues.

- You don't have to go through the hassle of shopping for a new car and obtaining a loan every few years. If your credit rating could use some improvement, generally qualifying for a lease is easier than qualifying for a loan because the lessor owns the car and assumes the risk of ownership, limiting your financial exposure.

- Allows you to drive a newer model car all the time.

- Doesn't normally require a large down payment, freeing up more cash for use in your business.

- Monthly payments are generally lower than if you purchase a new car, so once again, you have more cash on hand every month to help you advance your business.

- Eliminates hassles of selling a car when you're ready for a new one; you just turn in a leased vehicle. *Note: We should caution, however, that this is only true for a "closed-end" lease. An "open-end" lease, on the other hand, obligates you to purchase the car when the lease expires. While most leases are closed-ended, we strongly caution you to check the lease type before signing.*

## Disadvantages

- If you go over the annual mileage allowance you purchased in your lease, you are required to pay a mileage over-charge, which is usually $.10 to $.15 per mile. While you can purchase any number of miles per year, keep in mind that the lease payment increases as the mileage allowance goes up. Most leases include a 12,000 to 15,000 annual mileage allowance, so if you anticipate exceeding this amount, you should purchase more miles as part of the contract because it is less expensive to do so upfront.

- Tax saving depreciation calculations do not apply to leased vehicles.
- Sales tax is included in your lease payment, so in effect, you are always paying sales tax as long as you drive the leased vehicle. This expense is greatly reduced if you buy a reliable used car and drive it for several years, because you pay a moderate sales tax (as opposed to stiff new car sales tax) upfront once and do not have the expense again for a long time.
- Generally costs more overall than purchasing a new car of equivalent value because if you lease and then buy the car, you will pay far more than if you just buy a new car outright.

Other things to consider that may help you determine whether to lease or buy:

- If your financial income does not vary from year to year, leasing might be a bit better than buying a new car.
- If it is very important for you to drive a new vehicle in your business (if you are in sales or real estate for example), then leasing may suit you.
- If you don't like to own cars for more than four years, leasing has some benefits.
- If you hate auto repairs and dislike leaving your car at the shop, leasing has an advantage because it is a fixed cost that reduces your exposure and the economic risk of owning a car.

## Buying a Used Car

Unless you fit most of the descriptions above, we do not advise leasing a car as a tax-saving strategy. In addition, it's usually better to lease a car only if you're going to drive it for less than four years. Instead, we recommend buying a reliable used car that you keep for at least four years and drive into the ground. By so doing, you will get the maximum amount of tax write-offs. If you don't have to drive a brand-new car, buying a used car can be a great tax-saving strategy. We should note based on computer projections that buying a used car and keeping it 10 years is the best financial strategy in utilizing vehicles in your business.

First of all, a used car costs much less to purchase and doesn't usually require a large down payment, freeing up cash you may need for your business. Second, because used cars cost much less than a new car, they tend to get paid off more quickly, again, ultimately freeing up more cash. Third, once the car is paid off, you are not pouring money into a car payment or lease payment. Fourth, car repair expenses are tax deductible to the extent they relate to the business mileage driven. Fifth, you can obtain some tax savings from depreciating the car.

In the end, deciding whether to lease or buy depends entirely on your situation. We have found this decision to be highly emotionally charged (Money Mastery Principle 1) and there is no set hard and fast rule as to which is better. You should make your decision only after you have examined all the rules of leasing (Money Mastery Principle 5), looked at your overall financial picture (Money Mastery Principle 7), and have considered the volume of money that will be involved in either scenario. Remember Principle 10 and the velocity of money: You can only make more money in your business as you put your existing money into motion. You cannot put this money to work for you if it is tied up in an expensive new car payment or in a leased car that really doesn't offer any value to your business.

Choose carefully the best option. Overall, we feel the best approach in terms of tax savings is to buy a reliable car and keep it as long as possible, preferably 10 years or more.

## Claim Taxes and Interest on Car Purchases

If you purchase your business cars, which we recommend, here is another way you can increase the amount of deductions you can take for a business automobile. If you've purchased a new car that you use for a certain percentage of business, you can claim the taxes on the car and the interest on the loan you secured to get the car.[42] If you are in business, interest and taxes are deductible regardless of whether you use the IRS method or the actual method. If you have not claimed these deductions, be sure your accountant files amended tax returns for up to the last three years to get deductions on the taxes and interest you have paid previously.

## Depreciate Maintenance Equipment and Supply Costs

If you maintain your own car, you can deduct the cost of maintenance equipment and supplies in proportion to the car's business usage as part of the expense to your business of owning the automobile.[43] Identify everything you use on your cars and make a list of these items including battery chargers, cables, tire pumps, buffers, gas cans, hoses, tools, repair manuals, and so on. Then see if you have receipts to verify the cost of the items. If you do not, which is likely, pile all the equipment and supplies together and take a photograph; this will stand as documentation if needed.[44]

## Sell Cars That Produce Deductible Losses, But Trade Cars that Produce Taxable Profits

There comes a point when a car is no longer useful to a business and it's time to get rid of it. To avoid unnecessary taxation on the capital gains and ordinary income on some depreciation taken from the sale of a car, you may want to consider trading it in instead in order to defer gain over the life of the new auto you purchase. Consult with your accountant to determine whether you should trade or sell your used car to get the most tax savings.

# Make All Your Travel Tax Deductible

Wouldn't it be great if you could deduct some or all of your travel expenses, regardless of where you go in the world? Well, you can if you know what you're doing. If you operate a home-based business, you have the opportunity to write-off all kinds of trips that would not be possible if you were nothing more than a W-2 employee. That's because the tax laws governing travel deductions are fairly liberal (believe it or not!) for the self-employed.

Let's begin by defining what kind of travel is tax deductible. First of all, the IRS says travel must be "business travel" in order to claim it. Business travel occurs whenever you travel away from home, overnight, or for a period of time sufficient to require sleep.[45] "Aha!" you might be thinking, "I've been out of town on vacation in the last few years and had to sleep overnight. I bet all of that vacation would have been tax deductible." Well, no, it wouldn't be unless you conducted some business while on that trip. "Yes, but what about the time I went to Hawaii, and while I was there, I passed out my business cards?" Can you write off such a trip because you seemed to conduct "business" while there? The answer is probably not, because in addition to sleeping overnight somewhere, you also have to have a "primary intent to do business" *before* you go on the trip in order to claim the expense.[46]

Suppose, in order to do more business, you need to travel from Washington, D.C. to New York, where you must give a seminar during the day; let's further suppose that you then traveled home in the evening of the same day. Does that constitute business travel? No, because you didn't sleep overnight anywhere. What if you travel 70 miles down the road from your office to a nearby city to give an early-morning lecture and you sleep over in a hotel in that city the night before to be sure you make it to the lecture on time? Is that considered business travel? You bet. The IRS has no minimum mileage requirement for travel as long as your intent to do business was present before you made the trip and you slept overnight. You can travel 10 miles or 10,000 miles; it doesn't matter, as long as you sleep overnight in a bed other than your own.

How can you show "business intent" before you travel? The following example of a woman we'll call Loni spells it out:

Loni is a public relations consultant who just happens to love Las Vegas. When she found there was a trade show in Las Vegas where she could meet some potentially important editors to discuss one of her client's consumer electronics products, she decided it would be a perfect opportunity for her to take in some of the new attractions she had been dying to see. Before the trade show, Loni contacted by e-mail 10 different editors she wanted to speak with at the show and set appointments to meet them in her client's booth. She conducted press briefings with these editors on the first two days of the show, and on the remaining three days, spent her time having fun on the town.

Was Loni able to write off the trip to Las Vegas? You bet. That's because she met all of the business travel criteria:

- She was away from home overnight.
- She contacted business people in writing before her trip.

*Tip: Keep copies of letters or e-mails showing that you had some business intent before making the trip.*

Now, even though Loni was able to write off this trip because it was considered business travel, she still had certain IRS requirements to meet that dictated what expenses she could claim and what percentage of those expenses could be deducted. Let's take a look at the way travel is categorized for the purpose of making expense claims. Expenses are deducted in one of two ways, depending on what type of expense is incurred while traveling:

1. On-the-road expenses: Any and all costs necessary to sustain life while traveling for the purpose of doing business, except for transportation expenses.[47]

2. Transportation expenses: Expenses you incur in getting to and from your destination.[48]

## On-The-Road Expenses

You can deduct 100 percent of the cost of lodging, laundry, hairstyling and haircuts, dry cleaning, shoeshines, and even manicures[49] while on your business trip! So if you get your nails done while you are at a convention, for example, you can deduct 100 percent of that little trip to the salon!

Now what about food? Food is only 50 percent deductible.[50] You might also assume, because we have already noted that you cannot deduct meal expenses when you eat alone, that you should not be able to take even 50 percent of your meal expenses when you travel. Actually, there is an exception to the "eating alone" rule that does not require you to discuss business with a prospect or client while eating on the road, allowing you to deduct 50 percent of your meal costs.[51]

What about transportation? Costs to travel to and from your destination are not considered "on-the-road" expenses by the IRS, and as we have already noted, are governed by another set of rules that we will detail later in the chapter.

## "On-the-Road" Travel Deductions Rule

You do not need a receipt for travel expenses under $75 per expense.[52] There are two exceptions to this rule:

1. You must have a receipt for all lodging, regardless of the cost.
2. You should also try to have receipts for all transportation (this is not transportation for getting to or from your destination, but transportation once you have arrived such as rental cars, bus fares, train fares, and taxi fares). While not absolutely necessary, we recommend getting receipts for these expenses when you can. If you spend $100 on a cab that takes you from the airport to your hotel, must you have a receipt for that cost? Yes, because it's transportation and it cost more than $75.

After arriving at your destination, let's suppose you eat a nice buffet breakfast and spend $10 for it. Do you have to have a receipt for that meal expense? No, because you ate it while on business travel and it cost under $75.

When it's time to go home, you check out of your hotel and get the bill, which is $1,200. After you pay the bill (the hotel supplied free resuscitation), you are sure to take the receipt for that lodging expense because you will need it in order to substantiate your very nice tax deduction for that hotel bill.

The receipt rules are fairly simple: Remember to keep receipts for lodging and local transportation. Otherwise, you probably won't need a receipt for almost anything else you purchase on your trip because it's unlikely that any expense will exceed $75. And remember to write down all on-the-road expenses in your tax diary!

## Rule for What Constitutes a Business Travel Day

The IRS considers each day you are on the road traveling as a "business day." That means that you don't have to wait until you get to the seminar or that business meeting before you can deduct 50 percent of your food, and 100 percent of your other on-the-road expenses. You can begin deducting them the minute you get onto the road. Let's use Loni again as an example.

Loni decides to travel to Las Vegas by car from her home in Evanston, Wyoming. She gets in the car on Thursday afternoon at about 3 p.m. and begins driving towards Las Vegas; it will take her approximately eight hours to get there if she were to drive straight through. She stops about 6 p.m. to eat at a nice little roadside restaurant and pays $10 for the meal. She doesn't keep a receipt for her dinner but does write it in her tax diary. Even though she hasn't reached the trade show yet, her time on the road can still technically be considered a business day because she's making efforts to get to a place where she will conduct the actual business meetings, so all of her life-sustaining expenses are deductible.

Now, let's suppose instead, that Loni decides to leave for the trade show in Las Vegas about five days early so that she can stop in Salt Lake City along the way to ski and have fun with friends. The IRS has a rule that says she should try to travel at least 300 miles every day if she wants to count each of those traveling days as business days.[53] To figure whether you are within the bounds of this rule, take the number of miles you are driving to your destination and divide by 300. Round up for fractions. In Loni's case the total travel miles (if she did not stop in Salt Lake City) from Evanston to Las Vegas are 650 miles. She would take that 650 miles and divide by 300, which gives her a little over two days to get to Las Vegas if she wants to write off the expenses she incurs while on the road. Does she have time to stop in Salt Lake and ski? Maybe, but it would have to be a very quick trip.

## Rule for Deducting Spouse, Significant Friend, or Children's Travel Expenses

To understand how this rule works, let's suppose that Loni wants to take her husband with her to the trade show in Las Vegas. She certainly doesn't feel like traveling 650 miles alone. And besides, she has hired her husband, Kurt, to handle all her office and computer equipment, so she wants him to browse around the trade show and get new ideas for the best ways to update her home office. Because he's going to be at the trade show conducting his own business and he is her employee,[54] Loni can deduct all of Kurt's traveling expenses as well.

Now Loni decides that taking her three kids to Las Vegas would be fun too, so she packs up the whole family in the car. What can she deduct of the costs she will incur to take her entire family to the show? She can deduct anything she would have spent had she gone alone.[55]

## Loni's Deductions If She Takes Her Entire Family:

- **Gas:** Yes, she would have used fuel to drive either way. However, the rules that govern this deduction are covered under the "Transportation" category; refer to this section of the chapter for more information on how much of this fuel cost can be deducted.

- **Tolls:** Yes, she can take these no matter who travels with her.

- **Lodging:** Yes, if she has to stay in a room, then that hotel room is deductible, but only the portion that the hotel or motel charges for a single occupant.

- **Food:** Yes, but only 50 percent of her own meal costs; not those of her husband and three growing children.

- **Other:** Yes, anything she might have to purchase for herself, but not for those in her family. For example, let's say Loni wanted to get her hair done in Las Vegas at the hotel beauty salon. Could she deduct the cost of that haircut and style? Yes, at 100 percent. Now let's assume she also wanted to have her daughter come with her to get a trim. Could she deduct the cost of her daughter's haircut? No, because this is not an expense she would incur on her business travel if she were alone.

  Suppose Loni wanted to get some dry cleaning done while she was at the trade show. Could she take this laundry to the hotel cleaners and then write off the expense? You bet. Remember, the IRS rule says that you can deduct any and all expenses (except for food) that you would incur while on the road at 100 percent. The IRS has ruled that not only can you deduct the costs of laundry or dry cleaning for the clothes that get soiled while you are on business, but the first dry cleaning bill you incur when you get back home is also 100 percent deductible![56] How's that for a good tax law?!

## Rule for Deducting Cruise Travel

You may have heard that under some conditions, you can deduct a cruise as a business expense (if you attend a cruise ship convention, for example). It is possible to deduct some of the expenses for such travel, but the rules governing cruise write-offs are constantly changing. We recommend that you consult with your accountant or with the Tax Reduction Institute (TRI) for more information on how to meet the requirements for taking these deductions. (TRI contact information can be found in Appendix A.)

## Transportation Expenses

As we mentioned earlier, transportation costs to and from your destination are governed by rules separate from on-the-road expenses. Transportation costs include the expenses you incur in getting to and from your destination. These expenses include gasoline, airfare, train fare, and so on. In order to deduct these costs, you must take one of three kinds of business trips,[57] each one being governed by a separate set of rules:

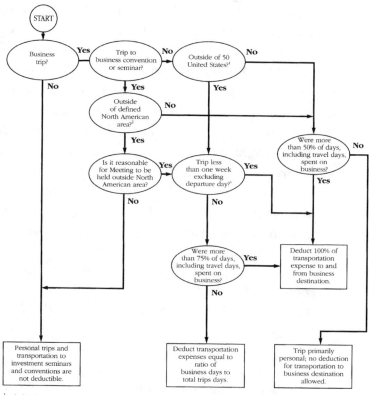

[1]Includes the District of Columbia but excludes U.S. possessions and territories.
[2]Trip outside Canada, Mexico, Jamaica, Barbados, Grenada, the U.S., its possessions, the Trust Territory of the Pacific, the Marshall Islands, the Federated States of Micronesia, Costa Rica, Dominica, Dominican Republic, Guyana, Honduras, Saint Lucia, Trinidad, Tobago and Palau. See Rev. Rul. 87-95, 1987-2 C.B. 79 and Rev. Rul. 94-56, 1994-36 IRB.
[3]Assuming one deductible business day during the trip; Reg. § 1.274-4(c).

1. Foreign business trips
2. U.S. business trips
3. Convention trips

The flowchart above summarizes the transportation rules for each of these three kinds of business trips and tells you what percentage, if any, of the transportation costs are deductible.

## Rules that Govern Transportation Deductions for Foreign Business Trips

Suppose you want to take a business trip to Montreal, Canada, because you speak French and know that you can find prospective business there. But while there, you also want to have some fun. So, you decide to spend one day doing business and the other five days having fun. Now, using the flowchart, let's see how much of the transportation costs for that six-day trip to Montreal will be tax deductible. From "Start":

- Is this a business trip? Yes (follow the arrow to the next question).
- Is this a trip to a business convention or seminar? No
- Is Montreal outside of the 50 United States? Yes
- Is the trip to be less than one week excluding the day of departure? Yes (because you will be gone 6 days total).

Follow the arrows to the appropriate box and you will see that the transportation expense to and from your business destination in Montreal is 100 percent tax deductible! Isn't that great? Aren't you glad to know that you can spend just one day doing business in Montreal and spend another five days enjoying yourself while deducting all of the transportation costs to and from Montreal?

*If you are on a foreign business trip and you are back in less than one week, you can deduct 100 percent of your transportation regardless of the number of days worked.*

Okay, let's consider a different scenario. Let's say you don't want to come back in less than one week. Let's say after you conduct your business in Montreal that you want to go to Vancouver or Prince Edward Island and you spend one day of business and nine other days having fun. How much of your transportation costs can you deduct? Using the flowchart, you will see that this trip is:

1. A business trip.
2. Not a convention or seminar.
3. Outside the 50 United States.
4. Takes more than one week.

Now following the arrows, answer the next question:

5. Were less than 75 percent of days, including travel days, spent on business?

How do you answer this? Well, for starters, don't forget when calculating time spent on actual business that you can count the days traveling to and from your destination as "business days." So, in this case, it takes you one day to travel to Montreal and one day to travel back home, plus one day actually conducting business. So you have really spent three days doing business, and seven days having fun. Do three days constitute more than 75 percent of your 10-day trip? No. Following the arrow on the flowchart, you will notice that the transportation costs that you can deduct in this case are equal to the ratio of business days to total trip days. So, if your business days are three out of a total of 10 trip days, the amount of transportation you can deduct is only 30 percent. That's two-thirds less expenses you can deduct because you didn't make it home in less than one week. Therefore, the tax saving tip you should get about foreign business trips is:

*Come back in less than a week so you can deduct 100 percent*
*of your transportation costs.*

## Rules for Deducting Transportation Expenses for a Business Convention or Seminar

To understand these rules, let's use Loni again as an example. Remember, Loni was traveling to Las Vegas to attend a trade show (convention). She planned to work the tradeshow for two days and play the other three days of the convention. Loni took one day to travel the 650 miles from Evanston, Wyoming to Las Vegas, and one day to travel back. Those two travel days can also be considered business days, so Loni spent four days on business and three days playing, for a total of seven days.

Using the flowchart, follow the arrows to the appropriate box to determine how much of Loni's transportation costs to the Las Vegas convention can be deducted:

1. Is it a business trip? Yes.
2. Is it a trip to a business convention or seminar? Yes.
3. Is Las Vegas outside the defined North American area? No.
4. Were more than 50 percent of trip days, including travel days, spent on business? Yes (four days is more than 50 percent of seven days).

### SO

Loni's gasoline and other car transportation expenses to and from the Las Vegas trade show are 100 percent deductible.

The thing to remember about travel for conventions or seminars is:

*Spend more than 50 percent of your days on business*
*and you can deduct 100 percent of your transportation costs.*

## Rules for Deducting Transportation Costs for Trips in the United States

Let's say you settle on San Francisco as a place to conduct some business in order to promote your home-based business. You love San

Francisco, especially the great food. While there, you will talk to distributors and meet with potential clients you have set appointments with in writing before you leave on the trip. You will leave on Thursday and conduct some meetings on Friday and Monday. Based on this information, how much of your transportation costs to San Francisco are tax deductible?

Using the flowchart, follow the appropriate errors. You will discover that because you spend more than 50 percent of your trip days on business (don't forget that travel days are counted as business days), you can deduct 100 percent of your transportation costs to and from San Francisco.

The tax saving tip to remember for U.S. travel is:

*If you are on a U.S. business trip, spend more than 50 percent of your days on business and you can write off 100 percent of your transportation costs.*

You can see that the flowchart on page 252 can be very helpful in planning any trip. It summarizes about 38 pages of IRS regulations and rulings into one easy-to-use chart. Using this tool, you can make sure to plan your trips to mix business with pleasure while writing off the maximum amount of travel expenses allowed by law.

In addition, from the examples we have used, you can also see that knowing how many days of a trip are considered business days is very important, because the number of business days will dictate how much of your transportation costs can be written off. Let's discuss in further detail the rules that determine what can be considered a business day.

## Rules for Determining What Constitutes a Business Day

Many people ask how much time they have to work in a day in order for it to be considered a "business day." The answer: Not much. There is no prescribed work time requirement. If you can get everything done in one minute, that will make all 24 hours within that day count as business. The IRS says that if you are there for a bona fide business reason, there is no time limit.[58] The key is, you need to be meeting with others for a specific business reason in order to count the day.

The rule for seminars or conventions is a bit different. You must spend a majority of your work day attending meetings.[59] Remember that you must spend 50 percent of your travel days on business if you want to deduct 100 percent of your transportation costs, so that means you would need to attend meetings a little more than half of a federal eight-hour work day, or four hours and one minute (this includes lunch). This is called the "Four-Hour-And-One-Minute" rule.

## Rules That Govern Which Days
## Out of the Week Can Be Considered Business Days

*Weekdays:* Obviously any business you conduct on a weekday is going to count.

*Travel Days:* As we have already mentioned, the days you take traveling to your destination are considered business days. But let's suppose, for example, that you want to take a ship to your business meeting in Hawaii because you're a nervous flier. "I'll take a plane to Los Angeles if I have to, but from there to Hawaii, I don't want to fly over the ocean. I'll take a cruise ship for $1,400, and then when the meeting is over, I'll take the same boat and cruise back." If you do so, you will add several extra travel days to your total trip—time that would not be required if you flew. Can you do this and still count those travel days? The IRS has said that you can take any means of transportation you want—boat, plane, car, train, and so on, but the route has to be reasonably direct.[60] That means if you want to go to Hawaii by cruise liner, you can't go up the West coast to Alaska to get there. You must take a ship that is on a fairly straight course to your destination.

*Note: Cruise ship travel is a funny bird with regards to travel law and is figured differently than any other kind of travel. Congress views such travel as luxury transportation and for the purpose of figuring the tax deductions for it, has assigned the highest federal per diem rate multiplied by two. Consult with your accountant for more information on how to deduct this type of travel.*

*Weekend Days:* The IRS says that if you meet two rules, you can count Saturdays and Sundays anywhere in the world as business days and write them off.[61]

- *Rule #1:* You stay over Saturday and Sunday between business days.

- *Rule #2:* It must be cheaper for you to stay over (no matter where you are in world) than it would be for you to fly home and back again for the Monday meeting.

Let's examine this "weekend" opportunity more closely to see how it works. Suppose you have meetings planned in Anchorage, Alaska on Friday and another meeting on Monday. Both Friday and Monday are then considered business days. The Saturday and Sunday of the weekend are sandwiched in between those two business days, so you can write off all of your on-the-road expenses for Saturday and Sunday,[62] and you can count them as business days for the purpose of calculating your overall transportation deductions.[63]

Here's another example: One of our clients, Shannon*, who lives in Buffalo, New York, wondered how she could write off her trips to Honolulu, where she vacations frequently. After learning about these tax-saving travel strategies, Shannon contacted some distributors in a home-based business similar to hers to find out when there would be seminars taking place in Hawaii. She found a seminar that took place on a Friday in Honolulu. She left Buffalo on the earliest possible flight on Thursday at 6 a.m., and arrived in Honolulu at 6 p.m. She spent the rest of the day playing golf. Of course, based on the travel day rules we have already outlined, Shannon could count Thursday as a business day because she spent it getting to her business destination (even though she got in nine holes of golf before the sun went down!).

On Friday, Shannon went to the seminar. This day, naturally, counted as a business day. Saturday she spent on the beach, and Sunday she spent playing 18 holes of golf. Monday she had set up an interview with a potential distributor (in writing before she left on her trip) to get more information about a new product she planned to sell. After the meeting, she played more golf with some of these business contacts. Because she had sandwiched a stay over on Saturday and Sunday between business meetings on Friday and Monday, both weekend days counted as business days. Tuesday, Shannon spent the whole day on the beach until 6 p.m. She then took a late flight back to Buffalo. Tuesday was also considered a business day because she traveled home from her business destination. In six days, Shannon got in a lot of golf and sun and was able to legitimately deduct 100 percent of her transportation costs to do it. Remember:

*If you sandwich Saturday and Sunday between business days, you can add them to the number of days you can use to calculate your total transportation deductions.*

To summarize the rules that govern transportation expenses, remember to plan your trip according to the type of business meeting you will attend, where it will take place in the world, and make sure to take advantage of any and all days that can be considered "business days."

## Other Rules to Consider for Travel Expense Deductions

We should note that you can deduct travel expenses to maintain out-of-town rental properties or seek a new employment opportunity. Consult with your accountant for the rules governing these travel expenses if they apply to you.

## Bullet-Proofing Your Documentation for All Business Travel

We have already discussed the kinds of receipts you need to keep in order to prove your on-the-road expenses. In addition to these, you need to have the appropriate documentation before, during, and after your trip for all travel expenses including food, lodging, transportation to and from your destination, and so on. Keeping copies of letters or e-mails you sent to potential business contacts is one way to document the intent to do business before taking a trip. Another way is to keep copies of reservations or seminar applications or tickets, I.D. badges, or other proof that you attended an event. To further prove that you actually attended a seminar, conference, or business meeting, keep workbooks and notes and date them. Keep all such records for at least three years after the meeting, and guard your tax diary carefully. We recommend carrying no more than two months documentation around with you in your diary. If you use a PDA (personal digital assistant) to keep track of expenses, it is vital that you back up the information on the PDA every week to a hard drive or storage back-up device.

What should you be writing down about your business travel in your tax diary?

- Amounts spent daily on food, lodging, taxi fare, haircuts, laundry, and so forth.
- Dates of departure and dates of return.
- Destinations to which you traveled.
- Your purpose for making the trip.

Remember, the IRS will not allow you to make approximations.[64] What do you think happens to those deductions you forget to write down? They are lost forever because you can't go back and try to reconstruct a paper trail later. (Refer to Appendix A for more information on how to obtain Tax Reduction Institute and Money Mastery tax organizer items.)

As you can see from everything we have outlined in this chapter, there are many ways to deduct your meals, fun, entertainment, car expenses, and travel. Simply follow the guidelines we have outlined exactly as noted and be sure to document your activities daily. By following this advice, you can put thousands of extra dollars in your pocket each year. Plus, you'll never have to worry about an IRS audit again!

## Challenge #15

# Review Checklist Regarding Deductions, Entertainment, Automobile, and Travel

1. This week, review the following checklist to ensure that all of your meals and entertainment are being properly expensed:

   ✔ Pick a "trigger" that will help you remember to write down each of the substantiation requirements for meals, entertainment, and travel on the day the meal, event, or travel took place. Be sure to obtain a tax diary or use your spending booklets to track such information if you have not done so already. (Refer to the Appendix for more information on how to obtain Money Mastery Spending Booklets or the TRS Tax Diary.)

   ✔ Eat in a location conducive to business, i.e, where a contract can be signed. Remember, no floor shows.

   ✔ Remember, you cannot deduct meal expenses when you do not attend the gathering or when you take your spouse out to eat alone. Feed and entertain your spouse along with other prospects.

   ✔ Deduct Dutch-treat meals; document personal meal costs to support your Dutch-treat deduction.

   ✔ Talk business either before or after entertaining a prospect or client and document in the same 24-hour period.

   ✔ Deduct home entertainment by talking business with guests at small dinner parties.

2. Get the most out of your automobile by reviewing the following automobile deduction checklist:

   ✔ Figure your car expenses using either the "Actual" method or the "IRS" method.

   ✔ Figure your business mileage by keeping a daily log, a 90-day log, a weekly log, or through the "no hassle" method.

   ✔ Determine whether you should use two cars in your business.

   ✔ Decide, based on your particular business situation, whether you should lease or buy a car.

3. This week, get the most out of your travel by reviewing the following checklist to be sure you plan your next business trip appropriately:

   ✔ Make weekends deductible by sandwiching Saturdays and Sundays between business meetings on Friday and Monday.

   ✔ Mix business with pleasure by planning meetings around play time in a destination of your choice.

   ✔ Locate seminars, conventions, or courses related to your line of work that are being held in a city to which you would like to travel and plan a trip around them.

   ✔ Hire your spouse so that you can deduct his or her expenses when they travel with you on business.

4. Using the flowchart found in this chapter and the tax saving strategies we have covered, plan your next vacation so that you can deduct 100 percent of your transportation costs, 100 percent of your on-the-road expenses, and 50 percent of your food costs.

# Chapter 16

# Income Shifting:
# Tax Secret of the Wealthy

Since the inception of the income tax, people have been developing methods of shifting income within family groups in order reduce excessive taxation. The concept is simple: Spreading income among several people, especially among those in lower tax brackets, is much cheaper when it comes to paying taxes, than having one person pay tax on all the income. Thus, income shifting is a technique wealthy people often use to protect valuable assets from over taxation. But income shifting is not just for the rich; anyone can take advantage of various aspects of this tax-saving strategy—married people, single people, single individuals with children, it doesn't matter.

 ## Tax Strategy #6: Shift part of your income to family members by hiring and leasing from them.

Most of the income-shifting opportunities we will outline in this chapter have the potential to put from $500 to $1,000 in saved tax dollars in your pocket—some even more.

## Income-Shifting Methods

### Hire Your Spouse in Your Home-based Business

If you are a sole proprietor, partnership, C Corp, or LLC, and you employ your spouse in your business, remember that all wages you pay your "employee" spouse are subject to Social Security tax (FICA)[1]—taxes that can eat into your business profits. The best way to avoid all those extra taxes is to pay your spouse a minimum wage and then give him or her as many tax-free fringe benefits as possible.

In order to take advantage of the tax-free benefits we will outline in this chapter, the hiring of your spouse must be legitimate and bona fide.[2] Don't be tempted to just call your spouse an employee without evidence of actual work performed.

## Pay Your Employees' Medical Expenses

Once you have legally hired your spouse, take advantage of their employment with a plan to pay his or her medical insurance premiums and deductibles and your children's medical expenses. That way you can deduct 100 percent of your family's medical insurance expenses.

Here's how it works:

Suppose you are a sole proprietor paying $400 a month for a high-deductible, catastrophic medical insurance policy, the only policy you can get as a small self-employed business owner. If you do not hire your spouse and set up a medical benefit plan for her, then you can only deduct 60 percent[3] of your family's medical expenses, which is $240 per month out of the $400 per month premium. In order for you to get a tax deduction on the remaining 40 percent, those expenses must exceed a certain threshold (which in 2001 was 7.5 percent of your adjusted gross earnings).[4] Unless you have lots of medical expenses in a year, it's doubtful that the remaining 40 percent of your $400 a month premium will be deductible.

But what if you hire your wife part-time? Even if she has a regular W-2 job but works for you as your bookkeeper, she is still considered an employee of your business by the IRS. As your employee, you make her the primary insured on your medical plan and select to have her covered along with your children on that plan. Now 100 percent of your medical insurance premiums are deductible.[5] Why? Because these premiums are now considered a business employee expense; the IRS gives you a tax-free benefit for such premiums paid out through the business that it would not give to you if you were simply to take them as an itemized deduction as an individual on your Schedule C tax forms. In this way, you are deducting the expenses as an employee fringe benefit, and not as a regular itemized medical premium.

What if you aren't married? You do have some options for taking advantage of this medical deduction:

1. You can hire your kids, if you have children, and pay for their medical premiums, thus qualifying you to take these as a business expense at 100 percent.

2. You can incorporate as a regular non-Sub "S" corporation (either as a regular C Corp or as an LLC) and deduct all the premiums.

3. You can get married!

*Note: Remember from our explanation in Chapter 12, if you are structured as a Sub S corporation, you cannot deduct 100 percent of your medical insurance premiums by hiring your spouse. You must be either be a sole proprietor, a partnership, a Limited Liability Corporation (LLC), or a regular "C" corporation. In fact, if your business is structured as a regular "C" corporation, you don't even have to hire anyone from your family to take advantage of this medical deduction—as we outlined in Chapter 12, this is one of the very big advantages of incorporating as a regular "C" corporation.*

## Set Up a "Medical Reimbursement Plan" to Pay for All Other Expenses Not Covered by Insurance

A Medical Reimbursement Plan is a written plan whereby the employer (you) hires an employee (spouse) and reimburses that employee and any of his or her family members (your children), for medical expenses not covered by medical insurance.

Some of the healthcare needs that you and your family might have that are not covered by a standard medical insurance policy include:

| | |
|---|---|
| Eyeglasses | Hearing aids |
| Contacts | Insurance deductibles |
| Co-pays | Dental |
| Orthodontics | Medically-required cosmetic surgery |
| Preventive care | Routine physicals |
| Well-baby care | Chiropractic care |
| Acupuncture | Other non-traditional forms of medicine |
| Prescriptions drugs | Pre-existing conditions your policy declines to cover |

These expenses can be written off using a self-insured medical reimbursement plan. This type of plan is probably one of the best tax loopholes ever created. The IRS has ruled that amounts reimbursed under an accident and health plan covering all bona fide employees, including the owner's husband or wife and family, are not included in the employee/ husband or wife's gross income and are therefore deductible by the owner as business expenses.[6] You get a deduction and your spouse gets that reimbursement money tax-free. This money does not have to be included in the 1099 form or the W-2 statement. It is absolutely and completely tax-free! Now doesn't that sound nice?

### How to Set Up a Medical Reimbursement Plan

The plan works the same whether you are married or single with children.

- **Step 1: Hire your spouse (or a child) part-time.** Keep in mind that this will only work if you are a sole proprietorship, partnership, LLC, or "C" corporation, not an "S" corporation.

- **Step 2: Draw up formal paperwork for both a medical plan and a reimbursement plan.** This can be done through a good attorney for about $500 or you can do it yourself by referring to the toll-free number and kit materials available in Appendix A of this book. Such medical reimbursement packages will include properly drawn up employment contracts, independent contractor contracts and a legal self-insured medical reimbursement plan. If you use such packages, you may still want to have your lawyer tailor it to your needs.

- **Step 3: Make your spouse or child the primary insured on a written medical plan.**

- **Step 4: Have your spouse or child elect family coverage.** This means that you, your spouse, and your kids will be covered.

    *Note: IRS Regulation 1.105-5 states that a medical reimbursement plan for a sole proprietorship, partnership, or LLC can have as few as one employee. Thus, if your only employee is your spouse, you can still qualify for a medical reimbursement plan.*

## Establish a "Supper Money" Allowance for Hard-Working Employees

Another wonderful income-shifting benefit you can offer family members that can help reduce your taxes is "supper money" funds. Such funds are what you agree to pay an employee when overtime work is required. Under this allowance, you get a deduction and the employee, that is, your spouse, gets that money tax-free.[7]

First of all, you should be aware that you cannot pay supper money to yourself. But if you are a sole proprietor and you hire your kids and/or spouse and they put in overtime, you can pay them supper money.

Nothing in the IRS code dictates the amount you can pay in supper money. But the chief counsel of the IRS has said that their internal policy is no more than $20 a day, two days a month for every employee who works overtime. Thus, occasional supper money can be paid to any employee who works more than 10 hours and one minute a day (except yourself). That can mean tax-free money of up to $40 a month for your spouse and/or children.

## Set Up a Simple Pension Plan and IRA

Another way to shift income to family members is by adopting a simple pension plan. Without question, setting up a 401(k), or some other type of profit-sharing plan, is one of the best tax-saving strategies available to a home-based business owner.

Set up in 1997 by Congress in an effort to eliminate some of the cumbersome requirements of a qualified pension plan, the "simple" IRA plan is a written arrangement that provides you and your employees with an easy way to make contributions towards retirement. Under such a plan, any employee may choose between making salary deduction contributions or receiving a salary. Here's what you need to know about setting up a simple plan:

- Unlike a qualified pension plan, if you are a sole proprietor, you can participate in a simple plan.
- If you do set up a simple plan, you must make matching contributions on behalf of each employee if they contribute to the plan.[8]
- As the employer, you must make matching contributions to your employees' contributions of up to 3 percent of compensation* each year, or as little as one percent for two out of five years.[9]
- An employee, that is, spouse, can contribute a percentage of his or her salary, or you can contribute a percentage of your net income up to $7,000 per year (in 2002). In addition, you as the sole proprietor can match your own contribution of up to 3 percent of your net income. For example, let's say you net $60,000 a year from your home-based business. You can contribute to a simple plan as much as $7,000.[10] Plus your business can match

your contribution—up to another 3 percent[11] of $60,000, which equals $1,800 on top of that.

Simple plans have some important advantages:

1.  If you have any employees, you will not have to worry about covering them if they do not contribute to the plan. If, however, they choose to contribute, you must match any of their contributions up to 3 percent of their wages.

2.  There are no administrative costs or filing requirements with simple plans. Most qualified plans can cost anywhere from $1,000 to $5,000 per year to administer. But simple plans cost you nothing. The funds you contribute go directly to the employee's own IRA without requiring you to do any complex filing with the IRS.

While qualified plans have their own advantages, if you are a small business owner, you should check out simple pension plans, reviewing your options with your accountant where necessary to determine where the maximum tax benefits can be achieved for you.

### How to Set Up a Simple IRA

1.  Obtain IRS model form #5305 (5305-simple) by calling the IRS at (800) 829-1040.
2.  Fill out a copy of this form.
3.  Do not send back to the IRS; simply keep on file in case you need a record of it.

## Hire Your Dependent Children Age 7 to 17

If you are a sole proprietor with children or grandchildren that will be going away to college or getting married someday, this part of the chapter is for you.

Suppose you have a 12-year-old daughter named Nicole. If you pay for Nicole's college education, the tuition might cost you $12,000 a year or more. Or, if you pay for her wedding at some point, that bill could easily run you $25,000. Although college educations and weddings are not tax deductible, if you run a business you can deduct the equivalent of such.[12]

Here's how:

First, you hire Nicole to work with you in your business. You pay her a wage,[13] which is tax deductible because wages are one of the expenses of your business, and she then puts that money away in a college savings account. At 18, Nicole takes that money and uses it for her own college education. Essentially, you have paid for her education after taking a tax deduction for it. If she decides to get married, instead, she could use the money to pay for the wedding, allowing you to pay for it with tax-reduced funds.

The beauty of hiring Nicole is that if you are not incorporated, wages paid by parents to children under age 18 are exempt from Social Security taxes. If she is under 21, she would be exempt from federal unemployment taxes as well.[14]

## The Eller Case

Now, what if Nicole was quite a bit younger than 12? The IRS says you may hire Nicole as long as she is at least 7. Why does the IRS fix the age at 7? This law is based on what's known as the "Eller Case."[15] A man named Dr. Eller hired some of his children to work in his business. One of those kids was just 7 years old. When Dr. Eller filed his taxes, the IRS audited him, stating that they didn't think it was possible for Dr. Eller to legitimately use any 7-year-old child in his business. The case went to trial. The tax court ruled that as long as the child did some sort of physical labor and Dr. Eller documented it, that he could hire the child.

Let's suppose you hire Nicole to work in your business at age 7; the older she gets, the more you can pay her. So you raise her wages from age 10 through 18. By age 18, when it's time for Nicole to go away to college, all those wages plus the interest they have collected over the years totals $30,000. She then says to you, "Dad, thanks a lot. I don't think I want to go to school, I want to buy a Porsche." Can she do that? Absolutely, when she turns 18, the money legally became hers. So what can you do to avoid such a catastrophe?

Employ a technique we like to call "Find the Money If You Can!" This technique can be accomplished by hiring Nicole in your business, and letting her know about only some of the money she is earning, which she can put away and use as she likes; the majority of the money you then take and put in a savings account without telling her where it is. If she makes the decision to go to school, you then simply liquidate the account and give her the money for tuition. If, on the other hand, she wants to buy a Porsche, you can say to her, "Okay honey, find the money if you can!" This is a very powerful technique and we suggest you implement it.

## Hiring Older Children

If your kids are between 18 and 21, you can still get some benefit from hiring them because their wages, although not exempt from Social Security, are exempt from federal unemployment tax,[16] and the wages would be fully deductible at your tax bracket, which is presumably higher than that of your child.

Now you may be thinking, "Yeah, I'd like to hire my children, but what about child labor laws?" Parents who hire their own children are exempt from any state child labor laws. In addition to the tax-saving benefits of paying your children wages, hiring your kids to help you work your business can teach them resourcefulness, the value of work, and can start them on the road to better financial management at a young age.

The IRS and Congress have said that you may hire your children and the first $4,700 (in 2002) you pay them in wages is tax-free.[17] Why is this? Let's say you are going to pay Nicole $4,700 in wages for 2002; you can then deduct that $4,700. In addition, Nicole will be exempt from Social Security taxes and federal unemployment tax. Wages for Nicole are reported on her W-2 as $4,700, but she then gets to deduct that entire $4,700 on her tax return as the standard deduction for that year. The result? You get a tax deduction, and she gets the money tax-free. You can also claim your children as an exemption if they bank the money and use it for college later on.

*Tax Tip: If you want to pay your kids more than $4,700 per year, set up a Roth IRA for their wages and put away up to an additional $3,000 per year (in 2002). The money is not tax deductible, but is tax-free when used for their education.*

What if you don't want your children anywhere near your home-based business? Hire them to do their daily chores such as making their bed, washing the dishes, and taking out the trash. These wages cannot be claimed as a business expense because these chores have nothing to do with your business. However, if their total wages are under $4,700 (in 2002), they will be tax-free because they can deduct the entire amount on their tax returns. If you pay them $2,000 to do their chores, they should be eligible to put that full $2,000 into a Roth IRA, which will be tax-free when used for their college education.

## Setting Your Child's Wages

Unlike your spouse, you want to pay your children under 18 as much as possible because there's no FICA taxes on such wages. But, the salary or wage you pay must be "reasonable" in order for you to take them as deductions.[18] This means that the amount you pay for services must be similar to amounts paid for similar services by similar businesses under similar circumstances.[19]

So let's say you hire Nicole to do some filing and bookkeeping in your business at a salary of $100,000 a year. Is this reasonable? Hardly. A reasonable wage is what you would pay an outside agency to do the same thing.

When setting the wages or salary, be sure to allow for the experience (or inexperience) and ability of your child. Also, consider the 10 factors the IRS uses to examine whether wages are reasonable:[20]

- Duties performed.
- Volume of work.
- Type and amount of responsibility.
- Complexity of work.
- Amount of time required for work.
- General cost of living in the area.
- Ability and achievements of the child.
- Comparison of amount of salary with amount of business income.
- Your pay policy regarding all employees (if there are others).
- Pay history of the child.

The IRS does not care who your hire in your business, except when it comes to your children. Then you need to be a little more careful about the way this takes place. The IRS will not audit you simply because you employ your children (hundreds of thousands of people do it each year), but if you ever get audited for any other reason, you must be ready to prove that your children really did work for you and at a reasonable wage. How do you prove it?

## How to Properly Document
## and Pay Your Spouse or Children's Wages

1. Have all relatives working for you fill out a weekly timesheet. To get your deductions for wages, you must prove what work was actually performed.[21] Each day your spouse or child works, the timesheet should show:
   - Date.
   - Description of tasks performed.
   - Hours worked.
2. Always pay your spouse and children by check. Follow this advice meticulously; don't be tempted by any of this "under the table" nonsense. One of the biggest mistakes home-based business owners make is paying their family members in cash.

They think, "Oh well, here is some cash Tommy, go have fun, you've earned it this week." Bad mistake. Never, ever, ever pay by cash. Always pay your spouse and children by check. By doing so, you will establish an audit trail from you to your child to your child's bank account.

3.  Fill out and file the right forms. When hiring anyone, even spouse and children, you will need to complete the proper paperwork before you can take full advantage of the income shifting tax deductions we have outlined in this chapter.

4.  Obtain a federal I.D. number. Use IRS Form SS4 to do this.

5.  Obtain Employee Wage Reporting Forms. You will need IRS Form W-2, W-4 + W-2.[22] These forms are for reporting tax withholding. If you pay your spouse or child $600 or more, you must give your employees a copy of IRS Form W-2 and file it along with IRS form W-3 with both the IRS and the Social Security Administration.

6.  Obtain IRS Form 940.[23] This form is related to Social Security unemployment tax payments. Although you are not liable for unemployment taxes on wages paid to your child, you must file IRS Form 940 at the end of the year. If your child is under age 21, is your dependent, and your only employee, you simply enter your child's wages as "exempt" from unemployment tax and return the form to the IRS.

7.  Obtain IRS Form 941.[24] Use this form quarterly to report withheld income taxes and deposits.

These forms are usually available at a payroll service; or you can have a service prepare all the forms for a monthly fee. In addition to filling out the proper forms, be sure to document your children and spouse's work activities in your tax diary.

Moreover, complete an employment contract between you and your spouse or children. This contract should pay them on an hourly basis and note what fringe benefits will be available such as the self-insured medical reimbursement plan. We should note that an employment contract is included in the Tax Strategies System provided by the Tax Reduction Institute; refer to Appendix A for more information on how to obtain it.

Finally, remember that in order to hire your children, they will need to have a Social Security number.[25]

# Other Ways to Save Taxes Through Income Shifting

What if you have a child who is not old enough to work or you have a college-aged son or daughter away at school who is never home long enough to work in your business? There are three ways to shift income to family members, even if you can't hire them or don't want to:

1. Gift to Push Taxes.
2. Gift with Lease-Back.
3. Sale of assets and Lease-Back.

## Gift to Push Taxes

This technique is one of the most powerful methods in the country used to shift income to other family members. In fact, this technique is so powerful that if everyone in the country knew about it, we could reduce the taxes paid into the U.S. Treasury by over $2 trillion dollars! The bad news is that 99.99 percent of the people who should be using this technique, don't even know about it!

Gift to Push Taxes allows you to give away to lower tax-bracketed relatives (like your children or grandchildren) property that has gone up in value. They subsequently sell the property and become taxed on the gain at their lower tax bracket.

Suppose John makes a tremendous amount of money in his business, we'll say in excess of $1 million a year. John also just happens to be an online stock trader. On top of all this, he also pays $20,000 a year for each of his three kids to attend college. John, who is normally a very smart person, is doing a very dumb thing. As a person in an extremely high tax bracket (50 percent), rather than paying all that money in tuition, he should be giving each of his kids stock. They can then take that stock and sell it and use it for their college tuition. Naturally, they will be taxed on the gain, but only at a 15 percent tax bracket. By doing so, John would save 35 percent in taxes by letting the kids pay the taxes on the stock and use the gain to pay their own tuition. Such gifts can be given to relatives in the form of stocks, bonds, valuable collectibles, real estate, and so on.

What's more, there are no income tax consequences for making such a gift.[26] There are, however, some gift-tax implications. If you are single, you can give away up to $10,000 per person (in 2001) per year gift-tax free.[27] If you are married, you can give away $20,000 per person per year gift-tax free.[28] In addition, you can give away up to $675,000 as a lifetime exemption from gift-tax. In addition, the recipients of your gift will receive the same basis[29] and the same holding period as you did when you first purchased it. For example, if you paid $20 a share for some stock and today it's worth $45 a share, when you give it to your child, it's basis is $20. When they sell it, they pay taxes on the $25 gain.

Can you see how powerful this is? What happens if you have real estate worth $100,000, or stocks that have gone up substantially in value? When you consider that the stock market alone has gone up in total about $4 trillion over the last eight years, not counting all the appreciation that has resulted from collectibles and real estate, this technique has the potential for massive tax savings.

Because it is such a good technique, Congress tried to kill it with something called the "Kiddie Tax." Children under 14 can only earn up to $1,500 of investment income and have it taxed at their lower bracket.[30] Anything over $1,500 (in 2001) is taxed at the higher bracket of the parent. With that new limitation in place, the Gift to Push Tax technique works best with children older than 14 or investment income up to $1,500.

## Gift With Lease-back

This technique is one of the most powerful financial planning methods ever created. It provides a way of writing off all your business equipment twice. For example, if you have a car that will eventually fully depreciate, you can give that car away to your kids, and then lease it back from them. By doing so, you have put your kids in the leasing business. You are now deducting the lease payments you are giving your kids. In other words, you get to deduct that car twice.

What about computer equipment that becomes obsolete very quickly? After you fully depreciate a computer, can you give it away and lease it back from your kids? Sure. Now you are deducting the computer twice. How about copy machines, fax machines, desks, filing cabinets, bookshelves, cell phones, and phone systems? You can use this technique with just about any property you use solely for business. Any equipment you use in rental property such as refrigerators, stoves, washers, and so on, can also be used as gifts with lease-back.

Equipment can be leased under a three-year contract for 40 percent of what the equipment is worth. So let's say your computer and its software is worth $1,800 this year if you were to sell it. You could give it to your kids and then lease it back from them for $720 a year, or 40 percent of its value under a three-year lease. Every three years you can re-value the equipment.

What about cars? The IRS has actually published leasing tables to help you figure the lease payments. You can get these tables from IRS publication 463, which tells you for how much you can lease a vehicle.

This technique is a perfect way to deduct more than once, items that you need today, but maybe won't need five or 10 years from now.

"But," you might be asking, "how does a 2-year-old grandchild own a computer? Or how does my 16-year-old daughter, a minor, own a car?" The answer is, they can't, so in order to use this technique properly, you will need to set up a trust. The trust, rather than your daughter, owns the car. You then lease the car back from the trust.

*Caution: We always recommend that you use a trust whenever you use the Gift with Lease-back technique. It's unwise to give away property that would produce a tax loss if sold. You will lose the tax deduction for the loss.*[31]

## Selling Assets and Leasing Them Back

You can give away your assets and then lease them back, but you can also sell them and lease them back. This is the number one financial planning strategy that Hollywood stars are using today. It also happens to work really well for home-based businesspeople. Although the concept can be fairly complicated, you need to be aware of this classic technique for not only saving tax dollars, but for putting Money Mastery Principle 10 to work for you. Selling assets and then leasing them back is a great way to get your money to do more than one thing for you at a time. Assets that are doing certain things for you can be used to do another whole set of tasks, thus setting your money in motion.

Here's a very simplified example of how it works:

This example assumes that one or both of your parents are alive and residing in a house that's paid off.

- **Step #1: Set up a joint bank account among you and all your siblings.** (You don't have to include your siblings on this deal, but if you don't, they'll hate you forever because it is so lucrative!). Each of you contributes to the account enough money to equal about $1,200.

- **Step #2: Offer to buy your parents' house.** Get an appraisal to be sure of the value of the house and get a mortgage to pay the full value for it. Let's say their house is worth $250,000— your parents will get top dollar for the house and there will be no commission involved. Because you are giving your parents a good deal, you are going to ask them to give you a good deal in return. Put $1,000 down on the house (from the money you collected from siblings) and ask your parents to be your banker. They are going to finance you to the tune of $249,000 at 7 percent interest (or whatever the minimum IRS rate is for mortgages at the time) for 30 years. You have now become the new landlord.

- **Step #3: Immediately lease the house back to your parents at fair market value rent.** Fair market value is whatever the going rate is in your area. Contact a Realtor in your community for information. Now every month you will receive a rent check from your parents out of the money you paid them for the house. Take that rent check and pay a portion of the mortgage off each month. You will want to set the rent a little more or a little less than the mortgage payment to offset the cost of the interest on the mortgage.[32]

The following illustration is a visual image of the above example:

#### Purchasing Parents' Home and Leasing It Back

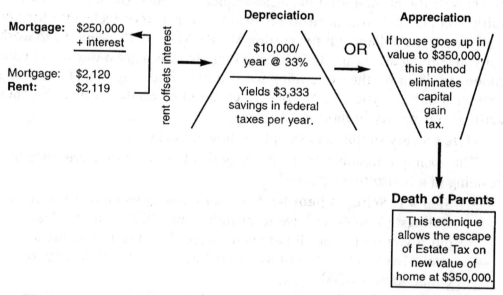

You can see from this illustration the tax advantages this technique affords you. Remember, you are the landlord; if your parents' house ever needs repair work, you can deduct those repair costs. You and your siblings may now depreciate your parents' house and take a portion on your tax returns. You and your siblings may each visit your parents as a tax-deductible caretaking expense. Upon the death of your parents, there will be no probate necessary for the house or furnishings because it is already in the children's estate. Finally, if the house appreciates, say $100,000 in value, you will have this appreciation amount locked into the children's estate and will not have to pay estate tax on the house.

Keep in mind that this technique does require that you dot your i's and cross your t's because there are a number of ways you can go wrong. Your lawyer should provide a letter stating your intent to sell and lease back the house.[33] Be sure to consult an attorney before attempting this method of income shifting.

*Tip: Even more effective than a mortgage note from a lawyer, have him or her draw up a private annuity. This will allow you to pay your parents for the rest of their lives, based on their life expectancy. Upon the death of your parents, there will be no estate tax on this annuity, and no income tax recaptured or recognized.*

## Challenge #16

# Examine Methods for Shifting Income to Family Members

This week, we challenge you to examine each of the ways you could shift income to family members in order to obtain the most tax savings. Review the following checklist to determine which techniques will work best for you:

- ✔ Hire your spouse.
- ✔ Pay your spouse's medical expenses.
- ✔ Set up a "Medical Reimbursement Plan" to pay for all other expenses not covered by medical insurance premiums.
- ✔ Establish a "Supper Money" allowance for hard-working family "employees."
- ✔ Set up a simple pension plan and IRA.
- ✔ Hire your dependent children age 7 to 17.
- ✔ Determine what property you may have that could be given away to lower tax bracket family members.
- ✔ Determine what property you can give away to lower tax bracket family members that can then be leased back.
- ✔ Determine if you are in a situation that would allow you to sell a family asset (such as a parents' home) and then lease it back.

# In Conclusion...

**W**e have discussed, at length, the power of change in the pages of this book. Our purpose in sharing the Money Mastery principles taught herein is to help you see that changing the way you look at money can totally change your life. Our personal convictions about the power of the Money Mastery principles and Tax Strategies are fueled by years and years of teaching these principles and seeing firsthand how they can totally transform people's lives. These principles are true! As Steven R. Covey has said, "There are basic principles of effective living, and ....people can only experience true success and enduring happiness as they learn and integrate these principles into their basic character."

That's what this book is all about...teaching a principled approach to money mastery. It's purpose has been to get you to look at yourself and how you think about money. We have, in many ways, asked you to shift your thinking away from what others teach about applying quick fixes and partial solutions to help solve financial problems. Instead, we have asked you to adopt a more grounded and fundamental approach that can help you build a solid foundation upon which you can stand, regardless of how your circumstances may change. When you are principled, then you are empowered to make better financial decisions, regardless of the situation you may find yourself in. A principled approach helps you see that it's not about the amount of money you make, but rather how wisely you use the money you already have. Only principle-based thinking enables the maximization of your financial power.

The Money Mastery concepts we have taught in this book are as old as time. They have been practiced by the great financial masters throughout the ages. These principles, while new perhaps in the way that we have presented them, are ageless and unchanging. They will always be true and unchanging whether you make them a part of your life or not. Again we quote Steven R. Covey from his book, *The Seven Habits of Highly Effective People*, "Principles are like lighthouses. They are natural laws that cannot be broken. As Cecil B. deMille observed of the principles contained in his monumental movie, *The Ten Commandments*, 'It is impossible for us to break the law. We can only break ourselves against the law.'...The degree to which people in a society recognize and live in harmony with [principles] moves them toward either survival and stability or disintegration and destruction." We must agree. The degree to which you apply the principles of this book will determine whether you thrive financially or not. The choice is yours.

In conclusion, we challenge you to memorize all 10 Money Mastery principles and all six Tax Strategies. Upon each decision to spend money, we encourage you to ask yourself which principle or strategy applies. We invite you to make the Money Mastery principles and Tax Strategies a regular topic of discussion at home and work.

In all matters of money, stick to the principles. In all matters of financial principles, make them a lens through which you can see clearly to make wise financial decisions today that will bring you the lasting happiness of tomorrow.

> *"Whatever you can do, or dream you can, begin.*
> *Boldness has genius, power, and magic in it."*
>
> — Goethe

# The 10 Money Mastery Principles

- **Principle #1:** Spending is Emotional.
- **Principle #2:** When You Track Your Money, You Control It.
- **Principle #3:** Savings is Actually Delayed Spending.
- **Principle #4:** Power Down Your Debt and Power Up Your Fortune.
- **Principle #5:** Know the Rules.
- **Principle #6:** The Rules Are Always Changing.
- **Principle #7:** Always Look at the Big Picture.
- **Principle #8:** Organizing Your Finances Enables the Creation of Additional Wealth.

- **Principle #9:** Understanding Taxation Enables You to Retain More of Your Money.
- **Principle #10:** Money in Motion Creates More Money.

# The 6 Tax Saving Strategies

- **Strategy #1:** If You Don't Have a Home-Based Business, Start One!
- **Strategy #2:** Consider How to Best Legally Structure Your New Business Venture.
- **Strategy #3:** Run Your Business Like a Business, and Not Like a Hobby.
- **Strategy #4:** If You Are Eligible For a Home Office Tax Deduction, Take It!
- **Strategy #5:** Properly Deduct Meals and Entertainment, Car Expenses, And Any Kind of Travel.
- **Strategy #6:** Shift Part Of Your Income To Family Members By Hiring and Leasing From Them.

# Appendicies

## Appendix A

### Money Mastery Products, Tools and Services:

- *Spending Planner Worksheet:* Available at no charge through the Money Mastery Web site: *www.moneymastery.net* or by calling the Money Mastery customer support toll free number: (800) 729-1057.

- *Financial Fitness Test:* Available at no charge through the Money Mastery Web site: *www.moneymastery.net* or by calling customer support: (800) 729-1057.

- *Spending Booklets:* Easy-to-use booklets contain a complete spending system, including a check register, a spending tracker, and a tax diary. Quantity of 12 can be purchased for $10.95 through Money Mastery by calling toll free: (800) 729-1057 or through the Web site: *www.moneymastery.net*.

- *Master Plan v. 5.0 Software:* Designed as a comprehensive tracking and forecasting tool, this software includes a money tracking system, a spending forecaster, debt management tools, and powerful financial calculation software. Spending Planner, Real Debt Reports, Get Out of Debt Reports, Retirement Worksheets, and Master Plan Worksheets help track how money is being spent on a monthly basis; how to track its spending in the future; how much interest will be paid on current debt; how quickly debt can be eliminated by applying Power Down principles; and how to plan for retirement by forecasting the value of investments over a long-term period. Price: $59. Available by calling Money Mastery Customer Support: (800) 729-1057, or ordering from the Web: *www.moneymastery.net*.

- *Coaching Services:* Mentoring packages include a personal, one-on-one relationship with a professional Money Mastery mentor. These services include a one-year consulting contract and include all the tools and techniques needed to maximize savings, control spending, and eliminate debt. Package also includes: Estate Organizer, Debt Elimination Video, a year's supply of Spending Booklets, the Master Plan v. 5.0 Software, Retirement Worksheets, *The Richest Man in Babylon* by George Clason, *Tax Strategies for Business Professionals*, by Sandy Botkin, *Money Mastery How To Manual and Workbook*, and a financial organizer which includes portable file system. To order Coaching Services, please call: (888) 201-2524.

- *Retirement Worksheet:* This tool is available through Money Mastery Coaching Services. To order these services, call (888) 201-2524.

- *Money Mastery Estate Organizer:* This comprehensive organizer includes everything necessary to get all financial and legal matters in order. From birth certificates to stock certificates, the Estate Organizer is the most complete guide to total financial organization on the market today. Available only through Coaching Services: (888) 201-2524.

## Tax Reduction Institute (TRI) Products, Tools, and Services:

- *TRI Audit-Proof Diary:* Includes everything needed to record all substantiating requirements for entertainment, travel, auto, and home office. Available through the TRI Web site, *www.taxreductioninstitute.com*, or by calling (800) TRI-0TAX (800-874-0829). Cost: $95.

- *TRI Tax Saver Module:* Version of the TRI Audit-Proof Diary that fits neatly into the Franklin Planner. Available for $79 through TRI by calling (800) TRI-0TAX, or through the Web: *www.taxreductioninstitute.com*.

- *TRI Tax Saver Software:* Generates comprehensive tax assessment for all tax expenses and summarizes them into easy-to-read reports for you or your accountant. Available for $80 through TRI: (800) TRI-0TAX or Web: *www.taxreductioninstitute.com*.

- *"Tax Strategies For Business Professionals"* and *"Tax Strategies for Home-Based Businesses"*: Audio tapes and workbook from

Sandy Botkin's national tax reduction seminars. Includes every-thing you need to audit-proof your tax return and save the most amount of tax dollars. Cost: $295 through TRI, (800) TRI-0TAX or Web: *www.taxreductioninstitute.com.*

- *"Tax Strategies for Residential Real Estate":* Audio tapes and workbook from Sandy Botkin's national tax reduction semi-nars. Cost: $195 through TRI, (800) TRI-0TAX or Web: *www.taxreductioninstitute.com.*

- *Tax Audit Protection Consulting Services:* Includes unlimited con-sulting for one-year; audit protection plus 100 percent coverage (accuracy guaranteed or TRI pays taxes and penalties); also in-cludes retroactive service for all previous tax years. Available for $349 by calling TRI: (800) TRI-0TAX. (Not available for purchase on the Web site.)

- *Tax Tool Box:* Payroll service for under five employees; includes Tax Saver module diary (for Franklin Planners); Tax Saver Soft-ware, "Tax Strategies" audio seminar and workbook, and Tax Audit Protection Consulting Services. Available for $575 and only by calling (800) TRI-0TAX.

- *Tax Reduction Institute Seminars:* Contact TRI if you would like to attend or sponsor a TRI Tax Reduction Seminar event, (800) TRI-0TAX.

- *Medical Plans and Self-Employed Medical Reimbursement Plan Kits:* Includes properly drawn-up independent contractor and employment contracts, and a legal self-insured medical reim-bursement plan. Available upon request after purchasing "Tax Strategies" audio seminar and workbook, (800) TRI-0TAX.

# Appendix B

## Checklist for Properly Structuring and Launching a Business

Following is a checklist of most of the required information for starting up a business and structuring it properly. *Note: This list may not be compre-hensive because each state has its own requirements.*

1. **Certificate of Occupancy:** If you are planning on occupying a building, you may have to apply to get this from your local city or county zoning department, especially if the building is new or you will conduct substantial improvements to the premises.

2.  **Business License:** Many states require licensing of a business. Sometimes the license must be obtained from the state, and other times it will be issued by the city or county. Many home-based businesses and network marketing ventures do not ordinarily need a license. Check with your state or city government.

3.  **Business Name:** If you use a name for your business or sole-proprietorship other than that of your own name, you must generally register the company name with the county.

4.  **Trade Name and Trade Mark Protection:** If you want to protect your trade name and any special trademarks that you want developed to brand your business, you will need to file a "Registration of Trademark or Service Mark" with the U.S. Department of Commerce. For further information or to reach the Commissioner of Trademark and Patents, call (800) 786-9199.

5.  **Copyrights and Patents:** If you have developed some special invention or have some written material that you don't want people to copy, you must file for a patent for invention or a copyright for written materials. This can be done by contacting the Commissioner of Trademarks, and the Patent and Copyright Applications office. Patent registration forms and questions: (800) 786-9199. To obtain copyright forms call (202) 707-9100. If you have a copyright question, call (202) 707-3000.

6.  **Business Insurance:** All businesses should have some form of insurance to cover them for theft of equipment and for liability issues. Most homeowner policies exempt business equipment from their coverage. Check with your property and casualty agent to see how extensively you are covered and what insurance you may need to obtain.

7.  **Sales Tax Number:** In many states, you may be required to collect and remit sales tax. Thus, you should get a sales tax number in the states in which you will be conducting business, especially your home state. Many network marketing companies take care of this for you with the state in which you will be working. If you are joining a multi-level marketing company, check with them about this number.

8.  **Unemployment Insurance:** If you have any employees or if you incorporate (incorporation assumes you are the "employee"), you will be required to pay both federal and state unemployment insurance. Contact your state unemployment insurance office for the forms and instructions. Also, you will need to get a

federal ID number from the IRS by filing form SS-4 with the IRS. This will set up withholding and federal unemployment tax for any employees.

*Tip: Use a payroll service to file all necessary employee forms such as W-2s, forms 940 and 941 for unemployment and Social Security, etc. These services are fairly inexpensive to use and if you have employees, will save you lots of trouble. A good payroll service will charge about $40 per month for all these services. You can also subscribe to the Tax Reduction Institutes's "Tax Tool Box," which will give you payroll service plus unlimited toll-free consulting and audit protection. (See Appendix A for more information.)*

9. **Immigration Act:** If you have employees, you will need to verify employment eligibility by filing form I-9 for each new employee other than yourself or immediate family. Failure to do so could result in sizeable penalties. For additional information, call (800) 755-0777.

10. **Health and Safety:** Be aware that there are many health and safety laws which apply to employees. The federal Occupational Safety and Health Administration (OSHA) has some standards and brochures of which you should be aware. Call them for information. If you plan to open a restaurant or a manufacturing facility and you will employ people, you will need to comply to OSHA's standards. In many cases, complying means posting some rules somewhere in your facility.

11. **Workers' Compensation:** If your business employs three or more people, Workers' Compensation Insurance must be carried to cover injured employees. The owner may usually exempt himself or herself from this if they wish.

12. **Minimum Wage Laws:** Be aware that there are minimum wage requirements for employees that must be honored. If you have employees, find out what these requirements are and stay abreast of any changes.

13. **Form W-4 for Each Employee:** Each employee must fill out IRS Form W-4 for withholding and for claiming exemptions. If withholding or exemptions change within a year, a new form must be filed for each year a change takes place. See IRS publication 505. Generally, for every $2,800 in new deductions that you expect such as housing interest, expected losses from business, or for each dependent, you may claim an exemption.

# Appendix C

## Essential Reading

- *The Richest Man in Babylon*, George S. Clason. To order call Money Mastery, (800) 729-1057.
- *Tax Strategies for Business Professionals*, Sandy Botkin. To order call the Tax Reduction Institute: (800) TRI-0TAX (800-874-0829).

All other books mentioned in Chapter 5 are available through your local bookstore by author name.

# Appendix D: Floor Plan Maximization Calculations for a Home Office Deduction

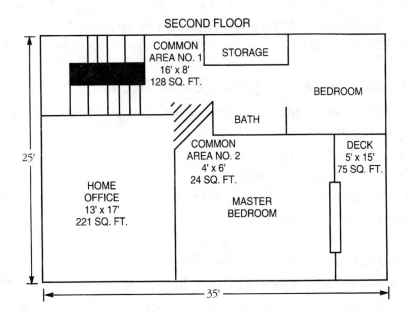

Using the above floor plan as an example, following are three ways you can determine the amount of space your home office occupies and the ways that space can be maximized:

# 1. Number of rooms the office occupies, divided by the total number of rooms in the house.

This is a simple way if your home office occupies an entire room in your house:

| | |
|---|---|
| Divide the number of rooms the office occupies | = 1 |
| By the total number of rooms in the house | = 8 |
| The percentage of the house that can be deducted using this method | = 12.5% |

# 2. Total square footage the office occupies as a percentage of the total square footage of the house.

This method allows you to maximize your square footage by getting a bit more detailed:

| | |
|---|---|
| Divide the total square footage of the home office | = 221 |
| By the total square footage of the house | = 1,675 |
| The percentage of the house that can be deducted using this method | = 13.19% |

# 3. Net square footage applicable to office use.

This method allows the most amount of square footage for your home office. To calculate net square footage:

Deduct common areas:

| | |
|---|---|
| First floor entry and stairway | = 128 |
| Second floor stairway and landing | = 128 |
| Second floor common area | = 24 |
| Deduct deck (not a common area) | = 75 |
| Your net square footage base | = 1,395 |
| Divide the square footage of the home office | = 221 |
| By this net square footage base number | = 1,395 |
| The percentage of the house that can be deducted using this method | = 15.84% |

Using one of these three methods will help you determine how much space your office actually occupies and will help you maximize the total amount of square footage you can deduct for tax purposes.

# Appendix E

## Deducting the Cost of Expensive Cars

Following is a chart outlining the 2001 rates depending on the method of depreciation used. Notice that the IRS places a "luxury limit" on the amount you can depreciate an expensive vehicle.

| Year | MACRS (or Accelerated) | Straight Line | Luxury Limit |
|---|---|---|---|
| 1 | 20.00% | 10.00% | $3,160 |
| 2 | 32.00% | 20.00% | $4,900 |
| 3 | 19.20% | 20.00% | $2,950 |
| 4 | 11.52% | 20.00% | $1,775 |
| 5 | 11.52% | 20.00% | $1,775 |
| 6 | 5.76% | 10.00% | $1,775 |

Say you purchase a $20,000 car and use it 75 percent for business. How much can you depreciate your car in the first year?

## Accelerated (or MACRS) Method:

- $20,000 (cost of car) x 20% (MACRS) x 75% (business use)
  = $3,000

## Straight Line Method:

- $20,000 (cost of car) x 10% (S-Line) x 75% (business use)
  = $1,500

## Luxury Limit:

- $3,160 (luxury limit) x 75% (business use)          = $2,370

You can see from this chart that, although the depreciation limit for a luxury car in the first year is ordinarily $3,160, when you multiply that figure by the percentage of the car you used for business (which remember is 75 percent), then the most you can depreciate this luxury car in the first year is $2,370. If there were no luxury limits, you could have depreciated the car at the MACRS (modified accelerated cost recovery system) rate for $3,000. With this luxury limit law in force, how long will it take you to write-off a car that costs say, $55,000? Roughly 25 years — hopefully you and the car will both live long enough to do it!

# Appendix F

## Calculating the Average Cost of a Meal at Home or Fast Food Restaurant

1.  Count the number of people living in your household.
2.  Determine what your overall grocery bill for one month is by consulting your spending planner.
3.  Using the 50-30-20 rule which deems 50 percent of a grocery bill for dinners, 30 percent for lunches, and 20 percent for breakfast, figure how much of that grocery bill equals the meal you are eating Dutch-treat. For example, suppose you spend $150 a week on groceries for a two-person household. What percent of that $150 equals dinner expense? Fifty percent, or $70.
4.  Divide seven nights of the week into $70 and the cost of eating dinner at home each night is $10.
5.  Divide the number of people in the house into $10 and that gives you $5 per person. This $5 is the average cost to eat dinner at home. Now when you go Dutch-treat at a business dinner, anything over $5 is deductible at 50 percent.

# Notes

## Introduction

1.  1990 U.S. Census.
2.  *Forbes* "Other Comments" page, quoting *Barrons*, (May 17, 1999), p. 36.
3.  Ibid.
4.  U.S. Economic Development Committee statistics as quoted by Ron Pierre, Department Head of Salt Lake County Aging Services, (April 2000).
5.  "Drowning in Credit Card Debt," *Bankrate.com*, (May 18, 2001), Web page: Special Report.
6.  Ibid.
7.  Diane Hales, "Smart Ways To Get Yourself Out of Debt," *Parade*, (February 13, 1994), p. 20.
8.  Walter Williams, "The Legitimate Role of Government in a Free Society," *Imprimis*, (August 2000), p. 3
9.  The Tax Advisor quoting the National Taxpayer Foundation, (May 2000), p. 43.
10. Ibid, p. 43.
11. Walter Williams, "The Legitimate Role of Government in a Free Society," *Imprimis*, (August 2000), p. 3.
12. Ibid, p. 3.

# Chapter 1

1.  Interview with Richard A. Feinberg, Purdue University, (December 5, 2001).
2.  American Bankruptcy Association Meeting, (November 1998), Boston, Massachusetts.
3.  Interview with Jim Christensen, Chairman of the Board, Christensen & Combs, (December 5, 2001).

# Chapter 2

1.  "NBA Labor War," *Associated Press*, (October 20, 1998).
2.  Douglas LaBier, "Modern Madness," (New York: Simon and Schuster, 1989).
3.  Jane Bryant Quinn, "How To Live On One Salary," *Woman's Day*, (November 1, 1994), p. 13
4.  Tony Pugh, "Americans Tap Credit Cards, Are Ill-prepared for Retirement," *Mercury News*, (April 25, 2001).

# Chapter 3

1.  Tony Cook, "Secrets From the 'Millionaire Next Door,'" *Reader's Digest*, (November, 1997), p. 132.
2.  Jill Jedlowski, "Today's Seniors Find Fulfillment Via Family, Work, Volunteerism," *Deseret News*, Senior Living Fall Edition, (October 19, 1999).
3.  U.S. Economic Development Committee statistics as quoted by Ron Pierre, Department Head of Salt Lake County Aging Services, (April 2000).
4.  Owen Ullmann, "Billionaire and Activist Give Kids Same Advice: Avoid Credit Cards," *USA Today*, (October 12, 1999), p. 5A.

# Chapter 4

1.  U.S. Bureau of the Census, Statistical Abstract of the United States: 1998, p. 523.
2.  James L. Clayton, "Global Debt Bomb," (New York: M.E. Sharpe, 2000), p. 11.

3.  Ibid, p. 13. *Clayton references Federal Reserve Board, Bureau of Economic Analysis, as compiled by Hoisington Investment Management Co., Austin, Texas; World Economic Outlook, February 1997.*

4.  Ibid, p. 50.

5.  Ibid, p. 47.

6.  Ibid, p. ix.

7.  Ibid, p. 83.

8.  Ibid, p. 90.

9.  Dennis Lythgoe, "Compelling 'Global Debt Bomb' Carries a Most Urgent Message," *Deseret News,* (December 19, 1999).

10. "The Best Deals In the Cards," *Consumer Reports*, (January 1996), p. 34.

11. Dennis Lythgoe, "Compelling 'Global Debt Bomb' Carries a Most Urgent Message," *Deseret News*, (December 19, 1999).

# Chapter 5

1.  Lynn Brenner, "What We Don't Know About Money Will Hurt Us," *Parade*, (April 18, 1999).

2.  Ibid.

3.  Carma Wadley, "Living Resourcefully," *Deseret News*, (August 11, 1997).

4.  "The New Rules of Borrowing," *Consumer Reports*, (July 1999) , p. 14.

5.  Ibid, p. 16.

6.  Ibid, p. 14-15, (italics added).

7.  Ibid, p. 15

# Chapter 6

1.  Walter Williams, The Legitimate Role of Government in a Free Society," *Imprimis*, (August 2000), p. 3.

2.  Ibid, p. 3

3.  Associated Press, "Talk of Simplification Aside, Tax Forms More Complex," *Salt Lake Tribune*, (February 19, 1999), p. 6.

# Chapter 7

1. Denise M. Topolnicki, "The Five Threats To Your Retirement," *Money*, (November, 1993), p. 66.
2. U.S. Department of Health and Human Services, Publication #: 13-11871, (June 1990).
3. Ibid.
4. John Pierson, "Thirty Years of Retirement," *Fortune*, (1993).
5. Social Security Administration, "Going Broke" chart, *USA Today*, (June 6, 1996), p. 1.
6. Ibid, p. 1.
7. Anne Willette, "For Boomers, Social Security Is Near Bust," *USA Today*, (June 6, 1996), p. 2B.
8. Kenneth S. Apfel, "A Message From the Commissioner," Your Personal Earnings and Benefits Statement From the Social Security Administration, (1998).
9. John Pierson, "Thirty Years of Retirement," *Fortune*, (1993).
10. Charles E. Gerrard, "Long-Term Care – Act Now," *Deseret News*, (April 18, 1999).
11. John Pierson, "Thirty Years of Retirement," *Fortune*, (1993).
12. Charles E. Gerrard, "Long-Term Care – Act Now," *Deseret News*, (April 18, 1999).
13. Jonathan Clements, "Ten Problems That Often Hit Investors If They Lose Track of the Big Picture," *Wall Street Journal*, (March 10, 1998) "Getting Going" column.
14. Denise M. Topolnicki, "The Five Threats To Your Retirement," *Money*, (November, 1993), p. 73.

# Chapter 8

1. Thomas J. Stanley, "Why You're Not As Wealthy As You Should Be," *Medical Economics*, (July 20, 1992), p. 107.
2. Ibid, p. 107.
3. Ibid, p. 108.
4. Loveridge & Associates, as quoted by Michael R. Loveridge, attorney at law, Salt Lake City, Utah, (1999).
5. Norman Vincent Peale, "A Guide to Confident Living," Norman Vincent Peale, (1976).

6. Ibid.
7. American Institute for Economic Research, "How to Avoid Financial Tangles," *Economic Education Bulletin*, (Great Barrington, Mass.), p. 147.

## Chapter 9

1. The Tax Advisor quoting the National Taxpayer Foundation, (May 2000), p. 43.
2. Bart S. Croxford, "Using Life Insurance To Fund Retirement Has Many Benefits," *Salt Lake Tribune*, (November 20, 1996).
3. Loveridge & Associates, as quoted by Michale R. Loveridge, attorney at law, Salt Lake City, Utah, (1999).
4. "Wills of the Famous," Chief Justice Warren Bruger, *Court TV*, (*www.courttv.com*).

## Chapter 11

1. The Tax Advisor quoting the National Taxpayer Foundation, (May 2000), p. 43.
2. Jane Bryant Quinn, "How To Live On One Salary," *Woman's Day*, (November 1, 1994), p. 13.
3. David Darcangelo, "Wealth and Home," (New York: McGraw-Hill, 1997), p. 13.
4. Section 172 of the Internal Revenue Code.
5. Ibid.
6. Section 172(b)(1)(A) of the Internal Revenue Code and the Income Tax Regulations.
7. Small Business Administration, *Small Business Research Summary*, No. 194, (March, 2000).

## Chapter 12

1. Section 172 of the Income Tax Code (IRC).
2. Section 172(B)(1)(A) of the Internal Revenue Code.

## Chapter 13

1. Section 183 of the Internal Revenue Code and the IRS Publication 535, p. 5.

2. Ibid.

3. Section 183(d) of the Internal Revenue Code.

4. Section 183 of the Internal Revenue Code.

5. Section 1.183-2 of the Income Tax Regulations. See also Floyd Fisher, TC Memo, 1980-183 (1980), Moiruice Dreicer, 28 TC 642, AFFd, 702 F.2d 745 (CA Dist. Col. 1983).

6. Rugel v. Commissioner, 127, F.2d 393 (8th Cir. 1942).

7. Frank Suiter, TC Memo 1990-447 (1990); Charles Givens, TC Memo, 1989-529 (1989); Joseph Ransom, TC Memo 1990-381 (199) (Amway Distributor); Frank Harris, TC Memo 1992-638 (1992) (Mary Kay Distributor).

8. Ibid.

9. Section 183-2(a) of the Income Tax Regulations. See also Jonas Brayand vs. Comm., 928 F.2d 745 (6th Cir. 1991).

10. Harry Van Scoyoc, TC Memo 1988-520 (1988).

11. Section 1.183-2(b)(I) of the Income Tax Regulations.

12. C. Frank Fisher, 50 TC 164. Acq.

13. Sheldon Barr, TC Memo 1989-69 (1989).

14. Section 1.183-2(b) of the Income Tax Regulations. See also Joseph Ransom, supra; Abdolvahab Pirnia, TC Memo 1992-137 (1992).

15. Wenzel Tirbelmen, TC Memo 1992-137 (1992).

16. Sherman Sampson, TC Memo 1982-276 (1982).

17. Percy Winfield, TC Memo 1966-53 (1966).

18. Sections 165 and 183 of the Internal Revenue Code. See also section 1.183-2(b)(6) of the Income Tax Regulations.

19. Section 1.183-2(b)(6) & (7) of the Income Tax Regulations.

20. Joseph Ransom, supra., TC Memo 1990-381 (1990) (Amway Distributor).

21. Section 1.183-2(b)(8) of the Income Tax Regulations.

22. Section 1.183-2(b)(9) of the Income Tax Regulations.

# Chapter 14

1. Section 280A(C)(1) of the Internal Revenue Code.

2. Section 280A(C) of the Internal Revenue Code.

3. IRS vs. Soloman, No. 91-998. Supreme Court of the U.S., Jan. 12, 1993.

4. Section 932 of the Taxpayer Relief Act, which amended section 280(C)(1) of the Internal Revenue Code.

5. Section 280A(C)1A of the Internal Revenue Code and section 1.280A-2(C) of the Income Tax Regulations (ITR).

6. Section 280A-2(C) of the Income Tax Regulations.

7. Green vs. Commissioner, 707 F2d. 404 (9th Cir. 1983). See also Frankel vs. Commissioner, 82 TC 318 (9184) and section 280A-2(C) of the Income Tax Regulations.

8. Section 280A-s(C) of the Income Tax Regulations and Frankel vs. Commissioner cited above.

9. Section 280A(C)(1)(C) of the Internal Revenue Code.

10. Section 280A of the Internal Revenue Code and Jackson vs. Commissioner, cited above.

11. Gomex vs. Commissioner, 41 TCM 585 (9180); section 1.280A-2(g) of the Income Tax Regulations.

12. Huuer vs. Commissioner, 32 TC 947 (1959); see also Jackson vs. Commissioner cited above.

13. Section 280F of the Internal Revenue Code. See also Sherri A. Mulne TC Memo 1996-320.

14. Section 280A(C)(5) of the Internal Revenue Code.

15. Section 280F of the Internal Revenue Code. See also Sherri A. Mulne as cited above.

16. Section 179 of the Internal Revenue Code. (Note: As of this writing, Congress has passed legislation to increase this $21,000 limit to as much as $35,000. This has not been signed into law however.)

17. Section 1016(a)(2) of the Internal Revenue Code; and section 1.1016(a)(1) of the regulations.

18. Section 280A(C)(5) of the Internal Revenue Code.

19. Ibid.

# Chapter 15

1. Section 274(d) of the Internal Revenue Code and Section 1.274-5(C)(2) of the Income Tax Regulations(ITR).

2. Section 1.274-5(C) of the Income Tax Regulations; see also, IR 95-56; Pntice 95-50, 1995-42 IRB.

3. Section 274(a) of the Internal Revenue Code; P.L. 99-514, Section 142 (a)(2)(A) amending Internal Revenue Code 274.

4. Section 274(b)(2)(B) of the Internal Revenue Code.

5. Section 274(n) of the Internal Revenue Code.

6. Sections 1.274-2(f)(2)(I)(a) and 1.274-2(c)(7) of the Income Tax Regulations.

7. Ibid.

8. Section 1.274-2(d)(4) of the Income Tax Regulations.

9. Ibid.

10. Sutter vs. Commissioner, 21 TC 170 (1953) , acq. 1954-1 C.B. 6.

11. Section 274(k)(1)(B) and Section 274(k)(2) of the Internal Revenue Code.

12. Ibid.

13. Sections 1.274-2(b)(1)(i); 1.274-2(b)(1)(iii)(b) of the Income Tax Regulations.

14. Ibid.

15. Sections 274(a)(2)(C ) and 162(a) of the Internal Revenue Code.

16. Section 1.274-2(e)(3)(ii) of the Income Tax Regulations.

17. Sections 1.274-2(e)(3)(ii) and 1.274-2(f)(2)(i) of the Income Tax Regulations.

18. Sections 274(a)(3), 274(a)(1)(B), and 274(a)(2)(A) of the Internal Revenue Code.

19. Robert Matlock vs. Commissioner, TC Memo 1992-324.

20. Sections 1.274-2(C )(7)(ii) and 1.274-2(d) of the Income Tax Regulations.

21. Ibid.

22. Section 1.274-2(d)(1)(ii) of the Income Tax Regulations.

23. Revenue Ruling 63-144, 1963-2 C.B. 129, Q&A 50.

24. Section 274(L)(1)(A) of the Internal Revenue Code.

25. Section 274(b)(1) and Section 274(j)(3)(A) of the Internal Revenue Code.

26. Section 274(b)(2)(B) of the Internal Revenue Code.

27. Section 1.274-3(e)(2) of the Internal Revenue Code.

28. Section 1.274-2(C )(4) of the Income Tax Regulations; Steel vs. Commissioner, 28 T.C.M. 1301  (1969).

29. 1 Rev. Proc. 2000-48, IR 2000-8.

30. "Your Driving Costs," published by the American Automobile Association, 2000 Edition.

31. Revenue Ruling 90-23, I.R.B. 1990-11, modified and superseded by Revenue Ruling 99-7, IRB 99-5.

32. Ibid.

33. Ibid.

34. Ibid.

35. Ibid.

36. Section 1.274-5(C ) of the Income Tax Regulations (ITR).

37. Section 1.274-5T(C )(3)(ii)(C) of the Income Tax Regulations (ITR).

38. Ibid.

39. Sections 1.162-1(a) and 1.162-2 of the Income Tax Regulations (ITR). See also Commissioner vs. Griner, 71-2 U.S.T.C. Par. 9714.

40. Section 280F(a)(2)(A) of the Internal Revenue Code and Rev. Proc 99-14, 1999-5 IRB 56.

41. IRS Publication 535 and Section 280F-5T(e) of the Temporary Income Tax Regulations.

42. Rev. Proc. 2000-48, IR 2000-8. See also IRS Publication 535.

43. Sections 162 and 280F(d)(2) of the Internal Revenue Code. See also Section 1.280F-2T of the Income Tax Regulations and IRS Publication 17 and 535.

44. "Tax Strategies for Business Professionals," Sandy Botkin, (2001 Edition) p. 87.

45. U.S. vs. Correll, 389 U.S. 209 (1967); Revenue Ruling 54-497, 1954-2 C.B. 75, superseded in part by Revenue Ruling 75-432, 1975-2 C.B. 60; Revenue Ruling 75-170, 1975-1 C.B. 60.

46. Sections 1.162-2a and section 1.162-2b of the Income Tax Regulations. See also IRS publication 463.

47. Internal Revenue Code 162(a)(2); 62(2)(B); 1.162-2(a), (b) of the Income Tax Regulations.

48. Ibid.

49. Ibid.

50. Ibid.

51. See U.S. vs. Correll above.

52. Section 1.274-5( C) of the Income Tax Regulations.

53. IRS Manual Handbook HB 1763 314(4).

54. Section 274(m) of the Internal Revenue Code; see also Giodano vs. Commissioner, 36 T.C.M 430 (1977); Revenue Ruling 55-57, 1955-1 C.B. 315.

55. Section 1.162-1(a) and 1.162-2 of the Income Tax Regulations; Revenue Ruling 56-168, 1956-1 C.B. 93.

56. Endnote 5; also, Revenue Ruling 63-145, 1963-2 C.B. 86; T.R.-493, 7/24/63; conference, 3/29/63.

57. Ibid.

58. Section 1.274-4(d)(2)(ii) of the Income Tax Regulations.

59. Sections 1.274-4(d)(2)(iii) and 1.162-2(b)(1) of the Income Tax Regulations.

60. Section 1.274-4(d)(2)(i) of the Income Tax Regulations.

61. Internal Revenue Code 274 (C )(2)(B); 274 (c)(1); 1.274-4(d)(1); 1.162-2(b)(1) of the Income Tax Regulations.

62. Section 1.162-2(a)(b)(1) of the Income Tax Regulations.

63. Section 1.274-4(d)(2) of the Income Tax Regulations.

64. Conference Report, p. II-27.

# Chapter 16

1. Sections 3121(b(3(A) and Sections 3306(c(5) of the Internal Revenue Code(IRC). See also IRS Pub. Circular E.

2. Section 1.162-7(a) of the Internal Revenue Code.

3. Section 162(l)(1)(b) of the Internal Revenue Code.

4. Section 213(a) of the Internal Revenue Code.

5. Section 1.105-5 of the Income Tax Regulations(ITR) and ISP Coordinated Issue Paper (UIC-162.35.22).

6. Section 105(h)(5) of the Internal Revenue Code; Section 1.105-11(b)(1) of the Income Tax Regulations; IRS Technical Advice Memorandum IRS Letter Ruling 9409006. See also footnote 4, noted above and Revenue Ruling 71-588.

7. Sections 1.119-1 of the Income Tax Regulations. See also Revenue Ruling 71-411, 1971-2 C.B. 103; Revenue Ruling 71-267, 1971-1 C.B. 37 and IRS Pub 535.

8. Sections 408(k)(2)(A) and 408(k)(2)(B) of the Internal Revenue Code. See also IRS Pub. No 560, p. 4.

9. Section 219(g)(3)(B) of the Internal Revenue Code.

10. Ibid.

11. Ibid.

12. Section 162 of the IRC and Regulations thereunder.

13. Ibid.

14. Section 3121(b)(3) of the Internal Revenue Code.

15. Eller vs. Commissioner, 77 TC 934, Acq., 1982-2 C.B. 1.

16. Section 3121(b)(3) of the Internal Revenue Code and Section 31.3402(n)-1 of the Income Tax Regulations. See also IRS instructions in preparing form 941 and Form 940.

17. Revenue Proc. 2001-13, 2001-3 I.R.B. 337.

18. Section 162(a)(1) of the Internal Revenue Code and section 1.162-7(b) of the Income Tax Regulations.

19. Section 1.162-7(b)(3) of the Income Tax Regulations.

20. IRS Publication 535.

21. Section 1.162-7(a) of the Income Tax Regulations.

22. Section 1.162-7(a) of the IRS Regulations.

23. See IRS Instructions for Preparing Form 940.

24. Section 31.3402(n)-1 of the Income Tax Regulations and IRS Instructions For Preparing Form 941.

25. Section 6109(e) of the Internal Revenue Code.

26. Sections 2503(b), 274(b)(1), and 102(a) of the Internal Revenue Code.

27. Section 2503(b) and section 2513(o) of the Internal Revenue Code.

28. Sections 2513(a), 6019, and 2503(b) of the Internal Revenue Code. See also section 25.2513-1(c) of the Income Tax Regulations.

29. Section 1001 and section 1012 of the IRC. Section 1015(a) of the Internal Revenue Code.

30. Section 1(g) of the Internal Revenue Code and Rev. Proc 2001-13, I.R.B. 2001-3 (December 2000).

31. Section 1015(a) of the Internal Revenue Code.

32. Estate of Maxwell, 98 TC 39 (1992).

33. Matthews vs. Commissioner, 61 TC 39 (1973), rev'd 75-2 U.S.T.C. Par 967 (5th Cir. 1975); Frank Lyons Co. vs. Commissioner, 435 U.S. 561 (S.Ct 1978).

# Index

# G

# H

# I

# K

# P

# R

# About the Authors

## Alan M. Williams

Alan Williams currently serves as managing member of Time & Money, LLC, dba Money Mastery, a Utah-based service company specializing in the education and marketing of principle-based money management. He has 30 years of experience in successfully directing business growth and company development.

Mr. Williams has served as owner, director, CEO, president, and sales manager of a variety of companies in the United States and Canada, and has been heavily involved in the successful start-up, development, and sale of these companies.

In 1994, Mr. Williams combined his financial experience with that of Peter R. Jeppson, to form Time & Money, LLC. As a co-author of the Money Mastery program, Mr. Williams has been able to incorporate successful money management techniques into a format that can be easily applied to every person in America who spends money.

Mr. Williams has served his community as a member of service clubs, director of consumer-oriented lending institutions, senator to a university, and as a leader in his local church. Mr. Williams is a graduate of Brigham Young University.

# Peter R. Jeppson

Peter Jeppson is co-owner and author of the principle-based Money Mastery system. He has trained over one million people in over 5,000 seminars over the past 30 years on personal finances. He has sat at the kitchen tables of thousands of people, coaching them one-on-one with practical implementation on how to better control their spending, eliminate debt, and power up their savings. Mr. Jeppson is the author of three motivational audiocassette tapes and a book series entitled *How To Spend Your Way to Financial Success*.

Mr. Jeppson's community service includes serving on district, council, and national levels for the Boy Scouts of America. He has also served as Crusade Chairman for the American Cancer Society, and most recently as the National Chairman for the Fire and Burn Institute. He loves staying involved with his children by helping coach their various sporting activities.

Mr. Jeppson is a graduate of the University of Utah with a degree in finance.

# Sanford C. Botkin

Sanford Botkin is an attorney and certified public accountant. He currently serves as CEO and principle lecturer of the Maryland-based Tax Reduction Institute (TRI).

During the past 10 years, Mr. Botkin has taught more than 50,000 tax-payers how to legally and ethically save anywhere from $2,000 to $10,000 on yearly taxes through his seminars. Prior to joining TRI, Mr. Botkin spent three years in the tax department of the international accounting firm, Touche Ross. He has extensive financial and legal experience, including five years as a legal specialist in the Office of Chief Counsel for the Internal Revenue Service. He was one of eight attorneys selected by the IRS to train all new attorneys to the Internal Revenue Service's tax division.

Mr. Botkin has authored numerous technical articles for national publications, lectured to various professional and trade groups, and has served as an adjunct professor of accounting and law at the University of Maryland and Columbia Union College.

Mr. Botkin currently serves as "Of Counsel" to Doyle, Schultz & Sella, P.C., a certified public accounting firm in Rockville, Maryland. He is a member of the Florida Bar Association and the Florida Institute of Certified Public Accountants. He is also listed in Who's Who In Business.